JAMES R. GIBSON is a member of the Department of Geography at York University.

Andrew Hill Clark (1911-1975) was responsible for much of the recent rise of historical geography in North America. The focus of his research was the opening of New World lands by European peoples and this North American experience is the subject of this collection of essays written by eight of Clark's students. They examine the rôle of a new physical and economic environment — particularly abundant and cheap land — in the settlement of New France, the cultural and physical problems that conditioned Russian America, the transformation of cultural regionalism in the eastern United States between the late colonial seaboard and the early republican interior, the changing economic geography of rice farming on the antebellum Southern seaboard, the interrelationships of the European and Indian economies in the pre-conquest fur trade of Canada, differential acculturation and ethnic territoriality among three immigrant groups in Kansas in the late nineteenth and early twentieth centuries, the development in England and the United States of similar social geographic images of the Victorian city, and the erosion of a sense of place and community by possessive individualism in eighteenth-century Pennsylvania.

The essays are preceded by an appreciation of Clark as an historical geographer written by D.W. Meinig and are brought together in an epilogue by John Warkentin. The work is an unusually consistent *Festschrift* which should appeal to all interested in the patterns of North American settlement.

European Settlement and Development in North America: Essays on geographical change in honour and memory of Andrew Hill Clark

Edited by James R. Gibson

UNIVERSITY OF TORONTO PRESS
TORONTO   BUFFALO

© University of Toronto Press 1978
Toronto   Buffalo   London
Printed in Canada

The paperback edition is published
as a research publication of the
University of Toronto Department of Geography

Library of Congress Cataloging in Publication Data

Main entry under title:
European settlement and development in North America.

CONTENTS: Meinig, D.W. Prologue. — Harris, R.C.
The extension of France into rural Canada. — Gibson,
J.R. Old Russia in the New World. [etc.]
1. United States — Historical geography — Addresses,
essays, lectures. 2. Canada — Historical geography —
Addresses, essays, lectures. 3. United States —
Colonization — Addresses, essays, lectures. 4. Canada —
Colonization — Addresses, essays, lectures. 5. Clark,
Andrew Hill, 1911-1975 — Addresses, essays, lectures.
I. Clark, Andrew Hill, 1911-1975 II.   Gibson, James R.
E179.5.E94   911'.73   78-8335
ISBN 0-8020-5415-3
ISBN 0-8020-3357-1 pbk.

Editor's foreword

Festschriften do not seem to enjoy a glowing reputation, despite their good intentions. Uncritical adulation of the honoured, contributions of uneven quality, the lack of a unifying theme, a high price and small market – these are the most common shortcomings. I am hopeful, however, that this volume has to a large degree overcome such defects, and in no small measure because of Andrew Clark's own legacy of a concern for ideas, trenchant criticism, and high standards on the part of his numerous and productive students. Donald Meinig and John Warkentin, both colleagues and friends but not students of Clark, represent the two countries that most engaged his expertise and affection, and they offer dispassionate and fresh perspectives that his students would find difficult, if not impossible, to provide. Meinig critically appreciates Clark *qua* historical geographer, and Warkentin distils the essays, linking them not only to the teachings of Clark but also to the wider purposes and values of geography. The intervening essays themselves, which in their diversity demonstrate that Clark did not leave behind a particular 'school' of historical geography (except in the very broadest sense), are no less instructive, as attested by the colleagues and referees who assessed drafts. To these unnamed individuals go my thanks, as well as a complimentary copy of the book. It will be read by not a few others, thanks to the phenomenal growth of historical geography in recent years. Much of the credit for this upsurge belongs, of course, to Andrew Clark and his quarter-century of teaching and writing at the University of Wisconsin in Madison. The book's reasonable price arises from the generosity of the subscribers and the efficiency of the publisher. The overall theme is European settlement and development in North America – broad enough to touch Clark's own preoccupation with British expansion overseas and to embrace the research interests of those of his doctoral students who are represented here, and narrow enough to give some focus and coherence. That these essays display philosophical and methodological pluralism within this broad theme, as well as rigorous scholarly standards, and represent many of North America's most productive and most influential historical geographers, would, I think, have afforded Andrew Clark much satisfaction. But I also think that he was well aware of his impact before he died, and, as one of many who benefited a great deal from his tutelage, I am grateful for that.

I am also indebted to Jock Galloway and David Ward for their encouragement and suggestions, and to Bob Ryan for much redrafting of maps.

JAMES R. GIBSON
York University

Contents

viii Contents

EUROPEAN SETTLEMENT AND DEVELOPMENT
IN NORTH AMERICA

D. W. MEINIG

Prologue: Andrew Hill Clark, historical geographer

I first heard about Andrew Clark from an impeccable source at a chance encounter. One sweltering summer day in 1952 I came down from my little office loft in the old Geology Museum at the University of Utah to find a stranger in the hallway. He said that he was from England and that he was travelling across the country and had stopped by to see if there might be any geographers around. He identified himself as Clifford Darby. Well, I had certainly heard of him, and when he found out I was sweating away at a dissertation in historical geography there began a conversation that lasted many hours and a friendship that lasted ever after. One of the first things he said to me was, 'you must *get acquainted with Andrew Clark at Wisconsin; he is a fine scholar and full of zeal for historical geography.'*

With that prompting I soon did get in touch with Andrew Clark, first by letter and then by a visit to Madison in the winter of 1954 (a one-day visit which was prolonged to six by a fortuitous collision between my car and a taxicab as I was leaving town). And of course I found that Clifford Darby was entirely right on both counts, and more, for Andrew Clark proved to be a person of great warmth and generosity. I was never his student but I received his help in numerous ways, as did so many others.

I begin with this personal note because Andy Clark was a very special friend, and my commentary on him has inevitably been shaped by what I knew of the man as well as by what I have read in his work. Nevertheless, what follows is not a eulogy but as honest an assessment as I can make. It has been perfectly natural and comfortable to make it so because that is what he would want and expect. That was the kind of relationship we had over all those years. He was so honest

*about his own work and so ready for constructive criticism that what I have
written is not essentially different from what I might have said to him during a
leisurely talk about his work and about the status and prospects of historical
geography.*

I

Andrew Hill Clark was the dominant figure in American historical geography for
more than twenty years. It was an exemplary, creative, and benevolent
dominance, earned by his scholarship and his tireless advocacy of the field,
sustained by his position as a teacher at a major graduate centre, and ever
suffused with his great generosity to all with whom he worked.

The lineage of American historical geography, in its various guises, was first
set forth by Clark himself in the landmark volume *American Geography:
Inventory & Prospect*, published by the Association of American Geographers on
the occasion of its fiftieth anniversary in 1954.[1] He subsequently updated that
survey for the international inventory *Progress in Historical Geography*,
published in 1972.[2] His position as a leader was in some degree both reflected in
and enhanced by his authorship of the first item; by the time of the second that
leadership had long been widely recognized. Both works now appear dated and
deficient because they could hardly convey adequately his own enormous
significance to the development of the field he was writing about.

As I now review the emergence of historical geography in the period following
the Second World War, I can see how in one sense Clark filled a void created by
the sudden death of Ralph H. Brown. Brown's books, *Mirror for Americans*
(1943) and *Historical Geography of the United States* (1948), were distinguished
achievements, volumes of high literary as well as solid historical and geographical
merit, which, as Clark noted, 'marked the coming of age of American historical
geography.'[3] But Brown's death in 1948 at the age of fifty cut short any direct
building on that new foundation at the University of Minnesota. Thus when
Clark arrived at Wisconsin in 1951 there was no rival centre in the region and the

1 'Historical Geography,' in P.E. James and C.F. Jones, eds., *American Geography: Inventory & Prospect* (Syracuse 1954), 70-105
2 'Historical Geography in North America,' in Alan R.H. Baker, ed., *Progress in Historical
   Geography* (Newton Abbot 1972), 129-43
3 'Historical Geography,' 83. Of course Carl Sauer had spoken strongly on the topic in his
   presidential address of 1940, 'Foreword to Historical Geography,' in *Annals of the
   Association of American Geographers* 31 (1941): 1-24, but, as has often been remarked,
   Sauer rarely used the term and historical geography had no clear identity as a formal
   field at Berkeley; rather, an historical dimension was assumed to be inherent in the
   study of cultural geography.

need for a new impetus was clear. Historical geography lost a creative figure in Brown, but it gained a more powerful builder and forceful protagonist in Clark.

The chapter on 'Historical Geography' in *American Geography: Inventory & Prospect*, which would serve for years as the most obvious and succinct orientation to the field, bears the strong imprint of Clark's general stance and ideas.[4] The eclectic list of more than 150 studies by North Americans reflects his refusal to prescribe sharp limits to legitimacy and his eagerness to identify all works which might in any way represent a serious interest in the geography of the past. He noted a number of definitions and approaches, but his own predilection for thinking of the field as the study of 'geographical change through time' is apparent from the opening paragraph. So, too, his own training and experience show in the strong emphasis given to physical geography, field observation, and the mastery of documents as essential preparations for research in historical geography. Clark's survey gave the field a prominent identity, a general shape, a lineage, and a prospect. Such a statement in a volume of such central interest, following upon the publication of his own first book, together with his professorial position, made Clark the unrivalled American spokesman for the field in the 1950s.

In the 1960s his doctoral students began to provide compelling evidence of his qualities as a teaching scholar. A total of nineteen dissertations were written under his guidance; to date ten of these have been published as monographs[5] and have received critical acclaim in and well beyond geography.[6] Together they make an impressive body of literature in North American historical geography. Furthermore, if we seek a proper measure of his influence we must note his role as general editor of the 'Historical Geography of North America Series' of studies issued by Oxford University Press.[7] Clark initiated the plan for such a series, persuaded the publishers of its worth, and selected and worked closely

4 The preparation of each chapter in that book was the responsibility of a separate committee. Clark acknowledged the help of Herman Friis, Dan Stanislawski, J. Russell
   Whitaker, and Richard Hartshorne, but he specified that he had prepared the successive
   drafts and was responsible for 'the basic approach, organization, and final decisions on
   wording.'
5 See pp. 228-9 of this book.
6 The most notable example is James T. Lemon's *The Best Poor Man's Country*, which
   received the Albert J. Beveridge Award of the American Historical Association for the
   best book in American history published in 1972.
7 This series has been appropriately renamed 'The Andrew H. Clark Series in the Historical
   Geography of North America.' Volumes published so far are: David Ward, *Cities and
   Immigrants*; D.W. Meinig, *Southwest*; R. Cole Harris and John Warkentin, *Canada
   before Confederation*; Douglas R. McManis, *Colonial New England*; Hildegard B. Johnson, *Order upon the Land*; James R. Gibson, *Imperial Russia in Frontier America*.
   Several more, initiated by Clark, are in preparation.

with each author. He was a superb editor, using his wide knowledge of language as well as of geography and history to bring out the best in his authors through detailed constructive criticism.[8] He also had a major hand in creating the *Journal of Historical Geography*. Launched in January 1975, this transatlantic publication was the first in English to be devoted explicitly and exclusively to the field. He served as editor for the Americas until his death.

I think there can be little doubt that if we should line up on one shelf the books by Clark, by his students, those in his series, and the issues of the *Journal* which he edited, we would have before us one of the most impressive and coherent productions in the whole of English-language geography.

Clark was a gregarious and engaging person with wide contacts in the academic world. He had close working relationships with scholars in several subfields of history. He was often called upon to represent the historical geographer's point of view at interdisciplinary symposia.[9] He also became increasingly involved in Canadian-American study programs. He was a charter member and active supporter of the Association for Canadian Studies in the United States.[10] He was to have been the Claude Bissell Visiting Professor of Canadian and American Studies at the University of Toronto in the fall of 1975. In addition, he maintained close contact with many scholars and institutions in Britain and the Commonwealth.[11] As Cole Harris has aptly put it, 'he had practically become the fulcrum of historical geography in the English-speaking world.'[12]

These publications and appointments are only the most obvious marks of Andrew Clark as a leader and catalyst in his field (see pages 222-7 in this book).

---

8 He was also editor of the new Monograph Series of the Association of American Geographers from 1957 to 1961, getting it launched with Richard Hartshorne's *Perspective on the Nature of Geography* and carrying it forward with volumes by D.W. Meinig and Lewis M. Alexander.

9 See, for example: 'Geographical Change – A Theme for Economic History,' *Journal of Economic History* 20 (1960): 607-16; 'Some Suggestions for the Geographical Study of Agricultural Change in the United States, 1790-1840,' *Agricultural History* 46 (1972): 155-72.

10 He contributed a paper entitled 'Contributions of Its Southern Neighbours to the Underdevelopment of the Maritime Provinces Area of Present Canada, 1710-1867' to the 1971 conference of this group, and at the time of his death was a member of the planning committee for their Bi-Centennial International Conference on 'Revolution and Evolution' as comparative experiences of the United States and Canada.

11 In 1971-2 he helped establish the first American Studies Programme in a Scottish university at Dundee.

12 Harris, 'Andrew Hill Clark, 1911-1975: An Obituary,' *Journal of Historical Geography* 2 (1976): 2

His students and colleagues could readily extend this account by descriptions of many other ways in which he helped them and served the cause of geography and the academic world. But it is time to turn from his general role as a teacher of, and spokesman for, historical geography to an examination of his own work as a scholar.

II

Clark's first book, published in 1949, was based upon his doctoral dissertation on South Island, New Zealand. In the preface he stated that it was 'intended to be the first of a series of studies dealing with similar problems of the development of patterns and practices of land use in mid-latitude areas overseas which were settled by folk from the shores of the North Sea' (p. vi). He had already done some work on Maritime Canada before the chance to go to New Zealand arose, and he returned to continue that research. In 1959 he noted in the preface of his book on Prince Edward Island that it was 'the second major regional effort in what is planned as a series; a study of Nova Scotia is nearing completion and preliminary planning for investigations in Australia and South Africa is under way' (p. v). *Acadia*, published in 1968, covered only the French era in Nova Scotia. A second volume treating the British and Canadian phases after 1760 was uncompleted at his death, but three of his articles are clearly important parts of that work.[13]

These three books and the parts of a fourth, each a substantial and discrete study but conceived as successive volumes in a set and completed as stages in a lifetime program, constitute the body of work upon which his reputation as a scholar will rest. I shall consider these works first individually and then as a series, but it is worthwhile emphasizing at the outset that the very idea of projecting a coherent program of scholarly studies, of undertaking a lifetime of inquiry on a major topic, was virtually unheard of in American geography. While there had been a few major figures, geography as an intellectual enterprise was alarmingly underpowered and its shelf of major research studies was embarrassingly short. Persons of Andrew Clark's scholarly vision, quality, and industry were desperately needed.

---

13 'Titus Smith Junior and the Geography of Nova Scotia in 1801 and 1802,' *Annals of the Association of American Geographers* 44 (1954): 291-314; 'Old World Origins and Religious Adherence in Nova Scotia,' *Geographical Review* 50 (1960): 317-44; 'The Sheep/Swine Ratio as a Guide to a Century of Change in the Livestock Geography of Nova Scotia,' *Economic Geography* 38 (1962): 38-55

In 1940, while he was a graduate student at Berkeley, an invitation from George Jobberns, who was developing the first New Zealand geography department at Canterbury University, turned Clark from his preliminary research on Maritime Canada to antipodal South Island. He did field work while serving as a lecturer there in 1941 and 1942, returning to Berkeley to complete the dissertation (awarded in 1944). The general nature of the study is indicated in the titles of the two versions: 'The South Island of New Zealand: A Geographic Study of the Introduction and Modification of British Rural Patterns and Practices Associated with the Exotic Plants and Animals of the Island' (dissertation) and *The Invasion of New Zealand by People, Plants and Animals: The South Island.* The opening sentence of the latter states that it is 'a report on a revolutionary change in the character of a region' (p. v). The book sets forth an orientation to the 'primitive habitat,' the region as it was upon first European contact, and then treats successively the introduction, initial spread, and subsequent changes in the geography of people, sheep, cattle, some lesser animals, and animal pests, potatoes, wheat, several fodder crops, exotic trees and shrubs. It was justly claimed to be a 'pioneering venture,' a view of colonization as a process of transforming the land, with special attention to ecological problems arising therefrom. It certainly differed from standard histories and geographies of any land, and with reference to New Zealand it revealed that the generally held 'Britain of the South' interpretation was a simplistic idea which failed to convey the complexities of New Zealand as a rural culture, was mistaken as to implied processes of development, and ignored the significance of other source regions, especially Australia.

Clark's study was clearly a major work on New Zealand and a fresh kind of historical geography. It was the first detailed application of the Berkeley genetic approach to the study of European overseas colonization of such middle-latitude new lands during the nineteenth and twentieth centuries. It was an exciting beginning for the projected series.

Three Centuries and the Island: A Historical Geography of Settlement and Agriculture in Prince Edward Island, Canada was markedly different in organization and theme. Instead of tracing successively people, plants, and animals, the book depicts the detailed patterns of rural population and land utilization through a succession of five eras, plus two lengthy chapters on agricultural changes over the past century and a brief review and conclusions. This difference in method reflects a difference in purpose. Clark explained in the preface that in Maritime Canada he was especially concerned with investigating the relationship between 'cultural origins of the settlers' and 'specific character-istics of farming operations.' In Nova Scotia the analysis of such relationships was difficult because some of the culture groups were spread over different kinds of ground and had had different economic and political experiences. On Prince Edward Island, by contrast, a number of the same peoples lived in clearly localized areas on a nearly uniform physical base in 'an almost uniform distribution of economic opportunity and political institutions and pressures at any particular time' (p. vi). Thus the island could be used as a 'laboratory,' a 'control area' for the larger study.

The book presents an extremely detailed description and analysis, relying heavily on statistico-cartographic techniques (there are 155 maps) to demonstrate relationships and changing patterns. The analysis reveals that the distribution patterns of crops and animals were in constant flux, that even so small an area as Prince Edward Island could not be taken as a unit for the study of agricultural activities, and that the patterns of land use at any time were in close concordance with the distributions of culture groups. The book stands as a remarkably intensive study of the island and a major demonstration of a particular approach to presentation and analysis in historical geography.

Acadia: The Geography of Early Nova Scotia to 1760 was offered as another 'case study' (p. 3) but was also rather different in organization and emphasis. Following a description of the 'endowment of nature' and a very brief chapter on the Micmac Indians, mainland Acadia is described as it developed over the course of a century and a quarter. Cape Breton Island is given a separate chapter because it was so peculiarly involved in fishing and military activities. Unlike the New Zealanders the Acadians numbered but a few thousand and were scattered in small groups among several distinct districts. Thus much of the study is a detailed description of localities, making use of every available statistic on numbers of people, houses, livestock, acres of crop, and volumes of production and trade in order to reconstruct as exactly as possible the locational patterns of settlement and the changes in those patterns era by era. There is, however, always a concern for relationships among these localities and the main theme, enunciated in the preface and sustained by the book, is how 'the persistence of an exotic people and culture in a new home inevitably led to a new combination of nature and culture in the area and, thus, to the appearance of a new geographical entity' (p. 3).

It was, as Louis Gentilcore has noted, 'a formidable contribution to geographical and historical research in North America' and 'a definitive statement on the geography of Acadia.'[14] The Beveridge Award Committee of the American Historical Association obviously agreed, citing *Acadia* as the 'best historical study on Canada' published in 1968.

14 *Geographical Review* 60 (1970): 452

III

Three major books, each an unprecedented study of its area — what qualities do they have in common as literature in historical geography? First of all, they reflect a basic style and standard of scholarship. Clark once wrote that while 'there is no known formula by which one can write satisfactory history and geography ... at least one rule should be inviolable: both the history and the geography should be presented with the greatest possible clarity.'[15] He certainly followed that rule in terms of logical structure, organization of data, and clear prose. Clark was a highly literate person with a simple literary style. He admired 'vivid, compelling, and yet accurate verbal descriptions' and lamented his own 'all too limited' skill,[16] but he had no reason to be apologetic about his writing. What makes some sections of his books heavy reading is his 'penchant for thoroughness,'[17] the presentation of history and geography in the greatest possible detail so that at times the narration becomes congested with information, even though the meaning is always clear.

A more fundamental quality was the kind of scholarship represented. Clark's great strength was his mastery of field and archive and his ability to bring the two into mutual reinforcement. It is a quality apparent in all his work — less thoroughly perhaps in the New Zealand book, where he was under time pressures in dissertation research,[18] but almost overpoweringly evident in the Maritime Canada studies.[19]

Clark's first paper in a geographical periodical was 'Field Research in Historical Geography' (1946).[20] It is a rather strident piece, the young scholar expressing his scorn for the 'increasing predilection for the armchair or library

15 *Geographical Review* 55 (1965): 133
16 '*Praemia Geographiae:* The Incidental Rewards of a Professional Career,' *Annals of the Association of American Geographers* 52 (1962): 237
17 This is Gentilcore's phrase in the review cited in note 14. Similarly, his speeches and essays do not always flow easily because his lively, brimming mind so often led him to make allusions, emendations, and qualifications.
18 In 'Field Research in Historical Geography,' *Professional Geographer* (Old Series) 4 (1946): 18, he stated that he would have liked six more months in New Zealand.
19 This quality is much in evidence in his Foreword and Notes to the republication of Isabella Lucy Bird, *The Englishwoman in America* (Madison 1966), where his 190 annotations exhibit his meticulous scholarship and wide humanistic interests.
20 This paper was first delivered as an address to the Middle Atlantic Division of the American Society for Professional Geographers, a group formed during the Second World War out of dissatisfaction on the part of many younger scholars with the Association of American Geographers. The newer group merged with the older in 1948 and its new journal, *The Professional Geographer,* was continued as an AAG publication.

desk' (p. 13) that he discerned and insisting that American geographers not only needed 'to place more emphasis on field research' but also 'to conduct it with much greater care' (p. 23) and do so within the framework of some 'philosophic purpose' (p. 14). He was reacting to what he regarded as a widespread indifference to methodology and philosophy among many of the geographers he encountered during his wartime service in Washington, DC. Clark was speaking from an unusually rich experience in field work, first at Toronto with the indefatigable Griffith Taylor, next, and no doubt more important in relating field observation to problems and philosophy, with Carl Sauer at Berkeley, followed by his two years in New Zealand with George Jobberns. He would later speak glowingly of the great stimulation and pleasure of being in the field with these and other keen readers of the landscape. Such men assumed a thorough grounding in physical geography as an essential part of a geographer's training. Clark always considered it so and continued to teach an undergraduate course in physical geography for many years as a logical and enjoyable accompaniment to his historical courses and research.

His training and experience in historiography were no less solid. At Toronto he worked with a number of fine scholars, of whom Harold A. Innis, the great economic historian, was clearly a major influence. Innis was closely associated with the geography department and was the one who first encouraged Clark to undertake a study of Maritime Canada. Clark later described Innis as not only a master of documentary research but a fine field man: 'much of his writing was based on detailed research and experience *in situ.*'[21] Clark would later dig into many of the same archives as had his mentor, in Ottawa, Halifax, and London, and would lay even greater emphasis upon relating what he found therein to actual sites. Throughout his career he would stress that there was 'no substitute for seeing phenomena, in context, for oneself with well-schooled eyes.'[22]

This grounding of historical geography in extensive training in physical geography, historiography, and field observation was receiving similar emphasis in Britain, with H.C. Darby as the principal spokesman and exemplar. The close relationship which grew between Clark and Darby was of great significance to the development of the field of historical geography on both sides of the Atlantic. They occupied comparable positions, each the acknowledged leader in his own country, and they had much to share with one another. Darby was much concerned with methods of presentation, with how to structure writings in historical geography so as to cope with the difficulties inherent in trying to

21 The statement is from an obituary by Clark in the *Geographical Review* 43 (1953):
   282-3. Also see his reviews of two of Innis' books in this same volume (140-2).
22 *'Praemia Geographiae,'* 237

depict patterns both in time and in space. Although his British friend was more a colleague than an obvious mentor, especially in the 1950s Clark was, I believe, stimulated by Darby's attentions to such matters, and I would place Darby with Sauer and Innis as having an important influence upon the style and character of Clark's work.[23]

Thus a Clarkian historical geography — the work of the students as well as the master — emerged as a recognizable type, distinguished by intensive empirical research in archive and field and a thorough familiarity with the larger patterns of geography and history relevant to the region under study. It was a level of scholarship far from common in American geography.

IV

Each of Clark's books was offered explicitly as an example for historical geography.[24] They were, however, three quite different models, and I can now

23 Although nearly of the same age (Clark was two years younger), their early careers were so very different as to put them out of phase until the 1950s. Darby had an astonishingly early start and impact. He was grappling with theory and methodology in historical geography while Clark was working as an actuarial assistant in a life insurance company, and the landmark volume *An Historical Geography of England before A.D. 1800*, which Darby conceived and edited, was published in 1936, just after Clark had begun graduate work. Their careers only began to converge after Darby moved from Liverpool to University College London in 1949 and Clark from Rutgers to Wisconsin in 1951 and each began to create major graduate centres for historical geography. Darby's visit to Madison in 1952 initiated their close working relationship. At the time, Clark was just getting underway with his inventory of historical geography and Darby was giving close attention to the questions of structure and theme — cf. 'On the Relations of Geography and History,' *Transactions and Papers of the Institute of British Geographers* 19 (1953): 1-11; Clark's New Zealand book is particularly noted therein on p. 8. Two years later Clark was in London at Darby's invitation and gave a lecture series illustrating his latest attempts to handle problems of analysis and presentation (in the preface of *Three Centuries and the Island* Clark acknowledges Darby's critical help on that occasion and later on the manuscript). It may be noted also that each man gave sustained professional attention to the practice of, and to topics and problems in, historical geography on the other side of the Atlantic; Clark taught courses on the historical geography of Europe, Darby on North America.
24 'The writer would like ... to hope that this study might be exemplary of the themes of historical geography' — *The Invasion of New Zealand* (New Brunswick 1949), v; '... the method of study and presentation is also intended to illustrate and test an approach to the study of historical geography as the author understands it — *Three Centuries and the Island* (Toronto 1959), v; '... the author has illustrated as clearly as he can his conception of what a regional exposition of historical human geography should involve' — *Acadia* (Madison 1968), 394.

see those differences as both a response to different problems and a sequence showing a direction in his own development.

The Invasion of New Zealand uses a 'vertical themes' approach. The various elements (people, plants, and animals) are traced each in turn as to origin, entry, and spread, and no series of synthetic views of South Island is offered. *Three Centuries and the Island*, on the contrary, is structured around a sequence of such cross-sections alternating with narrations of developments during the intervening years. It is an experiment in combining chorological and chronological descriptions in the study of 'geographic change.' *Acadia* is organized so as to present in sequence the three main eras of French development, but the principal topics (population, settlement, the economy) are treated separately within each era, and no comprehensive chorological cross-section sample or summation of these eras is attempted.

We can see in this a shift from the Berkeley emphasis upon diffusion and ecological disturbance to a more distinctively Clarkian emphasis upon regional historical geography. The critical difference would seem to be a matter of focus, whether primarily upon culture or area. Although Clark had a rich knowledge of the societies he studied, and especially those of Maritime Canada, he was not engaged in an explicit examination of 'culture.' He did not, for example, describe Acadian culture as a set of phenomena, a configuration, a behavioural pattern, or even as a geographical entity or system nested among other cultures or systems. *The Invasion of New Zealand* gave much attention to cultural alterations of the landscape, but none of his studies is focused on 'the making of the cultural landscape' in any general sense.[25] It is telling to note that there are no photographs in the Prince Edward Island book and only five in *Acadia*, as compared with a total of 190 maps and 64 tables in the two. Clearly his main concern was 'area' and his main geographic method was to *map* populations, productions, and various elements in order to make a 'fine-grained analysis' of areal patterns and of changes in those patterns. His titles and subtitles indicate this shift in emphasis, from *Invasion ... by People, Plants and Animals* to *A Historical Geography of Settlement and Agriculture* to *The Geography of Early Nova Scotia to 1760*. He stated that his 'most basic concern' in *Acadia* was 'to set down as carefully as resources of time, facilities, and skill allow, the accurate record of relevant phenomena and events' (p. 371). The result is an extremely detailed historical geography which bears his own distinctive stamp.[26]

25 Cf. W.G. Hoskins, *The Making of the English Landscape* (London 1955), and the series of county volumes under his editorship.

26 It is interesting to note Clark's recognition of his divergence from the Berkeley tradition and the difficulties he had in trying to categorize that work in his inventories: 'The

V

Three major books, then, each exemplary, but each of a different kind of historical geography – yet each was also explicitly offered as part of a series of studies dealing with the overseas expansion of European colonists to middle-latitude 'new worlds.' How do they relate to one another as a thematic series?

In the preface to *Three Centuries and the Island* he stated that his book on New Zealand had had the 'same basic purpose although its particular problems suggested a different approach' (p. v). However, that difference in approach would seem to arise more from a difference in purpose, the one being a report on a revolutionary change in a region and the other a laboratory for the testing of a hypothesis. *Acadia* is also specifically related to the series as an example of one of the many areas 'invaded by an alien people with well developed and complex culture and their retinue of exotic plants and animals' (p. 379), and he goes on to specify a general comparative framework: 'The problem is ... to place the Acadians and Acadia properly in the extremely varied continuum of experience that the full catalog of such invasions represents' (p. 379). 'At one extreme' is the example of New Zealand: 'a vast alteration in the face of the earth.' At or near the other extreme is Acadia, where 'except for a few hundred square miles which the Acadians farmed (and most of that, reclaimed tidal marshlands) the landscape, flora, fauna, and pre-European culture and economy of Acadia had altered very little indeed by 1760' (p. 379). But the comparison is carried no further. Earlier in that chapter he listed the 'ingredients that contribute to the basic human geography' of these colonization areas: '... the natural characteristics, the antecedent cultural occupation and its effects, the nature of the invading culture, and the regional and world-wide contexts of the political, commercial, and strategic relationships of the region' (pp. 370-1). This statement is in the 'conclusion' of *Acadia* and these features have been described meticulously for that region, but no formal comparison with Prince Edward Island or New Zealand or colonization regions studied by other historical geographers is offered.

writer did not know in 1954, and still does not, quite how to relate the cultural-environmental interests, with their often strong anthropological overtones, which have derived especially from the Sauer era at the University of California at Berkeley, to the rest of the variegated body of historical work' ('Historical Geography in North America,' 138). He went on to refer to it as 'geographical culture history' in which training, supporting fields, and themes made it distinct from 'the more historiographically focused historical geographers.' He saw himself as being at home in both camps, not only in training but in practice as he continued to direct some dissertations of the Berkeley type.

Indeed, there is a conscious refusal to do so: 'In the historical geography of the overseas expansion of Europe there are scores or hundreds of such studies to be made and very few yet completed. Thus the next stage, or purpose, of historical investigation, to attempt some broad generalizations, may be premature – to say the least – for historical geographers' (p. 371). Such reluctance produced a sharp rejoinder from one reviewer: 'The notion that all facts must be ordered before generalization can begin has been pretty well exploded ... the process of generalization begins with the initial ordering of facts.'[27] That much, at least, of what was in total a harsh critique of *Acadia*, seems apt. Presumably the series he repeatedly referred to and which he was creating book by book ought to have led towards generalizations about colonization or at least about European colonizations of that era, but it seems to have led him in the opposite direction. That in itself was not necessarily wrong; he could leave such generalization to others, but it could not but limit his impact in his own chosen realm of inquiry. More serious was his failure to formulate a statement about colonization which might serve as a framework for comparative analysis. He devoted thirty years to what was ostensibly an enterprise in comparative studies, but he showed little appetite himself for making such comparisons; he offered no explicit formulation of how to do so, and his books are so varied in structure and emphasis as to provide no model. Other scholars have now made studies of several regions, especially in Australia and the United States, which added to Clark's three begin to offer the coverage he himself had originally hoped to complete. But without some basic formulation of elements and processes it is difficult to articulate these studies so as to deepen our understanding of colonization as a geographic phenomenon. That is certainly a kind of generalization that must take place 'with the initial ordering of facts' if we are to undertake comparative studies efficiently. Clark's failure to do so need not detract from his books as highly scholarly individual studies of regions, but it does seriously limit their significance as a set bearing upon their proclaimed common topic. Had he been able to complete more of his projected series one might speculate that he would have been ready to generalize about his findings, but there is much evidence in his writings to suggest otherwise.

VI

In the final chapter of *Acadia* Clark does briefly relate his work to some grand historiographic theses on American development, but he reiterates that

---

27 William A. Koelsch in *Economic Geography* 46 (1970): 202

'scholarly prudence does not allow broad generalizations from the few such studies yet undertaken in North America' (p. 380). *Scholarly prudence* – the more one examines the whole body of Clark's work, the more that phrase seems to resound as a key to an understanding of his career, the direction of his development, and the reasons for the sharp criticism he began to encounter in his last years.

It is interesting and instructive to have Clark's own description of how he happened upon his first major research topic. When he went to New Zealand he had hoped to find some sort of land use problem similar to that on which he had begun to work in Maritime Canada. However, nothing attractive or feasible seemed apparent until 'one day I listened to a bitter informal debate between two well-informed New Zealand scholars, one an Anglophile and the other an Anglophobe, as to the net effect of British influence on New Zealand. Both partisans took for granted that New Zealand was virtually a second Britain ... they differed as to the desirability of this fact.'

When Clark spoke of this similarity which had been produced in so short a time between two countries half a world away as a topic worth investigating, these and other colleagues tried to discourage him. 'To them no such problem existed. It had been intended, some said, to establish a Britain of the South Seas and it had been done. The climatic similarity, insisted the environmental determinists, required a parallelism of development. More than 95% of the people were of original British stock, others pointed out, and had simply transported their culture with them.' Drawing thus upon general theories either of environmental determinism or 'unilinear cultural descent,' they told him that he would be 'wasting time on such a study.' But Clark felt that he had '... just enough knowledge of the history of land use ... to be extremely doubtful of these easy explanations. Indeed, the real problem seemed to be the maintenance [of], or eventual arrival at, similarity with so many factors seeming to work in the opposite direction. With the conviction that a satisfactory answer to the problem had not been given, I resolved to study it from a geographical viewpoint.'[28] His study offered an answer not in the form of a better general theory but in a conclusion based upon a careful examination of field and archival evidence relating to cultural diffusion in a very specific historical and geographical context.[29]

28 'Field Research in Historical Geography,' 17
29 A summary of his conclusion is presented in his first professional paper, 'The Historical Explanation of Land Use in New Zealand,' *Journal of Economic History* 5 (1945): 215-30. Relating his approach to his own background I might characterize it as the methods of Carl Sauer and Harold Innis (whom Clark described as 'one of the great empiricists of our time') correcting the kind of facile determinism characteristic of Griffith Taylor.

One of his earliest papers read before the Association of American Geographers, entitled 'Legend and Fact in Historical Geography' (1948), was a similar kind of refutation of a simplistic environmentalist interpretation of the history of the Lunenburg colonists in Nova Scotia.[30] This subjection of standard 'easy explanations' of man-environment relationships to fresh scrutiny became a strong pattern in the Clarkian approach to historical geography, most notably represented by several of the dissertations done under his guidance. The published studies of Merrens, Harris, Lemon, Jordan, and Hilliard are good examples. They are a form of geographic critique in which long-held general interpretations in history are replaced by detailed expositions of the complexities of processes and local circumstances. In each case it is the geographer working intensively with the documents and in the field to make his own kind of locational and environmental analyses who provides the corrective. Such studies play an important role in the vitality of scholarship, and these in particular have helped to bind American historical geography solidly to history and gain it recognition as a respected dimension of the larger field.

A strong overt scepticism about generalization becomes a recurring refrain in Clark's writing. Very early we find him stating that 'generalisations which are not almost self-evident truths would seem to be highly speculative.'[31] In his contribution to the landmark symposium on 'Man's Role in Changing the Face of the Earth' he explicitly restricted his commentary to regions with which he was personally acquainted; he was critical of many common assumptions about processes of change ('we really do not have the evidence to be as dogmatic as we have [sounded] ... '); and he concluded that the topic of man's impact upon New World grasslands was so complex, so varied from region to region, and so inadequately studied that 'few generalizations can be drawn.'[32] This is 'scholarly prudence,' but it also reflects a view of 'generalization' as a conclusion, an end rather than a means. Furthermore, although he referred to such broad 'historiographic theses' as those of Innis and Turner as 'frames of reference,' he seems to have treated them more as formal hypotheses to be proven or

---

30 'Legend and Fact in Historical Geography: An Illustration from Nova Scotia,' *Annals of the Association of American Geographers* 38 (1948): 85-6. The 'legend' was that these Rhenish agricultural people dumped in an inhospitable environment turned to the rich seas for their livelihood. The 'fact,' according to Clark, was much more complex; they did develop some agriculture, and they did not abandon farming 'to embrace the fisheries at the firm beck of the environment.'

31 'South Island, New Zealand and Prince Edward Island, Canada: A Study of Insularity,' *New Zealand Geographer* 3 (1947): 150

32 'The Impact of Exotic Invasion on the Remaining New World Mid-latitude Grasslands,' in William L. Thomas, Jr., ed., *Man's Role in Changing the Face of the Earth* (Chicago 1956), 738, 755

disproven. Thus he insisted that Acadia was 'one of the segments of reality which any historiographic theory must accommodate' (p. 383). Because neither the 'metropolitan' nor the 'frontier' thesis (the two 'interpretive formulas that would seem most likely to be appropriate' to an eastern Canadian region) could adequately account for the Acadian case, a new formulation was needed, one which would include 'a fully adequate representation of the parameters of cultural inheritance ... Nor will such a model be comprehensively useful until it is so constructed as to take fully into account ... the locational co-ordinates of the phenomena it considers ...' (pp. 392-3). There is no hint that he would himself attempt such a formulation. Quite the contrary, for he was convinced that 'no amount of argument, in itself, is as likely to convince the thoughtful and informed reader as the clearest possible record of what happened ...' (p. 394).

VII

The tenor and tone of Clark's treatment of this issue in *Acadia* made him the target of an unusually harsh attack from two critics within geography. William A. Koelsch used the book to conjure an 'intellectual crisis in historical geography,' while Hugh C. Prince cited Clark's works prominently among some others to assert rather stridently the 'inadequacies of inductivism,' and it was probably Clark's insistence on 'the clearest possible record' and on the need for any theory to encompass that record which caused Prince to exclaim in some exasperation that 'The more fully and precisely the facts are known the more certain is the conclusion that no interpretation will exactly fit them.'[33]

Clark was stung by these comments, and his responses help to define his mature views of geography as a field, of the main role and value of historical geography, and of himself and his work. He now spoke of himself as fundamentally a regional geographer and interpreted these attacks as posing 'the place of regional historical study' as 'the most critical question for historical geography.' He agreed that scholars must 'search for broad generalisations (models, theory),' but that quest should not lead them 'to disparage the ordering of information in substantial, broad empirical studies.' Regional studies provide 'the indispensable contextual matrix from which more theoretical generalising concepts can emerge.'[34]

Such a rejoinder was an appropriate expression of his own predilections, but it could hardly serve as a prescription for a field. If the issue were simply the old

33 Koelsch in *Economic Geography* 46 (1970): 202; Prince, 'Real, Imagined and Abstract Worlds of the Past,' *Progress in Geography* 3 (1971): 23
34 'Historical Geography in North America,' 131, 132

'inductive versus deductive' argument, we might dismiss it as an assumed polarity that can only reasonably be seen as a complementarity. But the issue was not quite so clear-cut. Clark and his critics did not have a very effective dialogue on these matters because they differed fundamentally as to purpose and priority in their scholarship, and neither partly really understood, nor perhaps respected, the position of the other.

It seems clear that for Clark historical geography was part of a larger world of historical and geographical scholarship devoted to the study of times and places. The generalizations he was most concerned with were those relating to specific eras and areas. Generalizations were basically a matter of scale; they were larger patterns discernible when one took an overview of more local studies.[35] A major role of the historical geographer was to test the validity of broad historiographic generalizations against the detailed evidence of case studies. If the generalization was not supported by the case study, it was an impediment to be cast aside en route towards the goal of 'improved interpretation and a more acceptable larger synthesis.'[36] Such a view reflected 'a deep suspicion of historicism' and a conviction that the aim of history and geography was towards ever better understanding of the characteristics of specific times and places.

His critics were measuring his studies and his statements in a very different context. For them geography was primarily part of a larger realm of social science, not of history. Thus Koelsch rather contemptuously dismissed Clark's relation of *Acadia* to the theses of Turner and Innis because 'the interpretation of history is not, one would think, the primary concern of the geographer,' and Prince declared that studies which served 'only to demonstrate the inaccuracy of previous interpretations' were of little interest because they only resulted in an impasse.[37] The generalizations that these critics admired were hypotheses, theories, and laws of human behaviour. For them the overriding concern of geography must be to enlarge and perfect the body of such formulations; and studies of specific times and places were of significance only in so far as they could be articulated to that purpose.

35 His essays in the Jobberns and Evans *Festschriften* — 'Geographical Diversity and the Personality of Canada,' in M. McCaskill, ed., *Land and Livelihood: Geographical Essays in Honour of George Jobberns* (Christchurch 1962), 23-47, and 'The Canadian Habitat,' in R.H. Buchanan, Emrys Jones, and Desmond McCourt, eds., *Man and His Habitat* (London 1971), 218-46 — and that which he co-authored with Donald Q. Innis in the compendium prepared for the centennial of Confederation — 'The Roots of Canada's Geography,' in J. Warkentin, ed., *Canada: A Geographical Interpretation* (Toronto 1968), 13-53 — contain many examples of this kind of generalization.

36 'First Things First,' in Ralph E. Ehrenberg, ed., *Pattern and Process: Research in Historical Geography* (Washington, DC 1975), 12

37 Koelsch in *Economic Geography* 46 (1970): 202; Prince, 'Worlds of the Past,' 23

In the search for social science theory it may often be true, as Prince insisted, that 'large collections of facts' may become 'a barrier to new ways of approaching' a problem. It may also be true, as Clark retorted, that 'to arbitrarily restrict oneself to very limited categories of information ... may lead to a logically disastrous kind of special pleading.'[38] But such paradoxes and dangers are inherent in the very nature of scholarly activity. They need not be distorted into a disparagement of facts or an unwillingness to theorize. Published in 1968, *Acadia* was caught up in the intense swirl of unprecedented discussion and dissension relating to these issues. In the heat of such battles the one side is apt to speak rather contemptuously of 'the current fad' among the 'newest wave' of geographers,[39] the other to talk pretentiously about 'newer paradigms' and 'methodological cutting edges.'[40]

The real issue in this wrangle was not *Acadia* so much as Andrew Clark. His very strength and stature in the field, his repeated pronouncements about major themes and methods and the role of the historical geographer, made him the obvious main target for those who saw such things differently. That there was a growing number who did so was partly a result of the prosperity of the field for which he could take more credit than anyone else. The sheer growth in numbers and vitality of historical geography almost inevitably meant a greater diversity in outlook and interest and a lessened possibility for any one person to be so clearly the leader of the whole. But it must also be said that Clark generated some such criticism by the direction of his work and his definition of the goals he set for geography as well as for himself. His books were major regional studies conceived as being at once individual and comparative in purpose. But his 'scholarly prudence' had kept him from pursuing vigorously these purposes in balanced fashion, and as he more and more insisted on the primacy of regional geography and on synthesis as the ultimate goal of the whole field he was ever more firmly aligning himself with one side of the contending forces which emerged so strongly during his later years. Thus it was quite impossible for him to be the spokesman for American historical geography in the early 1970s to the degree that he had been in the 1950s.[41]

---

38 'Historical Geography in North America,' 137
39 *Ibid.*
40 Koelsch in *Economic Geography* 46 (1970): 202
41 For further treatment of such issues cf. Prince, 'Worlds of the Past,' R.C. Harris, 'Theory and Synthesis in Historical Geography,' *Canadian Geographer* 15 (1971): 157-72, and Baker, *Progress in Historical Geography.* An excellent succinct statement is David Ward, 'The Debate on Alternative Approaches in Historical Geography,' *Historical Methods Newsletter* 8 (1975): 82-7.

Furthermore, Clark's concept of 'geographical change,' which by repeated enunciation and demonstration he had made synonymous with his kind of historical geography, came under critical scrutiny. He often applied the term very generally to a variety of studies. It was his way of emphasizing that the main purpose of historical geography was not to reconstruct the geography of an area at some particular time (which had been the main emphasis of Ralph H. Brown) but to see human geography as an ever-changing thing. But he also made clear in several careful expositions that he considered the most effective method for such study was to focus on 'the geographical structure of change' which revealed differences in the patterns of phenomena between one time and another. Hence the map was his main tool, as exhibited in the major display of his method in *Three Centuries and the Island*. These maps show distributions of specific phenomena and of combinations of phenomena (usually expressed in ratios, such as of sheep to swine) at selected dates, and amounts of change between these dates. The accompanying text provides extensive discussion of contexts and some discussion of processes of change, and his knowledge of the geography and history of the island was so rich that his explications seem very satisfying. Koelsch hailed the book as 'an experiment in method' which 'makes obsolete the pedantic distinction between "static" and "dynamic" approaches in historical geography.'[42]

But can that distinction be so readily dissolved? Clark seems to have very often used 'geographical change,' 'geography of change,' and 'changing geographies' as interchangeable terms. But while they are in some sense interdependent they would not seem to be entirely synonymous. His sequences of maps are depictions of quantities of change in selected phenomena and of changes in certain features of the geography of the island between two dates, but none of the maps deals directly with the actual dynamics of change. They do not depict movements in space, such as the spread of a people or a crop. His New Zealand study was more directly focused on the 'invasion' of people, plants, and animals, and one chapter is devoted to the 'flow of settlement,' but the book contains no maps of such diffusions. Which is not to say that Clark was wrong in what he did, only that his exposition of 'geographical change' seems limited to a study of certain periodic results of change. As Prince notes, the Clarkian approach is basically morphological and structural—it measures amounts of change *between* times but it does not deal directly with change *through* time. The latter requires an understanding of the processes of change, of how migration and diffusion operate. Such understandings must come from behavioural, social, and natural

42 In *Economic Geography* 36 (1960): 92-3

science and presumably those with a research interest in geographical change might hope to contribute to those understandings.[43]

Such studies would lead towards hypothesis and theory, but Clark, as we might expect, was headed in the opposite direction. In his description of 'geographical change' as a theme for economic historians he warned that valuable as his type of sequential cross-sectional studies could be for their work, 'It is axiomatic to the geographer that any interpretation of the location of economic change, or the change of economic location, will be partial and dubious unless it goes hand in hand with similar studies of the regionalization of physical, political, social and cultural change.'[44] In other words, the study of change must ever be done in the full context of regional geography. Clearly Clark was much more interested in *area* than in *process*, and thus it probably would have been better had he made a clearer distinction and represented his studies as being more concerned with *changing geographies* than with *geographical change*. What might have seemed a minor semantic difference in the 1950s had become an issue of major methodological and programmatic concern in the 1960s.

VIII

In the final paragraph of *Three Centuries and the Island* Clark noted that his detailed analysis of Prince Edward Island had not been undertaken simply because it was a convenient laboratory for the testing of an hypothesis and the exposition of a method. He confessed that throughout his interpretations there ran 'threads of keen personal interest in the island, long familiarity with it and a deep and abiding affection for it' (p. 223). A major purpose was to help his readers to appreciate better the qualities of the place and especially to help those who like himself had personal connections with it to understand 'what we are a little better through a clearer view of what we have been.' In the last paragraph of the preface (p. vii) he had already written vividly of his own ties and memories:

The writer has spent many happy summers on the island since he was a small boy and has wandered over most of its highways and byways. Both of his parents and

---

43 'Worlds of the Past,' 23-4. Also see Alan Baker's opening chapter 'Rethinking Historical Geography,' in *Progress in Historical Geography*, 11-28, and especially the comments of Paul Wheatley on the 'Clarkian' view of change, quoted on p. 15. Louis Gentilcore in his review of *Acadia* noted that despite Clark's repeated reference to processes of geographical change, the processes were 'difficult to extract' from the text as they were given no explicit identity or treatment. *Geographical Review* 60 (1970): 451-3
44 'Geographical Change,' 612

three of his grandparents were Islanders born and his roots are as deeply set in its red soil as those of any of its English-speaking sons. With all of the concern with detailed statistics and precise locations the burden of the work was ever made lighter by a host of happy memories: days at sea with the cod or lobster fishermen, digging clams in the sandy mud of its estuaries at low tide, watching Wednesday-afternoon harness races on the little oval tracks, tucking into the unbelievably luscious fare of 'strawberry festivals,' of listening to ... the High-landers ... or the blurred patois of *les Acadiens*, or happily (in retrospect at least) joining with the enlarged family in singing hymns to the accompaniment of wheezing pedal organs in the little white churches on Sunday mornings.

As he would later write, much of the motivation and reward for intensive regional investigation came from 'the tremendous satisfaction of feeling that one has gotten under the skin of such a region and has at his command enough detailed knowledge of it ... to identify the more important individual threads of its character.'[45]

All of these statements sound more like a human being writing about life than a geographer striving to advance science. To explore the soil of one's own roots, to find reflective satisfactions in one's understanding of and feeling for the personality of a place, to seek to touch the lives of others by enhancing their sense of time and place is to put geography to a humane purpose.

It was characteristic of this large-hearted and appreciative man that on the special occasion when his fellow geographers invited him to speak his mind on whatever he would most like to share with the profession as a whole he chose not to display his latest research, or to make a solemn pronouncement on the state of the field, or in more than prefatory remarks to insist once more on the necessity for historical geography but to offer instead 'a sermon of thanksgiving' on the great good fortune of being a geographer. Clark's presidential address to the fifty-eighth annual meeting of the Association of American Geographers at Miami Beach on 25 April, 1962 was an evocation of his own pleasures and an invitation to all of his colleagues to reflect and be glad for those rich 'premiums' of knowledge, craftsmanship, service, and reflective imagination which ought to accrue naturally from their profession.[46] It was a celebration of geography as a vocation, in the older sense of a calling as well as a livelihood, a life in which business and pleasure were 'inevitably and inextricably intertwined.' His broad learning, his catholic taste for the full rich heritage of the field, his avid interest

45 *'Praemia Geographiae,'* 234
46 *Ibid.*

in the whole wide world of mankind were vividly apparent in this, his appropriately most idiosyncratic statement.

'*Praemia Geographiae*' will endure. Shunted aside by those who are concerned only to trace the lineage of ideas and search for clues of new paradigms, it will be rediscovered time and again by geographers who feel in their bones that same calling or have already shared in those same premiums. Someday American geography may attain sufficient security as a discipline and maturity as a field to foster a wider interest in its leaders as persons as well as purveyors of ideas. That will be a recognition that ideas and intellectual controversies about them have simultaneously an independent life and significance and a direct connection with the personalities and intimate human circumstances of the individuals who express them. '*Praemia geographiae*' will then become valued as a major document showing not so much what geography was thought to be as what it was like to be a geographer.

In March of 1974 Clark spoke at a symposium on 'The Humanistic Tradition in Geography' sponsored by the department at the University of Michigan. Not published until two years after his death, the paper now seems a fitting last testament.[47]

It is a very personal statement, in considerable degree an apologia in which he explains that a concern for methodology was 'neither an enthusiasm nor a forte' of his but something thrust upon him, in part by the sudden death of others (Brown and Whittlesey) and otherwise conscientiously assumed as a necessary burden: 'for what has seemed to me like rather a long time, as one of the corporal's guard of historiographically minded historical geographers in North America, and one of the few such making a major effort to train scholars and encourage scholarly efforts in that sub-discipline, I almost inescapably have been drawn, from time to time, into the methodological lists. I don't think my efforts have been particularly successful because, among other handicaps, my heart never really was in them.'[48]

There is a poignancy in that confession, but the overall tone of his remarks is one of characteristic tolerance and generosity. Noting that some of his fellow

---

47 'The Whole Is Greater Than the Sum of Its Parts: A Humanistic Element in Human Geography.' I have worked from a copy of his speech rather than the version edited for publication.

48 *Ibid.*, 3. He speaks of having been 'drawn in as a last-minute substitute' for Ralph Brown to head the committee on historical geography for *American Geography: Inventory & Prospect*, and that he 'again was drafted as a replacement' after the sudden death of Derwent Whittlesey, editor of the AAG Monograph Series, and spent nearly a year working with Richard Hartshorne on the first monograph, *Perspective on the Nature of Geography.*

geographers had challenged 'the whole genre of substantive work of the kind in which I have been engaged,' he nevertheless observed that 'it would be a moribund discipline indeed, in which internal dialogue was not bubbling with the constant ferment of new and conflicting ideas,' and that he would permit his 'hackles to rise' only when enthusiasts demanded rigid narrow limits as to what geographers must teach and practise.

The remainder of the paper deals with the topic of regional synthesis, of what it is and how it might be developed more effectively. His principal recommendation was to emulate some of the rules and procedures of literary and art criticism and he drew briefly upon his own recent experience with a major exhibition of Canadian landscape paintings. To celebrate the occasion of this unprecedented assemblage at the Elvehjem Art Center in Madison, Clark was invited along with an art curator, an historian, and two literary critics to make an attempt at relating the seventy-four paintings to 'the cultural identity of Canada.' He responded with obvious pleasure. His brief paper, 'The Look of Canada,' marks a new stage in his efforts to comprehend that country.[49] It is an avowedly personal interpretation, intermittently anecdotal, relaxing 'scholarly prudence' to draw upon a lifetime of experience and reflection to reach imaginatively for some grasp of the personality of Canada. It is far from a finished work and it offers no demonstration of a method for synthesis, but it does display a direction he was finding increasingly attractive.

If, in his later years, the grand project of comparative studies had faded, the chewing over of methodological matters had lost its savour, and the burden of leadership had become a bit uncomfortable, the zest of the man for the richness, the sheer joy of being a geographer, never waned. Furthermore, the presence, the challenge, of Canada was ever there. If we now set aside his more programmatic statements about his own work and about historical geography in general, we can perhaps best interpret his career as one anchored upon his continual fascination with and love for his native land. In describing his own filters through which he viewed that collection of paintings he stated that although his legal residence has been outside of Canada for more than thirty-five years, he had actually spent more days of his life in Canada than out of it, and in his mature years was spending as many weeks there as he could, especially in the only home he owned, on his beloved Minaki island astride the great historic waterway west in the woods of westernmost Ontario. He began his field studies in a small corner of the Maritimes, and except for the early interlude in New

49 I have worked from a copy of the typescript of his speech. The catalogue of the exhibition is *Canadian Landscape Painting, 1670-1930*, text and catalogue by R.H. Hubbard (Madison 1973).

Zealand all of his scholarly research was focused on Canada. Two monumental books, a dozen articles on other topics, half a dozen more general pieces, and an expanding academic role in Canadian studies were all part of that 'profound satisfaction' which he described as deriving from 'the deepest possible familiarity with individual areas and places,'[50] and all converged towards that grasp for the whole, 'the ultimate goal' of geography and history.

Few American geographers have had as productive and influential an academic life as Andrew Clark. And few geographers can have got more pleasure from their calling or radiated it so widely and warmly to others. His work endures, but for those who knew him well the stronger legacy will be the memory of the man himself. For the whole was so very much more than the sum of his academic parts that we shall often reflect that Andrew Hill Clark was the finest example we have known of what he himself had so vividly described[51] as that

special, indispensable class
of educated man,
the geographers.

50 *Praemia Geographiae,* 234
51 *Ibid.*, 232

R. COLE HARRIS

The extension of France
into rural Canada

The condition of rural life in the middle-latitude New World colonies of Europe in the seventeenth and to some extent in the eighteenth centuries presented a fundamental geographical contrast with the mother countries that depended less on differences in climate, flora, fauna, or topography than on the availability of land. Indigenous populations, usually hunters and gatherers, could be pushed aside and vast stretches of new territory opened for settlement. If a forest had to be cleared, sod broken, or marshes drained, this racking labour was usually accomplished; farmland became available and, in comparison with European land, it was relatively cheap. Although land was cheap, European markets were far away, and in the seventeenth century European agricultural prices were generally low and falling. Local markets in recently settled colonies were meagre. In these conditions the farmland that Europeans in the seventeenth century slowly won from new middle-latitude settings overseas became less a cog in a commercial economy than a place for ordinary Europeans to live. It was a setting in which European material life and social values would be reproduced but, given the sudden availability of land and the characteristic weakness of the agricultural market, reproduced in drastically simplified and relatively egalitarian societies. In the eighteenth century the rate of European population growth increased, agricultural prices improved, colonial populations grew, and markets for New World grain and animal products became larger and more lucrative. Agricultural land values rose, agriculture became more centrally commercial, and socio-economic differentiation increased as those in position to take advantage of rising land prices and improved markets did so. But even in the eighteenth century there were pockets of New World settlement where land was relatively cheap and agricultural markets poor. South Africa beyond the Cape was one such setting, much of the westward fringe of New England and the Middle Colonies was perhaps another, and Canada, its tiny population isolated in the interior of a continent and along the climatic margin of wheat cultivation, was a third.

The relationship between society and land in France and in early Canada could hardly have been more different. The France from which a few thousand people emigrated to Canada was densely settled, old, overwhelmingly rural, and profoundly local. There were almost twenty million French people, 90 per cent of them rural; the population density averaged almost forty per square kilometre. Although there had been some fairly recent reclearing of land abandoned during the Hundred Years War, most farmland had been worked for at least four hundred years. Village churches were more likely to be Romanesque than Gothic, and many village houses were also several centuries old. Houses in villages a few miles apart often reflected quite different local styles, each part of a material culture that was the legacy of a long past of a life *in situ*. Whereas intricate networks of cart roads and paths served local areas, ordinary people who did not live close to navigable water were isolated from most outside goods and people by the high cost of overland travel. Life was contained within a web of inherited local custom, some of it codified in *coutumes*, more acquired orally, much transmitted unconsciously by example. Custom differentiated place from place, creating the innumerable *pays* of rural France – those 'medals struck in the image of a people,' the products of retrospective rural societies each living in a restricted territory for a long, long time.[1]

In this old France land was still the basis of wealth and status. Almost everyone who lived in the countryside, even the artisan and the merchant, worked or controlled a little land. The peasants, the great bulk of the people of France, supported not only themselves and their families but also the small minority of prosperous and wealthy Frenchmen. An oppressive royal tax, the *taille*, that bore particularly on the peasantry, furnished half of the national revenue. Peasants' tithes supported abbeys and priories, while seigneurial charges of many kinds supported an increasingly effete nobility whose high living frequently led them into debt to an urban bourgeoisie – the careful managers and unbending creditors to whom many seigneuries were forfeited. Even this

---

1 These and subsequent remarks on seventeenth-century France are drawn principally
   from the following: Fernand Braudel, ed., *Histoire économique et sociale de la France*
   (Paris 1970), 2; Pierre Goubert, *The Ancien Regime: French Society, 1600-1750*
   (London 1973); and Fernand Braudel, *Capitalism and Material Life, 1400-1800* (New
   York 1975).

increasingly dynamic and powerful bourgeoisie was characteristically tied to land by the country houses it visited in summer, by its revenue from seigneuries and rotures, or by the many loans to peasants and seigneurs that would be turned eventually into cash or land. In this sharply stratified society to be landless was to be virtually without position, a beggar, *déclassé*. Day labourers clung to their garden patches. At the other end of the spectrum the king, as the seigneur from whom all seigneuries were held, was the ultimate landholder. This would not soon be an industrial country; the strength of seventeenth-century France lay in the peasant masses who worked a land that was scarce and valuable, avidly sought, and tenaciously held.

For Frenchmen the interminable Canadian land was wilderness – land without social meaning, without boundaries, and valueless except as it was cleared. The shock of the encounter with such land drove many soldiers and *engagés* (indentured servants) back to France when their terms of service expired. Most of those who stayed in a colony where the labour requirements of the fur trade were soon satisfied took up the lifelong work of clearing and farming as they found French purpose for, and imposed French meaning on, an alien land. There was no reason why they should not think and act in French terms. No radical ideas had propelled them across the Atlantic. Apart from the Indians with whom few settlers were in regular contact, no new population injected different ways of life. Officials administered Canada as an overseas enclave of France. Yet those who farmed along the lower St Lawrence would not reproduce the French rural landscape, if only because in Canada land for agricultural expansion would long be available for the ordinary person. The availability of land broke French rural life out of the restrictions inherent in its fixed landed base and created conditions in which one element of a French legacy – the independent nuclear family on its own land – would be accentuated while others would atrophy.

This basic geographical contrast between a Europe where land was scarce and expensive, and a New World colony where it was not, lasted in Canada through several generations, for whom agricultural markets were poor and agricultural prices were low. There was time to establish a European society within these conditions, time for it to acquire a tradition. The human landscape that began to emerge along the St Lawrence River near Quebec and Montreal in the middle of the seventeenth century was carved out of the fringe of the Canadian Shield in the middle of the nineteenth century. At the heart of this landscape was the farmhouse on a long lot – farm after similar farm in a row along river or road. Each of these farms was the setting for the life of a family, and the circumstances of one family were much like those of another. A setting where land was cheap and markets were poor had provided an admirable base for the expansion of the self-reliant, nuclear household, with very ordinary people establishing families on their own land, and had weakened or eliminated all other elements of the social heritage of French rural life. French rural society had been pared down to a simple remainder not because a fragment of it had crossed the Atlantic but because conditions in rural Canada had exerted strong selective pressures.

THE FRENCH BACKGROUND OF IMMIGRANTS TO CANADA

Except in Brittany and in parts of the Auvergne, regions from which almost no settlers came to Canada, the nuclear family was the basic unit of French rural life in the seventeenth century. The ideal of rural life, approached by only a few prosperous farmers, was a family secure in its own house and in control of lands yielding enough to avoid debt – in short, a peasant family able to *vivre de la sienne.*[2] For most peasants such independence was quite unrealizable. There were too many people on too little land, agricultural technology was too inflexible, and the exactions of royal treasury, seigneury, and church weighed too heavily on them. Inevitably the ideal was compromised. At worst the family was driven off the land and scattered in a drifting population of beggars. More commonly sons and daughters left home at an early age to become day labourers, apprentices, or servants. In much of France collective constraints on individual agricultural freedom, imposed by the village community, protected the individual family's access to pasture. Access to stubble fields after harvest *(vaine pâture)* and to common pastures and waste lands was closely regulated so that each peasant family might support a cow, perhaps a few sheep. In places, and at times of particular poverty, constraints such as these loomed larger; where life was a little easier the constraints were relaxed, and the family assumed more independence. The primacy of the family could be strikingly expressed on the landscape in the form of the dispersed farmstead, but even where, as in most of France, rural settlement was still agglomerated, the family often closed itself in behind the thick walls of its house, offering a latched door but not a window to the village street and opening out only into its own interior yard. French civil law, too, in all its local variety, built legal walls around the rights and responsibilities of members of the nuclear family.

The essential support of the family was the garden, often tiny, always enclosed, virtually a part of the house to which it was attached; together with farm buildings it went under a single name: *mazure* in Normandy, *mas* in

2 Pierre Goubert, 'Les cadres de la vie rurale,' in Braudel, *Histoire*, 88-9

Languedoc.[3] Apart from cereals the garden produced the bulk of the household's foodstuffs – its vegetables, fruits, and poultry, unless they had to be sold to pay debts. In the garden flax, hemp, or even a few vines might be grown, their products intended partly for sale. This crucial, heavily manured plot paid no tithe, only the seigneurial *cens*. For most peasants the garden was more nearly their own land than any other, an enclosed patch where members of the family could plant, harvest, and experiment as they wished. In much of northern France the arable, on the other hand, was worked in a three-course rotation, and individual holdings, scattered unenclosed within large open fields, were subject to the rhythm of the prevailing rotation and were opened to general pasture when the harvest was in. Pastures were few and small, animals scarce, fields underfertilized, and yields low, seldom more than five or six units of grain for each sown, often much less. Most families depended upon the collective regulation of arable and pasture for their survival, and only a prosperous few managed to enclose their land, thereby removing it from some form of collective control. In western France pastures were larger and more numerous, and there were more animals. Here, where standards of living were somewhat higher, many peasants worked their own, enclosed fields, but even the owners of enclosed fields usually depended upon commons in marshes, sparse forests, or wastes nearby. Few peasant families were able to extend the independence that they enjoyed in their gardens over the whole of their agricultural activities. The more prosperous were the more independent. The poor accepted the collective constraints that enabled them, without nearly enough land of their own, to exist on the land.

In all areas and among all peasants it was a struggle to acquire enough land to support the family. Usually the peasantry controlled less than half of the village land, the rest being in the hands of noblemen, churchmen, or the bourgeoisie, who let it to the peasants in various forms of leasehold or sharecropping. The land that the peasants did hold was divided very unequally. In most villages only two or three peasant families controlled enough arable to support a team of horses and a heavy plough. These families of *laboureurs*, well under 10 per cent of the peasantry, held enough land to live on. Most families had far less than the twenty to twenty-five acres that in a three-course rotation, and after many charges, would supply bread for the subsistence needs of a family. These peasants usually depended upon some form of collective control of arable and pasture, and upon supplementary work or rented land. The poorest became artisans, sharecroppers, or day labourers working for *laboureurs* or for tenant farmers on the large estates. Those who were a little better off rented land to

3 *Ibid.*, 92-3

increase their arable, and a handful of tenant farmers became *gros fermiers* (prosperous tenant farmers) on large estates, and they were the most prosperous of all the peasantry. But these arrangements – the sharecropping whereby the landowner supplied seed, stock, and tools and took half of the product, the renting of leaseholds for usually three, six, or nine years for fixed sums that amounted to about a quarter of the produce, and even the day labouring, which was commonly a means of repaying advances of seed or the use of a team and plough – created their own lines of dependence and, often, their debts. When the harvest was good, the year's charges might be paid; when it was not, debts accumulated, and most peasant families lived under a burden of debt that approached the value of their land and threatened the basis of their livelihood.

Other charges pressed in on the peasant family. Royal taxes – the *taille* and the *gabelle* (salt tax) – took 20 per cent of its gross product. Tithes varied, a tenth here, a twelfth there, usually about 8 per cent and always collected in kind in the field after the harvest. Seigneurial charges varied even more. In Beauvais they were low, about 4 per cent;[4] elsewhere they were usually much higher. In many ecclesiastical seigneuries, and in those cleared relatively recently, *censitaires* (*cens* payers) usually paid a *champart*, an exorbitant charge that amounted to a second tithe. Together all of these charges took a third to a half of the peasant's gross product. In addition, rent for leased land had to be paid, and at least 20 per cent of the grain had to be kept for seed. Even in good years little enough was left.

Living on the edge of misery, deeply in debt, always faced with the spectre of loss of land, the peasant family could count on little outside support. In principle the seigneur was the master of the village, and in the seventeenth century there were still seigneurs who interceded at court on behalf of their peasants, who supported peasant revolts against the crown, and who recruited soldiers from among their dependents. In these cases there were still personal bonds, often of considerable affection, between peasant and seigneur. But the seigneur or his appointee was also judge in the seigneurial court, even of cases in which he was also a plaintiff, and he was invariably a creditor. Especially as the bourgeoisie displaced the older seigneurial nobility, the seigneurial system became increasingly a fiscal system, a source of heavy charges for the *censitaire* and of revenue for the seigneur. The *curé* was usually far closer to the peasants than the seigneur. Cultivating a little land, probably the offspring of a *laboureur*, he was virtually a peasant. In a society of believers he could be the much loved leader of his parish flock, a man who sometimes sided with the peasants against seigneur or royal official, but who could do little to lighten their burdens, and who taught of duty, obedience, and humility. The *assemblée des habitants*,

---

4 Pierre Goubert, *Beauvais et le Beauvasis de 1600 à 1730* (Paris 1960), 181

usually the principal men of the village, met after Sunday mass to discuss such issues as church maintenance, common or woodcutting regulations, and, above all, the collection of royal taxes, for the *assemblée* had to appoint local tax assessors and collectors and furnish an annual lump sum to a royal collector. In some areas this village plutocracy exercised considerable power, even serving as a focus for anti-seigneurial feeling. More often it was dominated by the seigneur or his bailiff, but even when it functioned independently the *assemblée* could only apportion burdens originating in circumstances far beyond its control. In such circumstances the peasant family had few defences; there could be little upward mobility and always there was some dropping off as the most vulnerable peasant families slipped into the ranks of the perhaps half-million Frenchmen who wandered and begged.

Death or emigration were other escapes. During the peasant revolts in Normandy in the 1830s some of the dying were said to have assured their *curés* that they died in peace knowing that, finally, they would be exempt from the *taille.*[5] Some two hundred thousand French people worked in Spain. Canada was another alternative, but it was so remote and uninviting that few left with the intention of settling there – a few dozen families, and the women from Paris poor houses sent in the 1660s to be brides. In 1634 Robert Giffard had enticed several families from Mortagne in Perche to his Canadian seigneury of Beauport only by offering each of them a thousand arpents (840 acres) of land and part of the harvest from his own farm in Canada.[6] Most men came to Canada under a temporary contract as soldiers or *engagés.* But such contracts were also escapes that drew if not from the beggars at least from the desperately poor in the lowest strata of the peasantry.[7] The majority of immigrants to Canada were people of this sort. When their contract expired or their regiment was recalled many returned to France, but more than half stayed to form the principal male stock of Canada's rural population.[8] There were also bourgeoisie, clerics, and

5 Michel Caillard, 'La révolte des nu-pieds,' in Caillard *et al., A travers la Normandie des XVIIe et XVIIIe siècles* (Caen 1963), 102

6 Caillard notes a contract of 14 March 1634 between Giffard and Jean Guyon and Zacharie Cloutier. *Ibid.,* 102n

7 It can be said, I think, that the very poor but perhaps not quite destitute people whom André Corvisier found to be the principal recruits to the ranks of the French army were also the sort of people who came to Canada. *L'armée française de la fin du XVIIe siècle au ministère de Choiseul* (Paris 1964), 1: 473-506

8 On immigration to Canada, see Louise Dechêne, *Habitants et marchands de Montréal au XVIIe siècle* (Paris and Montreal 1974), chap. 2; R.C. Harris, 'The French Background of Immigration to Canada before 1700,' *Cahiers de géographie du Québec* 16 (Sept. 1972): 313-24; and Gabriel Debien, 'Engagés pour le Canada au XVIIe siècle vus de la Rochelle,' *Revue d'histoire de l'Amérique française* 6 (Sept. 1952): 177-233, 374-404.

people of noble blood among the immigrants to Canada. Considered overall, the immigrant population included almost all the elements of French society – minus, perhaps, the upper echelons of each stratum – but the people who settled the countryside came overwhelmingly from among the nearly destitute and virtually landless.

They came from western France, principally from the old provinces of Aunis, Saintonge, and Poitou in the hinterland of La Rochelle, and from eastern Normandy. A good many of the women came from Paris. In the early years, when Rouen was the principal port of embarkation for Canada, about a quarter of the emigrants were Norman. In 1663 they and their children, together with people from adjacent Perche, formed a third of the Canadian population.[9] Later, as commercial connections shifted to La Rochelle and as regiments that had been recruited in the southwest were sent to Canada, most immigrants came from south of the Loire.

These western lands had seen some of the bitterest peasant revolts in seventeenth-century France. In 1639 ten thousand Norman peasants, rising against increases in the *taille* that were forcing more of them off the land and into debtors' prisons, conducted a guerilla war against royal officials and soldiers until they were brutally put down by the king's army. This was a revolt of *nu-pieds* – the desperate poor against the fiscal exactions of the crown – and it originated in the type of people who predominated among those who went to Canada. Like most of France, these western lands were overpopulated. In spite of increasingly severe regulations that reflected the interests of crown and towns, the peasants had depleted the forest so much that in many areas scarcely a tree was over twenty years old. Land values had risen sharply, and nobles and bourgeoisie sought to control, and then to subdivide and sell, common marshes and wastes. The bourgeoisie had penetrated the countryside at the expense of both nobles and peasants. In many villages and parishes the great majority of peasants were landless day labourers, tenants, or sharecroppers on the estates of the bourgeoisie. Yet this was also the area where the deep-seated individualism of the French peasant, centred on the nuclear family, had found its fullest expression. Long before the right was codified in revisions of the *coutume de Normandie* in 1579 and 1585, Norman peasants had the right to enclose, which meant that they could use their land as they wished without the collective constraints of a common three-course rotation and of *vaine pâturage*. Many peasants lived in dispersed farmsteads amid their own fields. In parts of eastern Normandy fewer than 30 per cent of the farm houses were in villages. Even

9 Marcel Trudel, *La population du Canada en 1663* (Montreal 1973), 49, and *The Beginnings of New France, 1524-1663* (Toronto 1973), 257ff.

where poverty was most acute and settlement was largely agglomerated, there were prosperous *laboureurs* who lived away from the village on their own land. Along the lower Seine, source of many of the earliest emigrants to Canada, and here and there on the limestone plains nearby, dispersed farmsteads were aligned along riverbank or road while their land stretched behind in *terrior en arête de poisson.*[10]

RURAL SETTLEMENT IN CANADA

Most immigrants to Canada came as individuals. In the early years there was an acute shortage of women, but the crown sent almost a thousand women to Canada in the 1660s, and girls in the colony characteristically married at puberty. Later, women married at an average age of twenty or twenty-one, several years under the average age of marriage for their sex in France. These unions created the households of Canada. Even before 1663, when a few seigneurs had brought small groups of immigrants from the same parts of France, only a quarter of Canadian marriages were between people from the same French province.[11] Upsetting the profound localness of French rural life even more than a transatlantic crossing was the mixing from all over western France that took place within the early Canadian household. The effects on accent, tools, diet, clothing, buildings, agricultural methods, and social practices remain to be studied, but there can be no doubt that the overall tendency was towards cultural standardization as the sharp edges of French regional types quickly blurred and merged.[12] And whereas marriage in France took place within sharply defined social categories, thie hierarchy of status must have coarsened in Canada because of the initial difficulty of finding any mate, and because of the impossibility among largely destitute people of establishing their precise social fit in a distant society. Men misrepresented themselves to royal officials – calling themselves *laboureurs* when they had been *journaliers* (day labourers) and *journaliers* when they had hardly worked – and they could be equally dissembling when they married.

Most of the *engagés* and demobilized soldiers who married and settled down in Canada became farmers. The fur trade required a small white labour force.

10 The essential reference on evolving society and land use in Normandy is still Jules Sion's brilliant *Les paysans de la Normandie orientale* (Paris 1909).

11 Trudel, *Beginnings*, 262

12 Professor Dechêne has gone so far as to suggest that the close juxtaposition in Canada of different folk religions, none of them with many Canadian adherents, favoured the penetration of a purer Christianity. *Habitants et marchands*, 479

Very few people living east of Trois-Rivières ever engaged in it; by 1700 no more than 2 per cent of all Canadian men were in the west in any given year, and by 1710 not more than 12 per cent of them had spent a season there.[13] The towns employed relatively few artisans and labourers. Yet most of the people who settled in Canada did so voluntarily. They had no niche to return to in France, whereas there was land in Canada and the prospect of a farm. With not nearly enough wage labour in the colony to support its population, labour was always expensive; its price, because any employer had to pay enough to counteract the alternative of farming, was a measure of the attraction of land. The royal shipyards in Quebec near the end of the French régime paid several times French wages yet had difficulty holding Canadian workers. 'As he is a Canadian,' wrote the intendant Bigot of a worker who wanted to leave a yard, 'he prefers his liberty to being subject to a clock.'[14]

In the villages of coastal Normandy and along the lower Seine early in the eighteenth century a *journalier* worked four days to earn a single livre. A thousand livres bought two or three arpents of arable land.[15] In Canada at the same date a *journalier* earned one and one-half to two livres a day, and a thousand livres would buy an enormous tract of uncleared land – even an unsettled seigneury – or a farm lot with some fifteen cleared arpents, a one-room cabin, barn, and stable, and sixty arpents of forest. To generalize broadly, wages were at least five times higher in Canada than in France, and the price of cleared land in Canada, even after the high labour cost of clearing it, was five to ten times lower. Uncleared land, valuable in France, was almost worthless in Canada. A parcel of arable land that could be earned by a year's work in Canada might not be earned in a lifetime in France. In Canada almost any man could obtain a forested lot at any time.

Throughout the French régime seigneurs conceded farm lots without initial charge. Because a forested lot would not produce its first small crop until at least eighteen months after clearing began, a destitute immigrant might begin by renting a partially cleared lot that he would pay for with up to a third or half of its harvest. This was a temporary arrangement. The tenant also obtained a lot *en roture*. If crops on his tenancy were good, he might be able to hire a man to begin clearing his own land; at least he could hope to quit the tenancy with the

---

13 Much the best discussion of the habitant's involvement in the fur trade is *ibid.*, 218-25.

14 Quoted by Jacques Mathieu in *La construction navale royale à Québec, 1739-1759* (Quebec 1971), 57

15 For figures on the value of land and labour in Normandy in the early eighteenth century, see Philippe Guillot, 'Etude économique et sociale du front de côte entre Orne et Seulles,' in Caillard *et al., A travers la Normandie*, 324-31.

means to survive the first years of clearing. Permanent tenant farmers were uncommon except near Montreal and Quebec and on some seigneurial domains.[16] Sooner or later most immigrants settled on their own farm lots. Sometimes they were no more than forty to fifty arpents in size, more commonly eighty to 120 arpents of land,[17] which in the first years were cleared at a rate of some two arpents annually and then more slowly as farm work demanded more time. After a lifetime of work a man might have thirty or forty arpents of arable and pasture and hold twice as much forest. Often he would have acquired additional lots for his sons, one of whom would take over the family farm, gradually paying off his brothers and sisters for their equal shares in the inheritance.

In this way immigrants who left France in poverty eventually lived on their own land. The long, thin lots fronting on the river were introduced by immigrants from eastern Normandy (Pierre Deffontaine's surmise was correct[18]) but the more basic introduction from France was agricultural individualism centred on the nuclear family. After an Atlantic crossing, a period as a soldier or an *engagé,* perhaps a few years as a tenant farmer, and the trauma of clearing the forest, the French peasant's craving for enough land to support a family was satisfied on a farm lot along the St Lawrence River.

Immigrants who crossed the Atlantic to Canada moved towards land but away from markets. The crop varieties and livestock breeds of northwestern France that were raised in Canada never penetrated the French market in the seventeenth century, when prices were low, and rarely in the eighteenth century, when prices were better. The West Indies were also remote, twice as far away by water from Quebec as from Boston. Louisbourg, the naval base and fortress built on Cape Breton Island in 1718, provided some market for Canadian agricultural produce, and in the 1720s and 1730s there were fairly regular sales in the West Indies, but in the seventeenth and eighteenth centuries Canada was isolated by a severely continental location from sizeable agricultural markets in the North Atlantic world. Many of the quarter of the Canadian population who lived in the towns kept gardens and livestock, and members of religious orders were supplied directly by domanial farms in church seigneuries. There were regular market days in Quebec, Trois-Rivières, and Montreal. In the fall merchants toured the countryside near Quebec to buy grain. Eventually most habitants sold a little

16 Dechêne calculates that 20 per cent of the farmers on Montreal Island were tenants. *Habitants et marchands,* 279-81
17 Richard Colebrook Harris, *The Seigneurial System in Early Canada: A Geographical Study* (Madison and Quebec 1966), 117-19
18 In *Le rang, type de peuplement rural au Canada français* (Quebec 1953)

grain and perhaps a calf and some butter every year, but farming developed in Canada within a chronically depressed agricultural market. Wheat prices declined from 1650 to 1720, rising only slowly and irregularly thereafter.[19] Land prices were static and, after a flurry of land trading in the 1660s and early 1670s, there were few sales.[20]

For a time the brutality of the confrontation with the forest obscured both the benefits of cheap land and the constrictions of the market. A Canadian farm of fifteen cleared arpents met the bare subsistence needs of a family.[21] Unless a habitant cleared some of the land while he still lived with his parents, unless he hired labour or bought a partially cleared lot, he and his family would struggle to survive for almost a decade. Such people would fall into debt and would face scurvy each winter. A few might get back to France; many would die. Here, as elsewhere, the initial confrontation of European settlers with the land around the fringe of the Canadian Shield was a devastating experience tempered only somewhat in the early, most bitter years by the availability of fuel, fish, and game. But the habitant was warmer in winter than were most peasants in northwestern France, where wood was so scarce and expensive that bake ovens often burned matted straw. Fish and game, to which French peasants had steadily less legal access and which they poached at greater risk, must have saved many settlers from starvation during their first Canadian winters, and they remained an important part of the Canadian diet long after the stumps had rotted in the first clearings.

If the farm family survived long enough to clear twenty-five or thirty arpents, then certainly by the second farm generation living standards had risen above those of most French peasants. In 1712 the royal engineer Gideon de Catalogne noted that in Canada everybody ate the wheaten bread afforded by only the most prosperous peasants in France; and if Peter Kalm exaggerated when he wrote in 1749 that meat was the dietary staple of rural Canada, his remark does indicate something of the surprise of an educated European, familiar with the almost meat-free diets of most European peasants, at the amount of meat consumed by ordinary people in Canada. Canadian farms themselves reveal the improvement. A farm worked by the son of its first occupant would have thirty or forty arpents of cleared land. It produced one hundred bushels of wheat and some peas, oats, and barley and carried one or two horses, probably a pair of oxen, five or six cows, three or four pigs, some poultry, and a few sheep. There was a kitchen garden, some apple trees, and a sizeable woodlot, and there was

19 Dechêne, *Habitants et marchands*, 521
20 Harris, *Seigneurial System*, 57-62, 140-5; Dechêne, *ibid.*, 287-94
21 Harris, *ibid.*, 160

access to the river for fishing and to the forest for hunting.[22] This was unspecialized agriculture, characteristic of subsistent farms, but among the French peasantry only a few *laboureurs* and prosperous tenant farmers possessed more.

Yet Canadian farms did not grow much larger. In some Norman parishes a very few *laboureurs* held two hundred arpents of arable and pasture and owned as many as ten work horses and a hundred sheep.[23] Such men were considerable employers of agricultural labour; often they were creditors and money lenders, and their relative wealth and power set them apart in the rural community. No Canadian habitants worked such farms during the French régime, partly because of partible inheritance but principally because there was no market for the output of a larger farm. The function of farming in Canada was to provide for the subsistence of a family; when this need was met, there was little other function. Clearing stopped – only a handful of habitant farms in Canada contained a hundred cleared arpents – and much the same family farm passed from generation to generation. These subsistence farms created no wealth, but the standard of living of most Canadian farmers was comparable to the French *laboureur moyen* – well within the top 10 per cent of the French peasantry. Probably few French peasants aspired to more; they reached the nobility or the urban bourgeoisie only in their fairy tales. After a generation or two, and after much hardship, Canadians had met this limited aspiration. The independence that most French peasants enjoyed in their gardens and craved for in their farms came far closer to being a reality in a colony where there was land to meet a family's subsistence needs.

Higher living standards depended upon available land rather than upon improved techiniques. Livestock were as poorly bred as in France; because of the increased use of the forest for forage and browse, manure was even more rarely spread on the arable; and two-course rotations often replaced three. Some habitants planted fields for several years in succession before relegating them to prolonged pasture or fallow – a form of convertible husbandry used on marginal lands in western France. Average seed/yield ratios were as low in Canada as in France, and would likely have been lower but for the high initial yields of newly cleared land. There had been some drift in Canada towards more extensive agricultural practices as cleared land was substituted for scarce labour, but generally the tools and methods of tradition-bound French peasant agriculture in

22 Dechêne, *Habitants et marchands*, chap. 6; Harris, *ibid.*, chap. 8
23 Guillot, 'Etude économique et sociale,' 328; also see Marie-Claude Gricourt, 'Etude d'histoire démographique, sociale, et réligieuse de 5 paroisses de l'archidiacone du petit Caux,' in Caillard *et al.*, *A travers la Normandie*, 476-7

the seventeenth century, little changed since the late Middle Ages, were transplanted in Canada. Applied to more land than most French peasants controlled, they yielded a higher standard of living.

The Canadian habitant's relative position was further enhanced by the absence of royal taxes. Neither the *gabelle* nor the *taille* was assessed in Canada, and the modest royal demand for road work, a *corvée* of two days a year, was long meaningless in a virtually roadless colony. Royal taxes had been discontinued to encourage settlement, not to alleviate the hardships of the common people, but whether or not royal officials clearly understood the change, their absence reflected the difficulty, common to sparsely settled European colonies overseas, of imposing European charges on inexpensive land amid the fluid conditions of new settlement. In the improbable event that royal taxes had been imposed and collected – to have done so would have made Canada an even less populated colony – the Canadian habitant's standard of living would have remained relatively high, for access to land rather than freedom from taxes was the fundamental change in his situation.

The failure of *gabelle* and *taille* to penetrate the countryside of the lower St Lawrence reflects the relative autonomy of the nuclear family in rural Canada. However much the French peasant family valued its independence, it lived within the impinging influence of village, parish, seigneury, town, province, and state. The Canadian habitant's rough ease created a large measure of independence as, to some extent, it did for the families of *laboureurs* in France. In Canada there was another difference. Because there was little market for farm produce there was little commercial pressure on agricultural land. For this reason the whole institutional infrastructure of French rural life was enormously weakened.

The urban bourgeoisie's massive penetration of the French countryside did not take place in Canada. Even in seigneuries near the towns, habitant families held most of the cleared land,[24] and in remote seigneuries they held virtually all of it. Some merchants had a few farm lots and perhaps a seigneury but most of their energy went into the fur trade, and their impact on rural life was negligible. Faced with chronic agricultural overproduction, capital put into the development of large commercial farms was lost unless, as for the domanial farms on some church seigneuries, there was an assured local market. Land speculations were unprofitable. The few farm purchasers were usually families looking for homes rather than merchants looking for profit. Because of high transportation costs, high wages, and official discouragement of colonial manufacturing, sawmilling, gristmilling, and weaving never developed as export industries. Since

24 See note 16

the Canadian countryside rewarded neither speculations nor entrepreneurship, the bourgeoisie turned its attention elsewhere.

The seigneurial system faced the same difficulty. Except in a few church seigneuries, there were no large farms on seigneurial domains because there was no market for the production. Seigneurial charges were usually lower than in France – approximately 5 to 10 per cent of the habitant's gross income – and many specific charges, including the *champart*, were discontinued. The small population stretched along the St Lawrence River through almost two hundred different seigneuries, most of which remained unprofitable throughout the French régime. Accounts were poorly kept, and rents went uncollected for years. A few seigneuries, particularly Montreal Island which had by far the largest population of any Canadian seigneury and was managed fastidiously by the Sulpicians, began to produce considerable revenues well before the end of the French régime. In them the seigneur or his agents became a considerable presence, and the habitants, like their French counterparts, procrastinated as best they could in the payment of rents. More commonly the French seigneurial system, which even in relatively small French seigneuries required a manager, an attorney and an assistant attorney, a clerk, a sergeant, lieutenants, and even a gaoler, hung over Canada during the French régime in a state of suspended animation. Its legal structure remained essentially intact, but the conditions that would make it profitable and give it life were largely absent until growing population pressure on the seigneurial lowlands of Quebec in the nineteenth century gave it some of its intended teeth.[25]

Parishes also developed weakly, although Roman Catholicism had come with most immigrants to Canada as naturally as the French language. Often the habitants were served by itinerant priests through two or three generations until there were enough people in a given local area to support a *curé*. On occasion they resisted the bishop's plan to establish a *curé*, perhaps because of the cost (although the Canadian tithe was only 1/26th of the grain harvest), perhaps because of the priest's moral censures and increasingly alien French background, and perhaps simply because they did not see the need. In some *côtes* (short lines of settlement) a chapel or church had been built and *fabrique* (church vestry) organized to meet intermittently, long before the *curé* arrived. Such organization strengthened with his coming but never gained the power of the *assemblée des habitants* with which the *fabrique* tended to merge in France. Royal taxes did not have to be apportioned and, except where commons had been laid out in

25 For a discussion of the seigneurial system in post-conquest Quebec, see R.C. Harris and J. Warkentin, *Canada before Confederation: A Study in Historical Geography* (Toronto, London, and New York 1974), chap. 3.

riparian marshes, collective agricultural arrangements did not have to be worked out. Villages were virtually absent. A weak rural economy had not brought them into being, and settlers had seized the opportunity to live on their own farms. Men were expected to serve in the militia, but we cannot yet say how often it drilled or what social role, if any, it played in the countryside.[26]

In all of these ways the heavy French burden of institutional constraints and financial exactions on the nuclear family were lightened in Canada. The family stood more nearly on its own within a civil law, a system of government, and a set of customs, institutions, and social values that had come from France but had lost much of their force or had been differently combined and emphasized in a new setting where land was cheap and markets were meagre. As time passed, clusters of surnames began to appear along the *côtes*, adumbrating the intricate consanguineous ties in the rural society of nineteenth-century Quebec. The *côte* itself became a loose rural neighbourhood, but neither kin nor *côte* ever replaced the social primacy of the nuclear family. Unless he took over the family land, a son would eventually move away and – until early in the nineteenth century, when there was no more land and he was forced into the factory towns of New England, the lumber camps of the Shield, or the slums of Montreal, Trois-Rivières, and Quebec – reproduce the family farm and the relative freedom of his parents.

Rural society in Canada quickly became and long remained remarkably egalitarian. The extremes of the French countryside had been pared down to a common, minimal ease. During the entire French régime in Canada there was not a single really prosperous habitant farmer and hardly, after the first years, a rural family without some cleared land. The great majority of rural families held some thirty to fifty arpents of arable and pasture and a considerable woodlot. Rural Canada had been a clean social slate to which immigrants who settled on the land brought relatively similar backgrounds of poverty. Social differentiation had not been stamped on the countryside from the beginning, and the common exigencies of clearing land and establishing a farm undoubtedly elicited a relatively common response in the first generation of farms along a *côte*. Partible inheritance meant that the sons who took over the family farm took on a debt to his brothers and sisters that perhaps dampened his initiative. In the longer run rural society did not become stratified socially or economically because of the availability of land and the weakness of the commercial economy. Larger farms and genteel living were blocked by inadequate markets. Agriculture became

26 W.J. Eccles suggests that the militia extended military values strongly through the Canadian countryside, but until the militia has been thoroughly studied I would hesitate to attach this importance to it. *France in America* (London 1972), 69-70

primarily subsistent, clearing stopped when family needs were met, and new *côtes* were opened in response to demographic pressure rather than to increases in the price of wheat. Farm families lived in rough sufficiency, their lives dominated by the seasonal rhythm of the land, not by more powerful people who lived in other ways. Rural life in Canada had not developed the complex, interlocking hierarchy of French social relations. Habitant families worked out their friendships and their feuds, habitant society acquired a folklore derived and modified from French traditions, and many old people must have possessed a deep lore about the ways of the land. These were its complexities. Institutionally Canadian rural society was simple enough: nuclear families spread across the land in small subsistent farms with few and weak institutional constraints on their independence.

CONCLUSION

The ambition of the ordinary French family to live securely and independently on its own land had found a more common fulfilment in rural Canada than anywhere in France. Farmhouse after small farmhouse lined the St Lawrence River, each on its own land, each much like its neighbour – a simple landscape created by a simple rural society. In a setting where land was accessible but markets were not, the socio-economic complexity of rural France had been pared away until little more than the ordinary nuclear family remained. As long as cheap land was available the self-subsistent independence that had become the way of life of the Canadian habitant family could be perpetuated in *côte* after *côte* as settlement spread through the St Lawrence lowland and into the fringe of the Shield and Appalachian highlands. When land became scarce, as it did early in the nineteenth century, expansion slowed. Land values rose, the young were forced into non-agricultural activities, and society in the older *côtes* became more stratified. In the 1860s an aged Philippe Aubert de Gaspé could still describe the Canadian habitant as *l'homme le plus indépendant du monde*,[27] but when he wrote this the independence of the habitant family was fast nearing its end. After two centuries of agricultural expansion, the safety valve of cheap land along the lower St Lawrence was finally plugged, and the basis of the autonomy of the French-Canadian rural family had been undermined.

Were these Canadian developments put in a Hartzian perspective, it would be said that a French fragment, in this case the poorer peasantry, had worked out its own limited aspirations in a remote colony far from the entrammelling whole

27 In his *Mémoires* (Quebec 1885), 530

of French society.[28] While it is true that the great majority of immigrants who settled down to farm in Canada came from relatively common backgrounds of poverty in the lower echelons of the French peasantry, the difficulty with Hartz, I feel, is that he assigns far too passive a role to the particular conditions of environment and economy in New World settings. In Canada the facts that land was abundant and cheap and that the market for agricultural products was poor meant that, whatever seventeenth-century Frenchmen had tried to farm there, the extremes of wealth and poverty of the French countryside would have tended to diminish rapidly and the nuclear family – the basic unit of all French society – would have asserted itself strongly. A society that was a drastic simplification of rural France had emerged in Canada, but the impetus to simplify had come from Canadian conditions rather than from the fragmentation of French society. Some members of the nobility came to Canada and obtained seigneuries, but then neglected them. The members of the bourgeoisie who controlled the commerce of the Canadian towns had not found it worth their while to extend their hold into the countryside. Had agricultural land in Canada been scarce and valuable, and had there been a regular market for Canadian agricultural products, the very immigrants who came to Canada would have created a strikingly different rural society, undoubtedly more stratified and hierarchical, more representative of the socio-economic variety that characterized all parts of rural France.

The social change that took place in rural Canada in the seventeenth century, and that was sustained in French-Canadian rural society until well into the nineteenth century, would take place wherever northwestern Europeans encountered similar conditions. Cheap land had drastically altered the conditions of European rural life, favouring one element of European society and weakening or eliminating the rest. With the safety valve of such land, an egalitarian, family-centred, rural society would be able to reproduce and extend itself generation after generation. Yet Frederick Jackson Turner neglected the influence of the market and, writing before pre-industrial society in Europe had been rigorously studied, he did not understand that frontier conditions had accentuated and simplified a long process of social evolution in Europe. In medieval society ties of heredity and name among the nobility and of village community among the poor had tended to obscure the nuclear family. From late in the Middle Ages this compact, diverse society, in which people of different station lived in intimate social interaction and in which the family was often not a private setting for socialization, was slowly giving way to another in which social life drew back into the nuclear family, supported eventually by a sense of

28 Louis Hartz, *The Founding of New Societies* (New York 1964)

class. By the seventeenth century the sentiment of the family was widespread, and there was a general tendency, where conditions permitted, to push back ties of wider sociability in favour of the intimacy of the family. This massive social reorganization proceeded quite unevenly, more rapidly among the bourgeoisie than among the nobility or the poor, more rapidly in the principal than in the small towns.[29] In the countryside of middle-latitude colonies overseas Europeans inadvertently found a setting where the ordinary family could find an unusually autonomous existence.

In Canada, where for well over a century a tiny population lived with cheap land and poor markets, conditions particularly favoured the self-sustaining family. The social evolution of plantation colonies obviously was different, and in most middle-latitude colonies cheap land and poor markets were not conditions of settlement for several generations. South African rural society is the closest parallel to the French-Canadian; the stock farm on the veld and the small mixed farm along the lower St Lawrence were the same socio-economic response in different physical conditions to the long availability of land in a weak market economy.[30] But by its very extremity rural society in Canada reveals a social tendency inherent in the outreach of Europe to new lands far from European markets where, for a time, land was likely to be much cheaper and markets much poorer than in Europe. In such circumstances the independent, nuclear family would tend to emerge strongly within an egalitarian, family-centred society, a tendency that would be variously checked or modified by any protracted increase in the price of land or improvement in the market.

29 See particularly the study by the French demographer Philippe Ariés, *L'enfant et la vie familiale sous l'ancien régime* (Paris 1960).
30 R. Cole Harris and Leonard Guelke, 'Land and Society in Early Canada and South Africa,' *Journal of Historical Geography* 3 (1977): 135-53

JAMES R. GIBSON

Old Russia in the New World: adversaries and adversities in Russian America

As an historical geographer Andrew Clark was primarily interested in the establishment and development of British peoples and economies overseas, particularly in the New World. This transoceanic expansion was, of course, part of a larger imperial movement undertaken by the several maritime powers of Western Europe, including France and Spain. We may still need to be reminded, however, that North America was explored and settled not only from the east by seafaring Englishmen, Frenchmen, Spaniards, and others but also from the west by Russian landsmen, who followed the earlier path of the Paleoasiatic aboriginal migrants. The Russians came much later than their fellow imperialists from Western Europe, who had only uncharted waters and unpredictable elements between their homelands and New England, New France, or New Spain. The Russians, on the other hand, had to cross the Siberian land mass before embarking for the 'great land,' as the American mainland was known to the indigenous inhabitants of the Siberian shores of the Bering Sea. Admittedly, Siberia offered few obstacles to the eastward advance of Cossacks and *promyshlenniks* (fur hunters). The natives were not very numerous, advanced, or united; no foreign powers vied with Russia for the region; Siberia's dense network of interlocking rivers and generally slight relief facilitated the Russian conquest; and the taiga's abundance of fur bearers, especially its virtual monopoly on precious sables, proved an irresistible attraction. Nevertheless, the enormous longitudinal extent of Siberia (120°), plus the dearth of Russian colonists (owing to the immobility of serfdom), meant that the Russians did not reach the Pacific until the middle of the 1600s, nearly three-quarters of a century after having crossed the Urals. And it was not for another full century

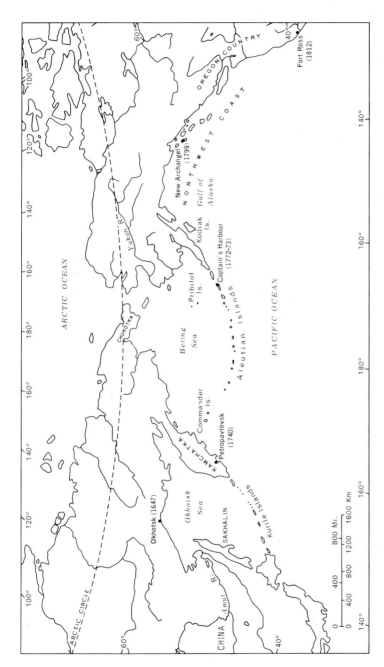

Russia on the Pacific

that they touched America, despite the misty stepping stones afforded by the Aleutians. The legendary Amur River Valley temporarily distracted Russian eastward expansion until China's ascendant Manchu Dynasty offered unyielding opposition. In 1741 Bering and Chirikov sighted Alaska and a new fur rush ensued. By 1773 – 165 years after the founding of Quebec and 166 years after the founding of Jamestown – the Russians had established their first permanent settlement in North America, probably at Captain's Harbour on Unalaska Island. In 1808 this initial colonial centre of Russian America was succeeded by New Archangel (Sitka).

Here the Russians had even more cause than in Siberia to complain that 'bad luck can take you across the Urals.' Siberia was miserable enough, what with its numbing winter cold, perennially frozen ground, 'roadlessness' during spring thaw, countless biting insects, short growing season, and widespread lawlessness. But Russian America was even more of a God-forsaken wilderness. Here, for example, the winters were not only cold but raw too, with much wind, rain, and fog. Supply of personnel and matériel was rendered more difficult by the greater distance from European Russia. Hunting was more dangerous because the maritime fur trade, unlike the continental fur trade of Siberia, entailed the hazards of navigation in the stormy waters of the far North Pacific, the habitat of the prized sea otter and fur seal. And the Russians were opposed more stubbornly by the Alaskan natives, particularly the Tlingits, than by the Siberian aborigines. The Tlingits were abetted by American and British traders. The presence of these foreign competitors was another obstacle that the Russians had not faced in Siberia. Little wonder that the Russian-American Company, which monopolized the exploitation and administration of Alaska from its chartering in 1799 until the American purchase in 1867, had difficulty obtaining and re-engaging employees.[1]

---

1 The Russian-American Company, which was formed by the merger of several private Siberian fur-trading concerns, was Russia's first joint-stock company. It came under increasing governmental control from the very beginning. In 1799 an imperial correspondent, and from 1804 a state council, directed the company's political affairs. Its St Petersburg-based head office, which consisted of four directors elected by the stockholders, managed commercial matters. The management of political affairs was returned to the head office in 1844, when in accordance with the company's third twenty-year charter the stockholders elected as directors one merchant and four military officers, who served as governmental representatives. Meanwhile, in 1811 the government had placed the head office under the jurisdiction of the Department of Manufacture and Domestic Trade, which in 1819 was subsumed by the Ministry of Finance. And from 1817 colonial governors were naval officers appointed by the government. So by the late 1810s, when international rivalry was peaking on the Northwest Coast, the Russian-American Company had become a state agency as well as a business corporation.

These problems are exemplified by the dismal state of affairs at New Archangel, which serves as a microcosm of Russian America's most serious shortcomings. Certainly the warrior archangel St Michael neglected the outpost that had been named after him. The settlement did occupy a commanding site and a scenic locale. Like almost all company posts, which were dependent upon the sea for shipping and hunting and which were surrounded by disillusioned natives, New Archangel (shown on pages 50-1) was situated atop a defensible promontory on an island (Baranof Island) off the tree-studded and mountain-backed coast. Also like most company settlements, it was undermanned and run-down. Governor George Simpson of the Hudson's Bay Company observed in late 1841 that 'Sitka, or New Archangel, situated in Norfolk Sound in Latitude 57° Longitude 136°, is the great depôt of the Russian American Company ...'; he added that 'Of all the dirty and wretched places that I have ever seen, Sitka is pre-eminently the most wretched and most dirty.' The residents, he noted, numbered but '... 400 officers and servants, which with families makes the population of Sitka upwards of 1200 souls, independent of a numerous Indian village situated immediately under the guns of the fort.'[2] In summer, at the height of the shipping and hunting seasons, New Archangel's population shrank to about one-quarter of its winter size.

The 'numerous Indian [Tlingit] village,' which contained 750 persons in the summer of 1838,[3] represented one of the most formidable adversaries of the Russian-American Company. During the last half of the 1700s, when the Russians were preoccupied with the fur trade of the Kurile, Commander, Aleutian, Pribilof, and Kodiak islands, the native inhabitants afforded little resistance. The low technological and political level of the Aleuts, the main group of islanders, made them easy prey for the determined *promyshlenniks* with their muskets and cannons. The Aleuts were reduced to servitude. Indeed, this condition was essential to the landlubberish Russians, for with their *baidarkas* (kayaks) and harpoons the Aleuts were matchless hunters of sea otters, whose pelts, according to Captain Otto von Kotzebue of the Russian navy, made '... the finest fur in the world ...'[4] even finer and dearer than sable. As a British

2 Simpson, *Narrative of a Journey round the World during the Years 1841 and 1842* (London 1847), 2: 190; Glyndwr Williams, ed., *London Correspondence Inward from Sir George Simpson, 1841-42* (London 1973), 69, 70
3 Lieutenant V. Z[avoiko], *Vpechatleniya moryaka vo vremya dvukh puteshestvy krugom sveta* [*Impressions of a Sailor during Two Voyages around the World*] (St Petersburg 1840), 2: 90
4 Von Kotzebue, *A New Voyage round the World in the Years 1823-1826* (New York 1967), 2: 46

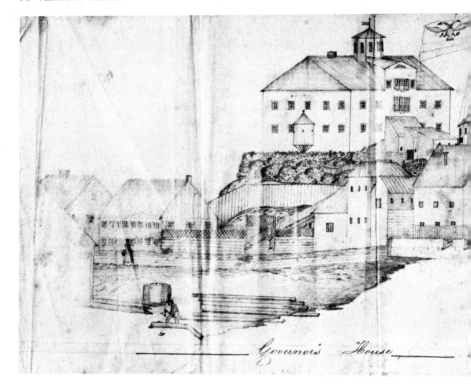

New Archangel *circa* 1840. By permission of the Hudson's Bay Company
Archives (F. 29/2), Winnipeg

Wharf at Sitka

seaman noted in 1807, the Aleuts '... are extremely expert in managing their canoes, and most ingenious in their modes of catching fish and other sea animals. They are excellent marksmen with the rifle and spear ...'[5] In 1820 a Russian naval officer, A.P. Lazarev, was surprised to find that the company's maritime fur trade was completely dependent upon the Aleuts, since no Russians had bothered to learn how to hunt sea animals.[6] So valuable were the Aleuts that they were exploited more than any tribe in Siberia, where the Russians could hunt sables as well as the natives. Not surprisingly, the Aleuts were drastically reduced in numbers; between the middle and the end of the eighteenth century their population was halved. Virtually every company post had a complement of these 'marine Cossacks' for hunting sea otters. By 1820 there were some one thousand Aleut hunters scattered among the company's far-flung posts.[7] In 1832 nearly one-third of all company employees were Aleuts.[8] The largest contingent was found at New Archangel.

The Tlingits at New Archangel were quite another matter. Like the Chukchis of extreme northeastern Siberia, the Tlingits were never fully subjugated to the tsar. Their bountiful temperate rainforest environment, which was particularly rich in fish and timber,[9] and their strong socio-political structure, which facilitated the formation of alliances, enabled these Northwest Coast Indians to resist fiercely Russian encroachment. Their resistance, which earned them the reputation of 'a warlike, courageous, and cruel race,'[10] was strengthened by firearms that they obtained in exchange for furs from American and British traders, who began to appear on the coast in the late 1780s. The American 'coasters' were especially unscrupulous; not only did they trade muskets and swords (as well as daggers and spirits) to the Tlingits but they also trained them in their use and urged them to use these weapons against the Russians. So the Tlingits became a pawn in the international rivalry between Russia and the United States over the Northwest Coast.

5 Archibald Campbell, *A Voyage round the World, from 1806 to 1812* ... (Honolulu 1967), 46

6 Lazarev, *Zapiski o plavanii voyennovo shlyupa Blagonamerennovo v Beringov proliv i vokrug sveta* ... [*Notes on the Voyage of the Naval Sloop Loyal to Bering Strait and around the World* ...] (Moscow 1950), 235

7 *Ibid.*, 234

8 Contre-Admiral von Wrangell, *Statistische und ethnographische Nachrichten über die russischen Besitzungen an der Nordwestküste von Amerika* [*Statistical and Ethnographical Report on the Russian Possessions on the Northwest Coast of America*] (St Petersburg 1839), 22

9 See Joan M. Vastokas, 'Architecture and Environment: The Importance of the Forest to the Northwest Coast Indian,' *Forest History* (Oct. 1969): 13-21.

10 Von Kotzebue, *New Voyage*, 2: 38

Already by the end of the century the Tlingits may have discarded their bows and arrows for firearms. An American skipper, John D'Wolf, observed in 1805 that among the Sitkan Tlingits 'Both sexes are expert in the use of fire-arms, and are excellent judges of their quality.'[11] This observation was corroborated a score of years later by Otto von Kotzebue, who remarked that 'No Kalush [Tlingit] is without one musket at least, of which he perfectly understands the use.'[12] About the same time another Russian visitor reported that the Tlingits used rifles and daggers 'very well' and that they even had small cannons.[13] These weapons emboldened and strengthened the Koloshes, as they were known to the Russians.[14] In 1802 they attacked New Archangel itself; the fort was looted and burned and the garrison was killed or captured. The company was unable to retake the colonial capital until 1804, and then only with the help of a Russian navy ship. In 1809 and in 1813 the Tlingits prepared to attack New Archangel, and in 1855 they did besiege the settlement. They remained a constant threat throughout the Russian period, although their hostility was weakened by the great smallpox epidemic of the last half of the 1830s (the Tlingit population fell from 10,000 in mid-1834 to 6000 in mid-1838)[15] and by the withdrawal of their American cohorts from the maritime fur trade after 1840. Unluckily for the Russians, New Archangel had been founded right in the heart of Tlingit territory. The Tlingits were particularly numerous around the settlement during the spring (herring) and summer (salmon) fishing seasons; in spring up to 2000 and in summer at least 500 assembled in Sitka Bay to fish. From 1841 many Tlingits also gathered at New Archangel in early spring for a fair; the 1846 fair, for example, attracted 1500 Indians.[16]

11 D'Wolf, *A Voyage to the North Pacific* (Fairfield, Wash. 1968), 48
12 *New Voyage*, 2: 54
13 Vladimir Romanov, 'O Kolyuzhakh ili Koloshakh voobshche' ['Concerning the Kolyuzhes or Koloshes in General'], *Severny arkhiv* 17 (1825): 7
14 Recently, however, it has been persuasively argued that the introduction of firearms did not significantly augment the military prowess of the Northwest Coast Indians, owing to the low quality of the guns (smooth-bore flintlock muskets), their unsuitability to hand-to-hand combat based upon stealth and surprise (which was preferred by the Indians to direct frontal attacks and pitched battles in the open), and their symbolic rather than utilitarian value to the natives as indicators of wealth, prestige, and power. See Robin Fisher, 'Arms and Men on the Northwest Coast, 1774-1825,' *BC Studies* 29 (Spring 1976): 3-18.
15 Z[avoiko], *Vpechatleniya*, 2: 90
16 United States, General Services Administration, National Archives, 'Records of the Russian-American Company 1802-1867: Correspondence of Governors General,' File Microcopies of Records in the National Archives: no 11 (Washington, DC 1942), 51: 188 verso

The inauguration of the spring fair formalized a mutual dependence that had begun as early as the 1820s. Paradoxically, the Tlingits supplied the Russians of New Archangel with sorely needed sustenance at the same time as they threatened to eradicate them.[17] Especially after the disappearance of their traditional American suppliers did the Tlingits come to rely upon the Russians for various manufactures, but even earlier they obtained some items, such as tobacco, pots, axes, beads, paint, linen, and calico, from New Archangel. In return the company particularly wanted fresh foodstuffs. There was a chronic shortage of provisions in the Russian-American colonies, thanks to the great distance and high cost of shipment from Russia and the environmental impediments to local agriculture. So any other source of food — including the dreaded Tlingits — was welcome. From the 1820s the Tlingits began to furnish New Archangel with halibut, shellfish, and wild mutton (from Dall mountain sheep?) in winter, the flesh and eggs of wildfowl and roots and herbs in spring, berries and snails (or slugs) in summer, and potatoes in autumn. In addition, hats, masks, pipes, rugs, and even timber were traded; from mid-May 1848 through mid-May 1849, for instance, the company bought 1360 logs (each 21 feet long and 6 inches thick) from the Tlingits.[18] But the provisions, particularly the fresh meat, fish, and fowl in winter, were much more important, if only to the officials and officers. During the last half of the 1840s the Tlingits supplied New Archangel with an astonishing average of 11 tons of mutton, 26 tons of halibut, and 56 tons of potatoes each year (Table 1). Thus, the long-standing and bitter enmity between the Russians and the Tlingits gradually came to be tempered by commercial concord.

The Russians of New Archangel had a similar relationship with their other major adversary — the Americans, who in the regional Chinook jargon were known as 'Bostonians' or 'Boston men,' since most of their ships were out of

---

17 They also provided the Russians with mates. Among the Russians the ratio of males to females was as high as thirty to one, and this sexual imbalance was one reason why the governor allowed the Tlingits to have a settlement outside the very gates of New Archangel. The offspring of Russian fathers and native (Aleut or Tlingit) mothers were called creoles, who came to form a special legal class and a sizeable pool of semi-skilled labour (although most of them died of tuberculosis by the age of thirty, and Governor Teben-kov opined in 1846 that it took three creole workers to equal one Russian *promyshlen-nik*). Winston Lee Sarafian, 'Russian-American Company Employee Policies and Prac-tices, 1799-1867,' PhD dissertation, University of California at Los Angeles, 1970, pp. 140-1

18 United States, 'Records,' 55: 142v

TABLE 1

Russian-American Company purchases of mutton, halibut, and potatoes from the Tlingits for New Archangel, 1842-66

Year*	Mutton (pounds)	Halibut (pounds)	Potatoes (pounds)
1842	?	?	127,875
1843	?	?	113,825
1844	14,445	?	30,225
1845	11,701	?	246,450
1846	32,466	56,986	23,715
1847	40,374	43,299	37,200
1848	10,473	27,482	140,895
1849	11,881	76,812	116,250
1850	3611	74,032	?
1851	903	138,096	104,625
	(head of sheep)		
1852	19	125,745	0
1853	70	107,075	0
1854	7	91,342	0
1855	15	34,223	0
1856	82	83,493	?
1857	339	50,654	?
1858	232	45,538	?
1859	1320	43,697	12,787½
1860	969	31,599	?
1861	2774	56,589	60,450
1862	1150	53,664	?
1863	634	94,616	?
1864	254	44,900	?
1865	77	22,269	?
1866	492	46,730	?

* The years extend from mid-May to mid-May for mutton and halibut and from mid-January to mid-January for potatoes.

Sources: Rossiisko-Amerikanskaya Kompaniya, *Otchyot Rossiisko-Amerikanskoy Kompanii Glavnavo Pravleniya za odin god ... [Report of the Head Office of the Russian-American Company for One Year ...]* (St Petersburg 1843-65), 1860: 44, 1861: 17, 1862: 28, 1863: 22; United States 'Records,' 47: 426, 48: 332, 50: 204-204v, 51: 187-8, 52: 326-326v, 54: 209v, 55: 125v-6, 56: 125, 57: 251v, 58: 189v, 59: 308v-9, 60: 25-25v, 61: pt 1, 85-85v, pt 2, 50, 62: pt 1, 63v, pt 2, 71v-2, pt 3, 47, 63: pt 1, 76-76v, pt 2, 40, 64: pt 1, 56v, 59v, pt 2, 42, pt 3, 15, 65: pt 1, 57v, pt 2, 33, pt 3, 53v

that New England port.[19] The Americans did not enter the 'Northwest trade' until the late 1780s, when they discovered that China would accept sea otter furs in lieu of specie in exchange for the tea, silk, porcelain, and bric-à-brac desired by American and European customers. By 1790 the lucrative 'golden round' of New England-Northwest Coast-South China-New England had been firmly delineated. By then, however, the Russians, who began taking sea otters in the early 1740s, had a half-century headstart. Moreover, they monopolized the sources of those varieties of sea otters with the best grades of fur – Kurilian, Kamchatkan, and Aleutian, whose hair was thicker than that of the Northwest Coast and Californian subspecies. Furthermore, the world's best hunters of sea otters – the Aleuts – were under Russian control. The Americans had to risk inshore trading with the unpredictable Indians, who occasionally overcame unwary trading vessels. But the Yankee skippers did outclass their Russian rivals in several respects. Firstly, they had better ships and better seamen than the continental Muscovites, whose vessels were notorious for being crudely built and poorly manned. Captain Von Kotzebue remarked in 1824 that '... North Americans are such clever sailors, that even when drunk they are capable of managing a ship.' The Russian-American Company admitted that during the first quarter of the nineteenth century the best ships in its colonial fleet were those that had been either built by American shipwrights in the company's employ or bought from American shipmasters. Secondly, the Americans were superior horse traders in their dealings with the Tlingits. They were simply more ruthless and more imaginative in their trading, as evidenced by their more attractive array of trade goods (including spirits and weapons). Captain Von Kotzebue asserted that '... no people in the world surpass the citizen of the United States in the boldness, activity, and perseverance of their mercantile speculations.'[20] Generally American trade goods were higher in quality and wider in variety than Russian ones. Thirdly, the American Nor'westmen had access to Whampoa Roads, which was closed to Russian ships. The only Chinese points of entry open to Russian traders were two small border towns deep inside the continent just to the south of Lake Baikal. By the time that Russian-American Company pelts had borne the expense of lengthy and difficult overland transport from the port of Okhotsk on Siberia's Pacific coast, they were undersold by American pelts at Canton. Moreover, Russian pelts were not as well prepared. Finally, the Americans could readily supply what the Russians badly needed – provisions,

19 The British, or 'King George's men,' did not seriously challenge the Russians until the 1830s, and this short-lived competition was soon resolved by an accord in 1839 between the Russian-American Company and the Hudson's Bay Company.
20 *New Voyage*, 2: 65, 64

including flour, groats, and butter from New England and rice, sugar, and molasses from the West Indies and Brazil, plus a few Yankee manufactures, in return for which they received mainly fur seal skins. These transactions greatly eased one of the principal weaknesses of the Russian-American colonies; indeed, during the first quarter of the 1800s American ships were the foremost provisioners of New Archangel.[21] This same spirit of collaboration was manifested in a number of joint hunting expeditions along the coast of New Albion between 1803 and 1813; the Russians provided Aleuts and the Americans furnished ships, the catch being evenly divided.

The Americans were also a threat to the Russians, however. For one thing, they deprived the company of many pelts in payment for provisions. More importantly, the same American ships that brought foodstuffs to New Archangel also sometimes brought Caribbean rum and New England knives and guns to the Tlingit settlements. Some American traders even showed the Indians how to use the firearms, including cannons, and incited them against the Russians. Inflamed by the firewater and firepower, the Tlingits attacked other Indians and Russian settlements and ships (and sometimes American vessels as well). They even succeeded in capturing New Archangel in 1802 and Yakutat in 1805; at least 200 Aleuts and 100 Russians were killed. Usually hunting parties of Aleuts in *baidarkas* suffered the most; not infrequently they were ambushed in the 'straits,' the myriad channels among the islands off the Alaskan panhandle. In Lieutenant Lazarev's words, '... not one summer passes without several of them falling victim while hunting. The least negligence on their part and the Tlingits suddenly appear and kill and capture them ...'[22] The hostility of the Tlingits, plus the unruliness of the *promyshlenniks* and from 1818 the officer rank of the governors, prompted the maintenance of strict military discipline at New Archangel.

American rumrunning and gunrunning became so serious that in 1821 the tsar signed a decree that barred foreign shipping (except in emergencies) from the Russian American coast north of 51°N latitude and from the eastern Siberian coast north of 45° 50'N latitude, as well as from the Aleutians and Kuriles. This ban did not last beyond 1824, however, because the Russian navy was too weak to enforce it and because New Archangel was too hungry to accept it. Besides, there was no holding back the aggressive and confident Americans; flushed with

21 The American vessels also profited by trade in Kamchatka. From 1828 until 1855 foreign ships were allowed to import goods (except liquor) into the peninsula duty-free. The ban on liquor was largely ignored.
22 *Zapiski*, 234

the success of their recent war for independence against Great Britain, they unabashedly regarded the entire North American continent as destined to be theirs.

By now, however, the Russians had less and less to fear from the American traders as they gradually forsook the depleted sea otter grounds of the Northwest Coast for the richer whale and seal fisheries of the Okhotsk and Bering seas; these waters saw 250 American whalers and sealers annually by the middle of the century.[23] Furthermore, regular shipments of grain and beef from Alta California, which opened its ports to foreign traders in 1821, made New Archangel less dependent upon the Americans for provisions. Another repellent for the Americans was increasing competition from the Hudson's Bay Company in the form of both coastal vessels and posts. The Russian-American Company, too, with its improved fleet was becoming more active in the Inside Passage. The American withdrawal mitigated the Tlingit menace to New Archangel. And the Tlingits themselves were becoming used to the permanent presence of Russian neighbours, who reached their maximum numerical strength around 1840, right after the Indians had been decimated by smallpox.

While the Russian-American Company was able to adjust to its two principal opponents, it never could compromise its two main physical obstacles, owing partly to their pervasiveness and partly to Russian technological backwardness. Certainly the elements were unchangeable, as well as execrable. Although nature was munificent in terms of flora (especially spruce, cedar, fir) and fauna (particularly salmon, herring, halibut), climatologically (and pedologically, for that matter) it was stingy. Russian Alaska's high latitude and proximity to the source of cold Arctic air and the Aleutian low pressure system; the nearby mixing of cool and warm ocean currents and cool, dry and warm, moist air masses; orographic intensification of cyclonic precipitation by coastal ranges — all of these factors combined to make the region cool, damp, cloudy, and foggy. These characteristics were especially prevalent on the coasts and islands, where most of the company's settlements were located. Particularly the persistent overcast impressed (or more accurately, depressed) employees and visitors alike. A fifteen-year resident of Russian America, Cyril Khlebnikov, who was the company's manager at New Archangel, wrote that 'According to numerous observations, it can certainly be said that in general two-thirds of the best years are foul weather and one-third is fair or mild weather, but there are times when

23 N.V. Sverdlov, 'K istorii russko-amerikanskikh otnosheny na Tikhom okeane i Dalnem Vostoke v XIX-nachale XX v' ['Towards a History of Russian-American Relations in the Pacific Ocean and the Far East in the 19th and Early 20th Centuries'], in Akademiya nauk SSSR, Otdelenie istoricheskikh nauk, Dalnevostochny filial, *Sbornik statey po istorii Dalnevo Vostoka* (Moscow 1968), 312

one-fifth of the days are fine; uninterrupted overcast, fine rain, and damp air are the norm ...'[24] And George Simpson, during a visit to New Archangel in the spring of 1842, complained that 'In all my experience, I have never seen anything so miserable as the almost constant damp, fog, and rain of the last three weeks ...'[25] These conditions are illustrated by the colonial capital's descriptive climatic record for 1831-67:[26]

	Winter	Summer
1831	?	'very rainy'
1832	'cold, clear, and, in comparison with previous ones, snowless'	'very good'
1833	'completely snowless and warm'	'unusually good, dry, warm'
1834	'not very regular' and 'fairly stormy'	'unusually cold and rainy'
1835	'snowless and milder than previous ones'	'very bad, cold and rainy'
1836	'extremely good and snowless'	'fairly rainy'
1837	'quite snowless and warm'	'fairly clear and warm'
1838	'not cold ... but clear and very regular'	'not one of the best'
1839	'snowless and warm'	'unusually rainy'
1840	'snowless and rather mild'	'extremely bad, cold and rainy'
1841	'snowless and warm'	'not one of the best'
1842	'not cold but very long and snowy'	'very inclement, rainy and cold'
1843	'very cold with frequent snowstorms and strong winds'	'very cold and inclement'
1844	'not cold'	'very good'
1845	'not cold but regular'	'fairly good'
1846	'rain, rain, rain'	'inclement'
1847	'snowy and cold'	'fairly inclement and severe' in the first half and 'dry and warm' in the second half
1848	'regular and extremely cold' and 'much snow'	'fairly dry and warm'
1849	'extremely cold'	'fairly cool and rainy'
1850	'long, regular, and very cold and snowy'	'not very warm but fairly dry'

24 [K.T. Khlebnikov], 'Zapiski o Koloniyakh Rossiisko-Amerikanskoy Kompanii' ['Notes on the Colonies of the Russian-American Company'], Archive of the Geographical Society of the USSR, raz. 99, op. 1, no 112, 28

25 *Narrative*, 2: 198

26 United States, 'Records,' 34: 203v-4, 35: 86v-7, 36: 214-214v, 37: 195v, 318, 38: 148v, 39: 246-246v, 40: 291v-2, 42: 306, 43: 220v, 45: 274, 46: 266, 47: 426-426v, 48: 332-332v, 50: 204-204v, 51: 186v, 188, 52: 134v, 325v-6, 54: 209-209v, 55: 125v, 56: 124v-5, 57: 251-251v, 58: 189-189v, 59: 308v-9, 60: 25, 123, 61: pt 1, 84v-5, pt 2, 50, 62: pt 1, 63-63v, pt 2, 71v, 63: pt 1, 76v, 195, pt 2, 39v, 64: pt 1, 59v, pt 2, 41v, pt 3, 14v, 65: pt 1, 57, pt 2, 32v, pt 3, 53-53v

	Winter	Summer
1851	'very tolerable, fairly dry and not very frosty'	'very warm and dry'
1852	'clear with little frost'	'fairly mild'
1853	'very short' and 'warm and clear'	'fairly mild'
1854	'regular' but somewhat mild	'fairly dry and warm'
1855	'fairly regular and cold with intermittent freezes and thaws'	'dry and warm'
1856	'quite non-existent' – 'quite warm weather with rain'	'fairly regular'
1857	'fairly cold and almost snowless until February'	'inclement'
1858	'unusually snowy and stormy'	'fairly good and not very rainy'
1859	'warm with unusually abundant snow'	'especially rainy'
1860	'non-existent,' that is, mild	'fairly good and warm'
1861	'very good' and 'clear with light frosts'	'unusually good and warm'
1862	'snowstorms with blizzards'	'unsatisfactory'
1863	'rainy and ... no frosts'	'bad'
1864	'non-existent' with 'rain and infrequent frosts'	'bad'
1865	'irregular' with 'rain and snow'	'bad' – 'rainy and cold'
1866	'non-existent' – 'mild'	'rainy and inclement'
1867	irregular	?

This raw climate appreciably conditioned company operations. Especially farming at New Archangel was adversely affected. Captain Von Kotzebue wrote: 'The climate of Sitka is not so severe as might have been expected from its latitude. In the middle of winter the cold is not excessive, and never lasts long. Agriculture notwithstanding does not appear to be successful here. There is not perhaps a spot in the world where so much rain falls; a dry day is a perfect rarity, and this would itself account for the failure of corn [grain]; the nature of the ground is however equally inimical to it.'[27] Even for hardy cereals and tuberous vegetables the growing season was too cool and too wet; only potatoes were grown with any success. Planting was delayed by late frost, growth was slowed by frequent overcast, and harvesting was impaired by rain. Usually grain did not ripen; vegetables fared better but even they tasted watery. Livestock were less sensitive to the raw climate. They also suffered, however, because of the difficulty of making hay for the winter months. There was ample grass for pasture but the foul weather thwarted the cutting and drying of hay. At New Archangel late summer and early fall rains often lodged standing hay and retted mown hay. For example, the settlement's hay crop was reported as 'limited' in 1836, 'normal' in 1837, 'sufficient' in 1838, 'very meagre' in 1839, 'extremely

27 *New Voyage*, 2: 43

poor' in 1840, and 'very poor' in 1841.[28] Enough could be cured for only half a dozen cattle, so that hay had to be imported (from as far away as California in the 1860s). Even the clearing of forest for agriculture was hampered by the dankness. The naturalist George H. von Langsdorff learned in 1806 that 'Several attempts have been made by the governor to burn a part of the forests in the neighbourhood of the settlement, but owing to the great moisture, these experiments have never succeeded.'[29] The inimical climate was probably the primary cause of the defeat of attempts to alleviate Russian Alaska's chronic shortage of food by means of colonial agriculture.

Farming was the main but not the sole victim of the climate. Shipping in and out of New Archangel was endangered by fog and gales which were strong enough to uproot trees. And canvas and rope were weathered by the 'ruinous' elements. So were wooden buildings, which lasted no longer than twenty and frequently only ten years, owing partly to the climate and partly to the fire hazard. In the late 1820s Captain Frederick P. Lütke of the Russian navy remarked that 'The wet climate, which is harmful to buildings and ships, is a disagreeable circumstance, but to avoid it would be to abandon the entire territory, for Kodiak, Unalaska, and all other places on the mainland and on the islands are scarcely much better than Sitka in this respect.'[30] Everyday living was made unpleasant, too. Work was slowed; at New Archangel during the winter of 1822-3, for example, outdoor work was interrupted by heavy rains, high winds, and hard frosts.[31] Considerable heating and drying were necessitated. More importantly, the coolness and dampness promoted sickness, which was also induced by malnutrition and overwork. Particularly respiratory and rheumatic ailments were not uncommon. In the 1820s and 1830s the daily number of sick company employees at New Archangel ranged from 25 to 45 in summer and from 40 to 60 in autumn, winter, and spring; smallpox and influenza raised the toll to 70-80 in the winter of 1835-6 and 150 in the summer of 1836.[32] Such a sizeable loss of manpower (as much as one-third of the settlement's company employees) must have been acutely felt in view of the colonies' chronic shortage of labour.

28 United States, 'Records,' 39: 246, 40: 291v, 42: 306, 43: 220v, 45: 274, 46: 266.
29 Von Langsdorff, *Voyages and Travels in Various Parts of the World* (Ridgewood, NJ 1968), 2: 102
30 Litke, *Puteshestvie vokrug sveta na voyennom shlyupe 'Senyavin' 1826-1829* [*Voyage around the World on the Naval Sloop 'Senyavin' in 1826-1829*], 2nd ed. (Moscow 1948), 59
31 United States, 'Records,' 28: 218v
32 Kapitan Kupreyanov, 'Donesenie o sostoyanii pogod v Novo-Arkhangelsk i proch. s predstavleniem Vedomosti, No. 303, Maya 10-vo dnya 1839' ['A Report on the State of the Weather at New Archangel, etc. with a Submission of a Record, No. 303, May 10, 1839'], Archive of the Geographical Society of the USSR, raz. 99, op. 1, d. 36, 1; United States, 'Records,' 31: 60v, 389v, 40: 190, 367v

New Archangel's other major adversity was 'space friction.' If, as Tsar Nicholas I is supposed to have said, Russia suffered from its distances, then Russian America must have been in agony. In Captain Lütke's words, 'The great distance from Europe and the infrequent and difficult contact with Europe constitutes one of the main disadvantages of life here [New Archangel].'[33] Russian America's remoteness was maximal; New Archangel was located on the opposite side of the world from the imperial capital of St Petersburg. Moreover, the land route via Siberia was obstructed by winter blizzards, spring break-up, summer flies and bogs, and autumn freeze-up, while via Cape Horn or the Cape of Good Hope the oceanic route, which was twice as long, was marred by calms, storms, and uncharted shallows. Consequently, the delivery of supplies, recruits, and instructions to the colonies and the shipment of products, superannuates, and reports to the motherland were hazardous, prolonged, and costly.[34] So rarely did New Archangel communicate with the company's head office in St Petersburg (usually once each year) that the event was celebrated as a special occasion.[35] Captain Lütke, who visited the colonial capital in the late 1820s, wrote: 'Mail is received once a year by ships coming from Okhotsk in August and September and bringing letters, magazines, and newly hired [men]. This important occasion stirs everybody for several weeks. The other important time (April) is the dispatch of ships to Okhotsk with answers to letters, departing employees, etc. The arrival of a navy or company ship directly from Europe is a holiday that does not occur every year.'[36] By contrast, Mexico received mail from Spain every month, and a courier went monthly from Mexico City to San Francisco. A 'London ship' reached Fort Vancouver every spring, and an overland express departed Fort Vancouver every spring for York Factory and returned every fall. Ships from either old or New England made the Northwest Coast in five or six months; Russian ships took a year.

33 *Puteshestvie*, 49
34 Transportation and communication were also problematical within the colonies themselves, which were anything but compact, being scattered around the northern arc of the Pacific from the Kuriles to the Farallones.
35 The directives from St Petersburg and the reports from New Archangel have survived. They became American property in 1867 and are now available on seventy-seven reels of microfilm at the United States National Archives, Washington, DC. Handwritten in legible Russian, this correspondence constitutes a rich and largely untapped source of varied information on Russian America. Almost all of the records of the company's head office have been lost, but considerable material on the company, especially from the Ministry of Finance, is found in the Archive of Russian Foreign Policy (Moscow), which, however, does not readily admit researchers or release documents.
36 *Puteshestvie*, 49

Thus, it was physically impossible for the board of directors of the Russian-American Company's head office in St Petersburg to keep a tight rein on its governors in New Archangel, who in turn could not ride close herd on the managers of the various districts of the far-flung colonies. Certainly the management of the Russian-American Company was less centralized than that of the Hudson's Bay Company, whose governor and committee in London was half as far from its overseas holdings. Because colonial officials in Russian America were rather loosely accountable to their superiors, they were able to act somewhat independently and sometimes arbitrarily. The Siberian saying that 'God is high above and the tsar is far away' was even more applicable to Alaska. As Governor Peter Chistyakov reported in 1830, 'The head office undoubtedly understands the ... uncontrollability of the conduct of subordinates, in a territory so remote from the motherland ...'[37] George von Langsdorff noted in 1805 that:

The stewardship in each single establishment is entirely despotic; though nominally depending upon the principal factory ... these stewards do just what they please, without the possibility of their being called to account. The ... Russian subject here enjoys no protection of his property, lives in no security, and if oppressed, has no one to whom he can apply for justice. The agents of the factories, and their subordinate officers, influenced by humour or interest, decide every thing arbitrarily, without the least apprehension of having to render an account of their conduct; for that their scandalous behaviour, their daily transgressions, should ever be noticed by their lords and masters of St Petersburgh, is a thing that does not enter into their ideas.[38]

Such abuses contributed to the general unpleasantness of life in the colonies. But the harsh conduct of the overseers seems to have been provoked in part by the low character of the *promyshlenniks*, whose baseness was in turn linked to their remoteness. In 1786 Captain Gabriel Sarychev of the Russian navy explained that 'Ochotsk is immensely remote from Russia, and the travelling by land no less toilsome than that by sea from thence to America, which must be undertaken in vessels altogether unfitted, either in bulk or tackling, for such a distance, and devoid of every comfort and convenience; whence it may be fairly concluded that few, except persons in desperate or low circumstances, will offer their services, and that among such an assemblage of people many will be found

37 United States, 'Records,' 32: 63v
38 *Voyages and Travels*, 2: 69-70

to abuse the power vested in their hands.'[39] Von Langsdorff concurred, asserting that 'The Aleutians ... are commonly under the superintendence of a Promüschlenik, which is, in other words, under that of a rascal, by whom they are oppressed, tormented, and plundered in every possible way.'[40] The quality of company employees improved with the reorganization of the colonies in the late 1810s but an appreciable disreputable element remained to neglect their duties and mistreat the natives.

Colonial isolation was also partly responsible for the inveterate problem of supply, particularly of provisions, which were both more essential to existence and more liable to spoilage than other supplies. New Archangel, which accounted for up to 75 per cent of colonial food needs, simply had to be fed. Local farming was unproductive, thanks mainly to the forbidding environment, be it the dank islands of the Gulf of Alaska or the foggy coast of New Albion, where an agricultural base (Fort Ross) had been founded in 1812. And the company was understandably reluctant to rely upon nearby competitors, be they American shipmasters, California missionaries, or British Hudson's Bay men. At least supply from the motherland was in Russian hands. This strategy had two variants: shipment by land and by sea from eastern Siberia via Okhotsk and shipment by sea from European Russia via St Petersburg around the Horn or the Cape. The second variant had the added advantages of training Russian seamen, showing the Russian flag, and furthering exploration and discovery. Both variants, however, were lengthy and risky, so that the provisions that were delivered to New Archangel were low in amount and high in cost. The Hudson's Bay Company was able to deliver supplies to New Archangel at one-third the cost of shipment via Okhotsk and one-sixth the cost of shipment via St Petersburg. Similarly, supplies received by New Archangel from St Petersburg cost twice as much as those brought by American traders. Thus, the Russians were inclined to depend for basic necessities upon their very rivals for the territory and resources of the Northwest Coast. Such a position was hardly a strong one.

In fact, Russia was simply overextended in North America. Siberia had been annexed easily, owing to the lack of forceful opposition from the backward natives and the isolationist Chinese and Japanese; neither the Manchu Dynasty nor the Tokugawa Shogunate was interested in Siberia, so Russia had a clear path across northern Asia to the Pacific. (Incidentally, this open frontier on Russia's eastern periphery made her less vulnerable than more central European powers to encircling alliances.) On the northwestern coast of North America,

39 Gavrila A. Sarychew, *Account of a Voyage of Discovery* ... (Amsterdam 1969), 2:12
40 *Voyages and Travels*, 2: 69-70

however, Russia found herself vying with both stronger natives and foreign powers – Great Britain, Spain, and the United States, whose supply lines were less lengthy and whose colonial outposts were less forbidding. In this sphere of keen international competition New Archangel – undersupplied and over-exposed – was simply in a less advantageous position than Fort Vancouver or San Francisco; besides, St Petersburg was preoccupied with European rather than Asian affairs. Russia's cumbersome imperialist system was put to the acid test by the extreme conditions – physical and human – of Russian America, and under these conditions the system faltered. By the middle of the century, with Manchu China in decline, Russia decided that her Pacific future lay not in the Far West of North America, where the bourgeoning power of the United States seemed irresistible, but in the Far East of Asia, where the promising Amur River Valley beckoned once again in the wake of Chinese disarray. What had started in Muscovy in the sixteenth century as a riverine continental empire in response to, in D.W. Meinig's words, 'a centrifugal pressure outward from the core of European Christendom,' ended three hundred years later in surrender to fellow imperialists of a seaborne maritime empire on the North American periphery; the 'moving frontiers of political control' had come full circle. And Russia had belatedly begun its 'shift from marginal seas and backcountry marchlands to the world ocean and continental interiors.'[41] The sale of Alaska in 1867 was but belated and formal recognition of the withdrawal of Russia from North America and the consolidation and enlargement of her position in Asia. The consequences of this geopolitical shift – Russia's incursion on China and the United States' squeeze on Canada – are still with us.

41 Meinig, 'A Macrogeography of Western Imperialism: Some Morphologies of Moving Frontiers of Political Control,' in Fay Gale and Graham H. Lawton, eds. *Settlement & Encounter* (Melbourne 1969), 216

ROBERT D. MITCHELL

The formation of
early American cultural regions:
an interpretation

A major problem in the geography of the early United States is how to identify and explain the diffusion of cultural traits and regional patterns west of the Appalachians. One of the most striking changes that occurred in early American society was the increasing cultural convergence of areas settled during the first few decades after the American Revolution. Prior to the Revolution we can identify a remarkable cultural and regional diversity in late colonial settlements; by the early nineteenth century we can discern a decreasing variation in cultural characteristics and a trend towards greater uniformity over extensive areas of the trans-Appalachian west. Previous attempts to conceptualize the processes operative in cultural transfer in the American milieu have focused largely on Turnerian ideas of frontier reductionism and reformulation or on ideas derived from the culture area concept, particularly the application of a core-domain-sphere model. Neither approach can account adequately for cultural change and variation in American society over time and space.

Any alternative approach that intends to explain the cultural consequences of early interior expansion, as this expansion has been reconstructed so far, must take into account the changing relationships among ideology, place, and material culture in areas undergoing initial American occupancy. A promising approach is to trace the interior patterns of population movement deriving from the late colonial seaboard and to view pioneer settlers as cultural vectors or agents in transmitting cultural traits and adapting to new geographical situations. Three major processes were at work in the creation of emerging frontier societies: the virtual *duplication* of seaboard culture hearth traits as a direct result of influences emanating from an adjacent hearth region, as occurred in the northern

Connecticut Valley and in western Maryland; considerable *deviation* from initial hearth characteristics because of local settlement circumstances, but not sufficient to create a viable alternative core, as in the case of Dutch settlements in the Hudson and Delaware valleys; and the *fusion* of traits from two or more hearths to produce a significant cultural reconfiguration that was influential in setting the tone and direction of further cultural diffusion, as was the case in parts of western Virginia and the Carolinas. The culture area concept has been concerned primarily with hearth initiation and degrees of duplication; the Turnerian approach has emphasized frontier deviation and subsequent duplication. However, it is the fusion process, aided by the appearance of symbols of national unity, that seems to have been most important in the cultural formation of the early trans-Appalachian west.

COLONIAL ANTECEDENTS

In his pioneering attempt to construct a map of modern American cultural regions Wilbur Zelinsky has recognized the significance of what he has termed 'The Period of First Effective Settlement.' He then added, with reference to the eastern seaboard: 'the cultural gradients tend to be much steeper and the boundaries between regions more distinct than is true for the remainder of the continent. There is greater variety within a narrower range of space as one approaches the older, inner regions, but greater blurring of cultural traits and confusion of identity in the reverse direction, toward the outer, new tracts.'[1] How did such gradients arise and what contributions were made during the change from colony to republic? More specifically, what formative processes were in operation prior to the Revolution that were reflected in early trans-Appalachian landscapes and how are we to distinguish their effects from those generated by an emerging national consciousness?

The initial European colonization of the eastern seaboard was a highly selective process. It involved a reduction and simplification of western European core cultures and an intensification of those traits and complexes that did survive in the United States in response to the ecological conditions encountered in the New World and the ideological aspirations derived from the Old.[2] In certain areas of seventeenth-century settlement these survivals were fused with

---

1 Zelinsky, *The Cultural Geography of the United States* (Englewood Cliffs 1973), 120, map on 118-19
2 The processes involved are discussed in George M. Foster, *Culture and Conquest: America's Spanish Heritage,* Viking Fund Publications in Anthropology no 27 (New York 1960), and Louis Hartz, *The Founding of New Societies* (New York 1964)

FIGURE 1.   Modern cultural regions

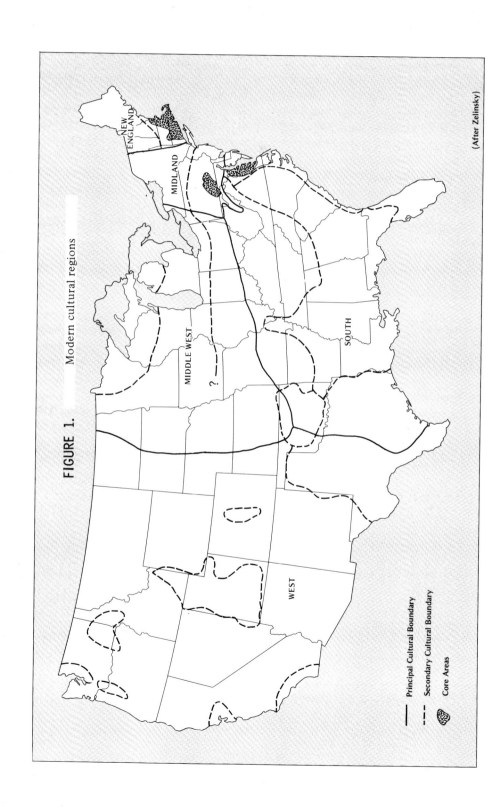

NEW ENGLAND

MIDLAND

MIDDLE WEST

?

SOUTH

WEST

(After Zelinsky)

——— Principal Cultural Boundary

---- Secondary Cultural Boundary

🖤 Core Areas

some aboriginal material traits to produce new cultural syntheses or hearths. At least three such hearths have been identified – southern New England, south-eastern Pennsylvania, and the western Chesapeake tidewater (Figure 1).[3] The two earliest hearths, New England and the Chesapeake, were initially the products of different fragments of the English cultural core. The Pennsylvania (or Midland) hearth, which developed a distinct configuration during the early eighteenth century, was a fusion of more pluralistic complexes of primarily English, German, and Scotch-Irish origins. All three hearths contained important regional subsystems (for example, tidewater Virginia and southern Maryland in the Chesapeake), a subject that requires more thorough geographical inquiry. Although they originated in the rural, agrarian, and commercial contexts of the early colonial period, both the New England and Pennsylvania areas contained strong traditions of mercantile urbanism. The Chesapeake lacked a dominant urban focus until the emergence of Baltimore during the last quarter of the eighteenth century. The relationships between town and countryside within these culture hearths, and between these mercantile centres and the creation of American culture after the Revolution, also remain to be explored.[4]

Regardless of the distinctive characteristics of these hearths, their occupants shared some basic values and traits that were to endure into the new republic and beyond the Appalachians. Liberalist, individualistic, and capitalist attitudes were entertained to a degree rarely encountered in Europe. A major goal of interior-moving settlers was a desire for secure material well-being, based upon property ownership (especially land), profitable enterprise, and wealth accumulation for immediate consumption and for transfer to the next generation, within a political context that placed the fewest impediments in the way of achieving such goals. Failure to appreciate the fundamental influence of market-place modes of operation on American society have prevented some students of American culture from identifying the most significant questions about continuity and change in westward expansion.[5] The articulation of such

3 Conrad M. Arensberg, 'American Communities,' *American Anthropologist* 57 (1955): 1143-60; Donald W. Meinig, 'The American Colonial Era: A Geographic Commentary,' *Proceedings of the Royal Geographical Society,* South Australian branch (1957-8): 1-22; Zelinsky, *Cultural Geography*, 117-28. The significance of the Carolina low country, centred on Charleston, as a fourth major seaboard hearth remains to be explored (as does the relationship of Savannah to this hearth).

4 Some interesting lines of inquiry on urban-national relationships are suggested in Allan R. Pred, *Urban Growth and the Circulation of Information: The United States System of Cities, 1790-1840* (Cambridge, Mass. 1973).

5 These points are made clear in Andrew H. Clark, 'Suggestions for the Geographical Study of Agricultural Change in the United States, 1790-1840,' *Agricultural History*

goals was clearly expressed in colonial rural landscapes in the form of irregularly shaped land assignment patterns grouped in individual farmsteads, a relatively rapid replacement of simple wooden housing structures by more substantial frame or brick dwellings, ubiquitous Euro-american crop and European livestock components, and road or stream access to local service centres, where courthouses, taverns, market places, and churches vied as focal points for social, economic, and political activity within primarily decentralized trading systems.

In the formation of new American societies the most fundamental institutional expression of Euro-american cultural tradition was the commercialization of the land. Because land was viewed primarily as a commercial commodity it was rapidly alienated from native control and redistributed among Euro-american owners, both occupant and absentee.[6] The resultant patterns of private land subdivision and population distribution produced a proliferation of discrete property units where none had existed before and an exponential rate of growth in the number and incidence of property boundaries, both recognized and asserted. Thus, the continuity of American continental space was broken by the super-imposition of European-derived cognitive and institutional organization on the land prior to actual occupance and utilization. Once occupied, it was those who owned the land who exerted the most formative cultural influences on the structure of the new society.

---

46 (1972): 155-72; Robert D. Mitchell, 'The Shenandoah Valley Frontier,' *Annals of the Association of American Geographers* 62 (1972): 461-86, and *Commercialism and Frontier: Perspectives on the Early Shenandoah Valley* (Charlottesville 1977), chap. 1. Also see Richard D. Brown, 'Modernization and the Modern Personality in Early America, 1600-1865: A Sketch of a Synthesis,' *Journal of Interdisciplinary History* 2 (1972): 201-28.

6 One of the most persistent Euro-american justifications for dispossessing native populations was that most land was, in legal terms, uninhabited 'waste' because the natives had not occupied and subdued it. Yet Indian sovereignty and property rights extended over most of the eastern United States. The land was not 'open' but covered with a comprehensive network of territorial claims totally incomprehensible to the Euro-american invaders. Especially useful studies of social and territorial organization are Fredrik Barth, ed., *Ethnic Groups and Boundaries: The Social Organization of Culture Difference* (Boston 1969), and Anthony F.C. Wallace, 'Political Organization and Land Tenure among the Northeastern Indians, 1600-1830,' *Southwestern Journal of Anthropology* 13 (1957): 301-21. For an overview of Indian dispossession, see Wilcomb E. Washburn, 'The Moral and Legal Justification for Dispossessing the Indians,' in J.M. Smith, ed., *Seventeenth-Century America: Essays in Colonial History* (Chapel Hill 1959), 15-32; for a recent and provocative interpretation, see Francis Jennings, *The Invasion of America: Indians, Colonialism, and the Cant of Conquest* (Chapel Hill 1975), chaps. 1, 2, and 8.

MODES OF EXPLANATION

Until very recently interpretations of the first phase of expansion into the piedmont and Appalachian interior, during the fifty years after 1720, have emphasized the reduced simplicity of interior societies. Renewal and rebirth were the essence of frontier expansion, 'a return to primitive conditions on a continually advancing frontier line,' as Frederick Jackson Turner phrased it.[7] Out of the ashes of forest clearance rose, phoenix-like, the configuration of a new American culture, with distinct sectional variations. From the point of view of its cultural applicability this traditional approach, and its more recent revisions, contains several critical flaws. Firstly, it presents a dichotomous subsistent-commercial gradient of economic evolution in which new societies first had to experience a period of subsistent economy to be replaced gradually, if at all, by a more commercial mode of operation. Most frontier societies were commercially oriented, although not commercially operative, from the beginning and it was their economic specialties for external markets that provided the clearest expression of emerging trans-Appalachian cultural patterns. Secondly, the traditional frontier model postulates severe distance constraints on the interactions between the seaboard and the developing backcountry, thus suggesting that frontier societies were consciously isolated socially and culturally from the external influences of the larger colonial and emerging republican worlds. Most frontier societies did not evolve in isolation for long, as a network of trails and roads developed to link backcountry and seaboard, and bring about an interchange of people, goods, and ideas that integrated newly settled areas into the emerging national scene. Thirdly, these assumptions of relative self-sufficiency and isolation have encouraged not only Turnerians but also many students of American culture to seek trans-Appalachian origins for the creation of a distinctive American cultural identity.[8] Implicit in this assumption is the idea that the cultural pluralism of late colonial settlements was reduced to a new American melting pot by local forces impinging on frontier settlers. Place took precedence over culture and ideology. Assimilative trends were certainly at work but they were ideological forces rather than spatial constraints. It was the virtually ubiquitous espousal of American materialistic ideology during a period

7 Turner, *The Frontier in American History* (New York 1920), 2
8 See, for example, Richard R. Pillsbury, 'The Urban Street Pattern of Pennsylvania before 1815: A Study in Cultural Geography,' PhD dissertation, Pennsylvania State University, 1968, Figs. 67-72, and 'The Urban Street Pattern as a Culture Indicator: Pennsylvania, 1682-1815,' *Annals of the Association of American Geographers* 60 (1970): 428-46.

of emerging national consciousness and almost non-existent immigration that provided the impetus for a renewed, rather than a new, cultural synthesis.

Except for the identification of original hearths, the culture area approach has been applied more thoroughly to the development of settlement and society in the nineteenth-century west than to the eighteenth-century east. The idea of a cultural region as a continuous or interrupted area of distribution of identifiable cultural elements or cultural groups has been most usefully applied to Mormon settlement in the west and, with modifications, in Texas.[9] An initial core area of new settlement is established that becomes the focus for the diffusion of the settlement's dominant cultural characteristics to adjacent areas. The influence of these core traits will diminish with distance, so that in a surrounding zone the initial culture remains dominant but with less intensity and complexity; this encourages the emergence of cultural subregions. Beyond this zone is the marginal and usually more extensive area of outer influence, the sphere, where bearers of the initial core culture represent a cultural minority in contact with others.

Implicit in the elaboration of such a system is a high degree of geographical isolation from external cultural influences, so that the core traits can be diffused in a non-competitive context. As Zelinsky has pointed out, such a condition is unusual in American expansion and he is correctly sceptical about the application of such a scheme to the eastern United States.[10] But he does not pursue the point further. The colonial culture hearths can be viewed as dynamic cultural regions with reasonably identifiable internal structures comprising 'cores' (Boston and adjacent eastern Massachusetts, Philadelphia and adjacent southeastern Pennsylvania, and the lower peninsula of tidewater Virginia) and adjacent 'domains' that undergo internal elaboration and change over time.[11]

9 Donald W. Meinig, 'The Mormon Culture Region: Strategies and Patterns in the Geography of the American West, 1847-1964,' *Annals of the Association of American Geographers* 55 (1965): 191-220, and *Imperial Texas: An Interpretive Essay in Cultural Geography* (Austin 1969)

10 *Cultural Geography*, 114-16. In a later essay Meinig anticipates such criticism. 'Although folk colonization is always selective and uneven in area, in the East the general tide of settlement was relatively comprehensive and local nuclei and salients in the vanguard were soon engulfed and integrated into a generally continuous pattern.' 'American Wests: Preface to a Geographical Interpretation,' *Annals of the Association of American Geographers* 62 (1972): 160

11 It seems unreasonable to exclude emerging urban influences within hearth areas, as if they were not an expression of the 'folk' culture of the hearth area. The Pennsylvania hearth is generally depicted as excluding Philadelphia, although why this should be so has never been explained satisfactorily. See Wilbur Zelinsky, 'The Pennsylvania Town: An Overdue Geographical Account,' *Geographical Review* 67 (1977): 127-47.

Because the diffusion of culture traits did not spread out from these hearth regions in a uniform manner, the duplication process tends to break down in the sphere zone, the area of contacts between different cultural traditions. It was in the early colonial spheres that competitive modes of living were encountered and selectively amalgamated, not automatically on the basis of distance from core areas but on the basis of land control, settler initiatives, and economic systems. Who owned the land and who settled it were as important as which areas were settled when.

Settlement beyond the frontiers of 1776 was a direct result of population movements from the eastern seaboard and from interior areas first occupied during the late colonial period. The relative significance of the contributions of these two migration sources depended upon three main factors: the numerical and cultural characteristics of the settlers comprising the pioneer generation, the specific behavioural and material traits that were adapted to the new location, and the timing of active settlement. Available evidence suggests that the pioneer generations on the earliest trans-Appalachian frontiers were derived less from the seaboard than from intermediate areas recently settled before the American Revolution.[12] By identifying the cultural characteristics of such areas we should be able to determine how they contributed to the cultural configuration of the early United States. Indeed, we may hypothesize the existence of specific areas within the interior spheres of the colonial hearth regions, regional 'way stations,' where significant cultural fusions occurred that directly influenced the development of early trans-Appalachian societies.

A few scholars have hinted at such an approach. Milton B. Newton, for example, has suggested the importance of a late colonial backcountry hearth area stretching from southeastern Pennsylvania (Lancaster) through western Maryland, Virginia, and the Carolinas to eastern Georgia (Augusta).[13] The Euro-american settlers of this region were viewed as the creators of a set of cultural preadaptations that provided the basis for extending the range of

12 Alfred P. James, 'The First English-speaking Trans-Appalachian Frontier,' *Mississippi Valley Historical Review* 7 (1930): 55-71; Thomas P. Abernathy, *Three Virginia Frontiers* (Baton Rouge 1940), 64 ff.; John D. Barnhart, 'Frontiersmen and Planters in the Formation of Kentucky,' *Journal of Southern History* 7 (1941): 19-36, and 'Sources of Southern Migration into the Old Northwest,' *Mississippi Valley Historical Review* 22 (1935): 49-62; Robert E. Chaddock, 'Ohio before 1850: A Study of the Early Influence of Pennsylvania and Southern Populations in Ohio,' *Columbia University Studies in History, Economics, and Public Law* 30 (1908): 1-155; Beverley W. Bond, Jr., *The Foundations of Ohio* (Columbus 1941), 275; Mitchell, *Commercialism and Frontier*, chap. 3
13 Newton, 'Cultural Preadaptation and the Upland South,' *Geoscience and Man* 5 (1974): 143-54

Upland Southern culture beyond the Appalachians to the Great Plains. Although it was not their primary purpose, Joseph E. Spencer and Ronald J. Horvath have been even more specific about the identification of distinct intermediate areas.[14] In their attempt to delineate the cultural and locational antecedents of Corn Belt agriculture, they have identified the Connecticut Valley and southeastern Pennsylvania as important source regions, and the Kentucky Bluegrass and the Nashville Basin as key areas bridging the gap between seaboard and Corn Belt. Their study is an illuminating discussion of the diffusion of certain agricultural traits, but the gaps that the authors try to bridge are too broad. Too much is left unexplained about the transmission of traits between Pennsylvania and Kentucky, for example. As Spencer and Horvath have pointed out, corn and hogs were not integral parts of the early agriculture of southeastern Pennsylvania and therefore their significance in Kentucky needs to be explained in some other fashion.

CATEGORIZATION OF EARLY AMERCAN CULTURAL REGIONS

Although more detailed research needs to be done, the existing literature does permit a tentative reconstruction of the spatial structure of early American diffusion patterns (Figure 2). The map is a suggestive rather than definitive statement of the regionalization of interior diffusion patterns by the early nineteenth century. Inland from the seaboard hearth regions at least two secondary areas, occupied during the late colonial period, appear to represent distinctive settlement experiences: western Virginia (specifically the Shenandoah Valley) and the northwest Carolina piedmont (focused on the area between Durham and Winston-Salem).[15] A case could be made for including southwestern Pennsylvania as a secondary centre, although a permanent civilian population had only existed there for a decade prior to the Revolution. A tier of significant tertiary areas appears to have existed by the early nineteenth century, ranging from west-central New York (the 'Burned-Over' District) through northeastern Ohio (the Western Reserve), southwestern Ohio (the Middle Ohio Valley), and central Kentucky (the Bluegrass) to central Tennessee (the Nashville Basin).

In terms of the cultural processes at work a further classification can be made according to the degree to which the transmission of cultural characteristics

14 Spencer and Horvath, 'How Does an Agricultural Region Originate?' *Annals of the Association of American Geographers* 53 (1963): 74-92

15 See Mitchell, *Commercialism and Frontier*; Robert W. Ramsay, *Carolina Cradle: Settlement of the Northwest Carolina Frontier, 1747-1762* (Chapel Hill 1964): H. Roy Merrens, *Colonial North Carolina in the Eighteenth Century* (Chapel Hill 1964).

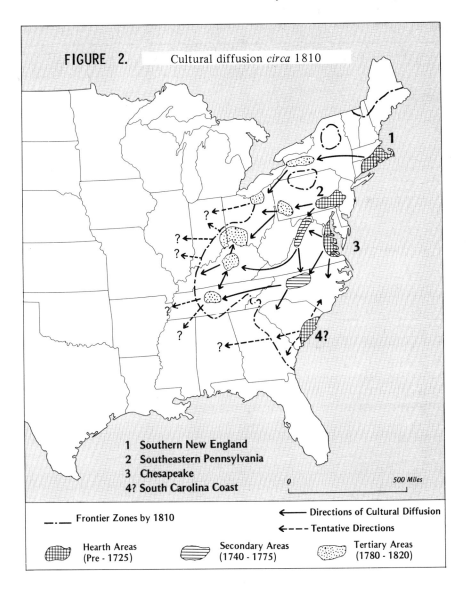

FIGURE 2. Cultural diffusion *circa* 1810

1 Southern New England
2 Southeastern Pennsylvania
3 Chesapeake
4? South Carolina Coast

0   500 Miles

_ . _   Frontier Zones by 1810   ← Directions of Cultural Diffusion
                                                  ←--- Tentative Directions

Hearth Areas   Secondary Areas   Tertiary Areas
(Pre - 1725)   (1740 - 1775)   (1780 - 1820)

from the hearth was a function primarily of duplication, deviation, or fusion. Thus, the western Virginia and northwest Carolina areas can be viewed as centres of trait fusion from the Midland and Chesapeake hearths. West-central New York, at least until the 1820s, and northeastern Ohio seem to have been relatively faithful reproductions of the New England hearth as it existed in the late eighteenth century.[16] Southwestern Pennsylvania was primarily a duplication of the Midland hearth with slight modifications (such as the minor importance of slaves) because of some population movement from western Virginia.[17]

Southwestern Ohio, central Kentucky, and central Tennessee are especially significant areas because they represent nodes of further fusion from both hearth and secondary source areas. Southwestern Ohio, influenced primarily by Midland traits, was moulded into a new synthesis because of selective influences from Kentucky and because of institutional changes generated at the national level during the 1780s and 1790s. The Kentucky and Tennessee centres, which were key locations in the interior expansion of upper Southern cultural landscapes, derived their main influences from the Chesapeake through western Virginia and northwest Carolina, respectively.

On the basis of such diffusion patterns and centres we can trace the geographical relationships between the eastern seaboard and the cultural delineation of the trans-Appalachian west as it had emerged by the second quarter of the nineteenth century (Figure 3). At a very aggregate level we can discern significant differences between a 'North' and a 'South' by the time of the American Revolution.[18] The former comprised the New England and Midland

16 Lois K. Matthews, *The Expansion of New England: The Spread of New England Settlement and Institutions to the Mississippi River, 1620-1865* (Boston 1909), 171-429; Ruth L. Higgins, *Expansion in New York with Especial Reference to the Eighteenth Century* (Columbus 1931); D.W. Meinig, 'The Colonial Period, 1609-1775' and 'Geography of Expansion, 1785-1855,' in John H. Thompson, ed., *Geography of New York State* (Syracuse 1966), 121-71

17 Solon J. and E.H. Buck, *The Planting of Civilization in Western Pennsylvania* (Pittsburgh 1939); Edward M. Burns, 'Slavery in Western Pennsylvania,' *Western Pennsylvania Historical Magazine* 8 (1925): 204-14

18 See the arguments advanced in Jackson Turner Main, *The Social Structure of Revolutionary America* (Princeton 1965), chaps. 1 and 2. For the colonial South, see especially Thomas J. Wertenbaker, *The Old South: The Founding of American Civilization* (New York 1942), and Carl Bridenbaugh, *Myths and Realities: Societies of the Colonial South* (Baton Rouge 1952). Also see the remarks on twentieth-century Southern landscapes in Wilbur Zelinsky, 'Where the South Begins: The Northern Limits of the Cis-Appalachian South in Terms of Settlement Landscape,' *Social Forces* 30 (1951): 172-8.

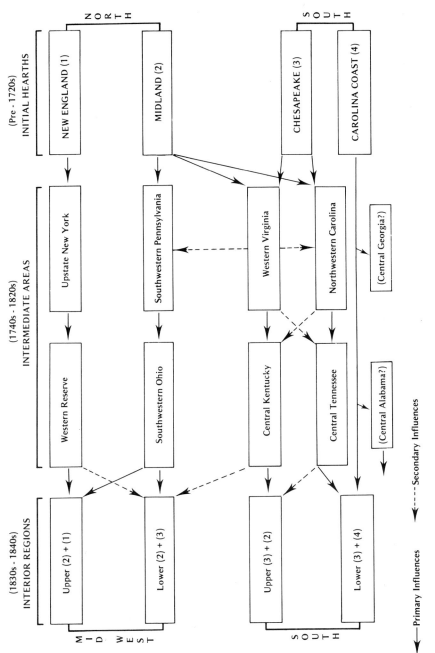

Figure 3 Patterns of diffusion before 1850

(Pre - 1720s)
INITIAL HEARTHS

NORTH

NEW ENGLAND (1)

MIDLAND (2)

SOUTH

CHESAPEAKE (3)

CAROLINA COAST (4)

(1740s - 1820s)
INTERMEDIATE AREAS

Upstate New York

Southwestern Pennsylvania

Western Virginia

Northwestern Carolina

(Central Georgia?)

Western Reserve

Southwestern Ohio

Central Kentucky

Central Tennessee

(Central Alabama?)

(1830s - 1840s)
INTERIOR REGIONS

Upper (2) + (1)

Lower (2) + (3)

M I D
W E S T

Upper (3) + (2)

Lower (3) + (4)

S O U T H

⟶ Primary Influences

---⟶ Secondary Influences

hearths, and the latter the Chesapeake and possibly the Carolina low country. Because of the migration and cultural linkages that occurred between interior centres during the period from the 1740s to the 1820s, the cultural configuration of the trans-Appalachian interior was characterized by only two major cultural regions: a Midwestern and a Southern extension of the seaboard South, both of which contained upper and lower subregions whose cultural ancestry can be determined reasonably well.[19]

The use of the terms 'upper' and 'lower,' as well as the multiple-nuclei approach of this study, runs counter to the tone of other recent interpretations of American regional culture. Zelinsky and Newton, for example, have used the terms 'lowland' and 'upland' to designate regional subdivisions within the South. For Zelinsky these subdivisions tend to correspond to topographic divisions. The Upland South corresponds generally with the southern Appalachian system, the Ozarks, and the adjacent lowlands of Tennessee, Kentucky, and the Ohio Valley. For Newton, who takes exception to 'upper' and 'lower' designations because they tend to be equated with political rather than cultural boundaries, the term 'Upland South' encompasses the entire South except for the tidewater zone. This would seem to be an exceptionally gross level of resolution, but it is consistent with his view that the culture complex that was preadapted to frontier living conditions emerged in the late colonial backcountry east of the Appalachians 'and was exported intact to the edge of the Great Plains.'[20]

TRAIT DIFFUSION IN A BORDER ZONE

In order to understand the emergence of the regional structure discussed in this study and to assess the formative factors influencing continuity and change, the similarities and differences between the late colonial landscapes of western Virginia and western Maryland and the early republican landscapes of central Kentucky and southwestern Ohio are worth examining. These are key border areas in delineating both the interior penetration and interaction of Midland and Chesapeake influences and the formation of Midwestern and interior Southern cultural regions during the early nineteenth century (Figure 4).

In the American ethos the forces that governed the creation and differentiation of interior societies and landscapes in the new nation were primarily social and economic in origin. The new settlement landscapes displayed to a

19 See the extension of such a scheme to Texas in Terry G. Jordan, 'The Imprint of the Upper South on Mid-Nineteenth Century Texas,' *Annals of the Association of American Geographers* 57 (1967): 667-90.
20 'Cultural Preadaptation,' 152

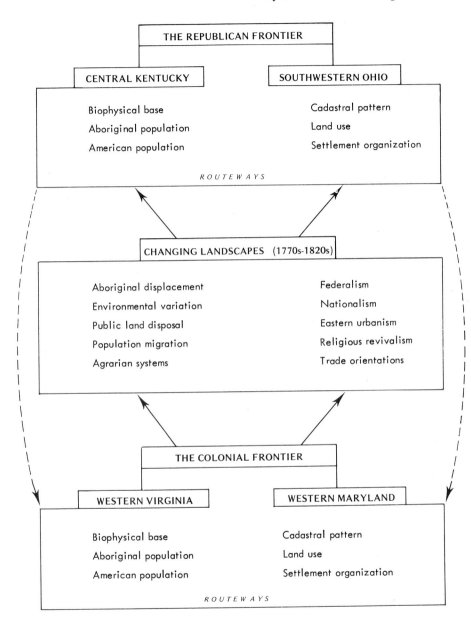

Figure 4 Transformational structure

considerable degree the operations of the socio-economic systems of the yeoman farmer, who was found almost everywhere in the eighteenth-century United States, and the planter, whose distribution was more restricted.[21] Consequently, in addition to the timing of settlement in the interior and the patterns of land assignment that were introduced, the most important forces influencing cultural patterns were those associated with agricultural specialization, population composition, and social organization.

These points are well illustrated in the contrasting settlement histories of western Maryland and Virginia. Although more topographic variation existed in western Maryland (piedmont as well as ridge and valley sections), both areas were relatively heavily forested, with growing seasons of similar duration (150-180 days) and an absence of aboriginal population at contact time. Both areas were occupied by western Europeans who had migrated from or through the Middle Colonies and who had established irregularly dispersed farms of 200 to 400 acres devoted to corn and to small grains and livestock from Europe. Yet they differed in one fundamental respect. Western Maryland, located adjacent to two major hearth regions, became an extension of Midland society and economy. Western Virginia, specifically the Shenandoah Valley, which was located farther from both hearths, became an area of fusion, at least in terms of population and land-use patterns if not fully in social patterns and religious affiliation.

Western Maryland failed to become an area of fusion not only because of its adjacence to southeastern Pennsylvania but also because of its delayed settlement.[22] Permanent settlement began during the mid-1740s, more than fifteen years after the first settlements in the Shenandoah Valley. Lord Baltimore had released his piedmont lands for settlement during the early 1730s, but border disputes with Pennsylvania and Virginia, misconceptions about land fertility, and large-scale speculation in land warrants by tidewater landowners discouraged immediate settlement. It was not until a few land developers

---

21 See particularly Robert E. Baldwin, 'Patterns of Development in Newly Settled Regions,' *Manchester School of Economic and Social Studies* 24 (1956): 151-79; Aubrey C. Land, 'Economic Behavior in a Planting Society: The Eighteenth-Century Chesapeake,' *Journal of Southern History* 33 (1967): 469-85; and Edward C. Papenfuse, 'Planter Behavior and Economic Opportunity in a Staple Economy,' *Agricultural History* 46 (1972): 297-312.

22 Frank W. Porter, III, 'From Backcountry to County: The Delayed Settlement of Western Maryland,' *Maryland Historical Magazine* 70 (1975): 329-49, and Porter, 'The Maryland Frontier, 1722-1732: Prelude to Settlement in Western Maryland,' in Robert D. Mitchell and Edward K. Muller, eds., *Geographical Perspectives on Maryland's Past* (College Park 1977).

actively sought settlers from Pennsylvania that the first, mainly German, families moved in. The great majority of the 45,000 settlers in the region by 1776 had come from the Middle Colonies. It was they who directed the area's economic specialization in the direction of wheat, cattle, and livestock products. The absence of the plantation system, tobacco specialization, and large-scale slavery can be accounted for by the timing of settlement and the behaviour of Maryland planters. It is true that it was more difficult to extend tobacco production onto the Maryland piedmont than the Virginia piedmont because of the absence of navigable, eastward-flowing rivers. But the best clue to planter behaviour was the response to the depression in the tobacco trade during the early 1730s and to the fluctuating prices of the later 1730s and the 1740s. Maryland planters were more diversified in their economic patterns than their Virginia counterparts and rarely as heavily committed to tobacco production. Rather than buy up western lands to extend tobacco cultivation, as the larger Virginia planters were inclined to do, wealthy Maryland planters sold off their western holdings to incoming yeoman farmers and extended long-term credit to smaller planters, thus encouraging higher rates of settlement persistence and greater economic diversification than might otherwise have occurred.[23]

In the Shenandoah Valley cultural fusion did occur because of the extensive ownership of lands in the northern half of the valley by tidewater planters and the immigration of small planters to the region between 1760 and 1800. The great majority of the 35,000 settlers in the valley by 1776 were yeoman farmers who had come directly from Western Europe and from the Middle Colonies. Land use was dominated by corn, wheat, rye, flax, and pasture and fodder crops for cattle, horses, and pigs. Settlement patterns were based upon individual farms whose Midland folk housing characteristics were elaborated to help create the saddlebag house and the crib barn that were to become a particular characteristic of the upper South (Figure 4).[24]

Distinctive Chesapeake traits were slow to diffuse to the region after 1760 and had to negotiate the already established yeoman-farmer matrix. The principal innovative traits were a heavy dependence upon both tenancy and

23 See Carville V. Earle, *The Evolution of a Tidewater Settlement System: All Hallow's Parish, Maryland, 1650-1783* (Chicago 1975), chap. 5; Aubrey C. Land, 'Economic Base and Social Structure: The Northern Chesapeake in the Eighteenth Century,' *Journal of Economic History* 25 (1965): 639-54, and Land, 'The Planters of Colonial Maryland,' *Maryland Historical Magazine* 67 (1972): 109-28.

24 Fred Kniffen, 'Folk Housing: Key to Diffusion,' *Annals of the Association of American Geographers* 55 (1965): 549-77; Fred Kniffen and Henry Glassie, 'Building in Wood in the Eastern United States: A Time-Place Perspective,' *Geographical Review* 56 (1966): 40-66

slavery, the plantation system, commercial production of tobacco and hemp, expensive tastes in clothing, domestic furnishings, food, and drink, and affiliation with the Anglican Church.[25] These traits were first established in the northern part of the valley and diffused selectively southward. Slavery and tobacco and hemp cultivation spread widely throughout the region; large-scale tenancy, the plantation system, and expensive consumption patterns were primarily restricted to the north, and the Anglican Church almost entirely so. Despite the commercial dominance of wheat throughout the valley by the early 1780s, the cultivation of tobacco and the use of slaves were more widespread after the Revolution than before, coinciding with their diffusion to pioneer Kentucky.

In trying to trace the emergence of such agricultural specializations westward, it is particularly unfortunate that we know very little about the emergence of agricultural regionalism during the late eighteenth century. That there have been few attempts to study this problem is evident in the recently published *Atlas of Early American History: The Revolutionary Era, 1760-1790.*[26] The major weakness of this fine work is the omission of agricultural land-use patterns for this critical period in the extension and transformation of American landscapes. Comments about the reconstruction of agricultural regions must be as tentative at this juncture as those suggested previously for the identification of trans-Appalachian diffusion centres.

An examination of the early settlement landscapes of central Kentucky and southwestern Ohio, the former initiated during the late 1770s and the latter a decade later, reveals some striking resemblances between central Kentucky and western Virginia, and between southern Ohio and western Maryland (Figure 4). Like western Virginia, and Maryland, central Kentucky had long been abandoned by aboriginal populations prior to American occupance; in Ohio, a refuge area for many displaced native groups, further displacement by force and treaty during the 1790s delayed active settlement outside of the Ohio Valley and the Western Reserve until the turn of the century. The extension of an upper Southern agrarian complex west of the Appalachians was virtually guaranteed by the migration of settlers from western Virginia to central Kentucky, a biophysical environment sufficiently similar as to require no major agricultural adjustments. Environmental factors were certainly significant at specific local sites, but throughout the eastern United States the only major examples of

---

25 Robert D. Mitchell, 'Content and Context: Tidewater Characteristics in the Early Shenandoah Valley,' *Maryland Historian* 5 (1974): 79-92

26 Lester J. Cappon, ed., *Atlas of Early American History* (Princeton 1976). But see Meinig, 'The American Colonial Era,' 1-22, and Spencer and Horvath, 'How Does an Agricultural Region Originate?' 74-92

agricultural selectivity produced by variable ecological conditions were the limitations imposed on the interior expansion of rice cultivation and the northward extension of upland cotton. Settlers who most clearly espoused a strong commercial orientation were most likely to avoid the hillier and more mountainous parts of the Appalachians and move on to more promising agricultural areas. Such cultural selectivity began to produce significant contrasts between the more progressive populations of the fertile limestone basin of central Kentucky and the middle Ohio Valley of southwestern Ohio, on the one hand, and the more traditional populations of the more remote, hillier parts of eastern Kentucky and southeastern Ohio, on the other.

Central Kentucky was first settled during the 1770s and 1780s by yeoman farmers and by small planters possessing from two to ten slaves.[27] The motivations of, and the interactions between, these two groups of settlers were critical in defining the cultural characteristics of the Kentucky frontier. The presence of slavery, backed by solid foundations in a staple economy, had a profound impact on many ambitious, socially mobile yeoman farmers. Many of these yeomen had been sufficiently exposed to plantation slavery in Virginia and North Carolina before the Revolution to be motivated to move into the ranks of the small planter in Kentucky, first specializing in hemp and then adding tobacco during the 1790s. Other yeomen, who were uncomfortable with the institution or who had come from non-slave areas of eastern Pennsylvania or western Maryland, tended to migrate across the Ohio River to the Old Northwest.[28]

Early Kentucky was characterized by a broadly based, mixed agricultural system in which corn, wheat, and rye were the dominant grains. Corn had been almost ubiquitous on the seaboard both as a human and as a livestock feed, but it was the large Southern gourd-seed varieties that formed the basis of the early livestock specializations in Kentucky and the Ohio Valley.[29] The fattening of

27 R.S. Cotterill, *History of Pioneer Kentucky* (Cincinnati 1917), 206; Barnhart, 'Frontiersmen and Planters,' 19-36; Eugene M. Brademan, 'Early Kentucky: Its Virginia Heritage,' *South Atlantic Quarterly* 38 (1939): 449-61. Pratt Byrd, 'The Kentucky Frontier in 1792,' *Filson Club History Quarterly* 25 (1951), 181-203, 286-94, examines the contrasting political outlooks of the two groups. According to the first federal census, just over 16 per cent of Kentucky's population of 73,677 was slave; few planters possessed more than ten.

28 Chaddock, 'Ohio before 1850,' 30-46; Barnhart, 'Sources of Southern Migration,' 49-62, and 'The Southern Influence in the Formation of Ohio,' *Journal of Southern History* 3 (1937): 28-42

29 Richard Lyle Power, *Planting Corn Belt Culture: The Impress of the Upland Southerner and Yankee in the Old Northwest* (Indianapolis 1953); Paul C. Henlein, *Cattle Kingdom in the Ohio Valley, 1783-1860* (Lexington 1959)

cattle on corn in open feed lots during the winter, a practice that laid the foundations of Corn Belt farming during the early ninettenth century, may have diffused to central Kentucky and southern Ohio from western Virginia.[30] Wheat specialization had emerged in southeastern Pennsylvania, western Maryland, the Shenandoah Valley, and northwestern Carolina prior to 1776, and it became an important commercial crop in early Kentucky, Tennessee, and Ohio. It was in southern Ohio in particular that it became an early staple; before 1820 total production was more than three times greater than corn.[31] According to the federal agricultural census, Ohio was the leading wheat-producing state in the nation by 1839 and remained among the top four states until 1860. However, over the long term corn was of greater importance in Ohio than wheat. Southern Ohio farmers shifted increasingly to corn growing and livestock fattening during the 1830s, and by the early 1840s total corn output had surpassed that of wheat. West of the Appalachians rye, barley, and oats declined as livestock feeds, but rye was able to survive because of its importance in whiskey production.

Flax, a common crop throughout the seaboard, was also widely distributed west of the Appalachians. However, in central Kentucky hemp became the first non-food staple after the Revolution, having been diffused from the Virginia piedmont and the Shenandoah Valley. By 1790 Kentucky had become the leading hemp-producing state in the nation (a position it retained until 1860) and eliminated effectively the older producing areas in Virginia.[32]

In terms of livestock specialization it was the steer-hog-horse complex, already well developed in western Virginia by the Revolution, that spread to central Kentucky and beyond to the Middle Ohio Valley during the last quarter of the eighteenth century.[33] In southern Ohio, where there was no competition from plantation staples, cattle, pigs, and corn were more thoroughly integrated into the local cash economy than in any other early republican frontier. This

---

30 Robert L. Jones, 'Ohio Agriculture in History,' *Ohio Historical Quarterly* 65 (1956): 229-58. For some contemporary observations on the importance of corn, wheat, and livestock fattening, see François-André Michaux, 'Travels to the West of the Allegheny Mountains (1802),' in Reuben G. Thwaites, ed., *Early Western Travels* (Cleveland 1904-7), 3: 239-41, and J.P. Cutler, *Life and Times of Ephraim Cutler* (Cincinnati 1890), 89-90.

31 Ohio Governors' Papers, cited in Edward K. Muller, 'The Development of Urban Settlement in a Newly Settled Region: The Middle Ohio Valley, 1800-1860,' PhD dissertation, University of Wisconsin, 1972, p. 92. Also see Paul W. Stoddard, 'The Economic Progress of Ohio 1800-1840,' *Ohio State Archaeological and Historical Quarterly* 41 (1932): 176-94.

32 James F. Hopkins, *History of the Hemp Industry in Kentucky* (Lexington 1947)

33 Jones, 'Ohio Agriculture,' 229-58

complex, combined with wheat, so dominated patterns of agricultural development north of the Ohio that the commercial agriculture of the Middle West became more specialized and simplified than that of the upper South.[34] After distinct agricultural specialties had emerged in Kentucky and Ohio, exports of wheat and flour, hemp, tobacco, livestock, and livestock products, either down the Ohio to New Orleans or across the Appalachians, began to compete in seaboard markets with the produce of the interior uplands occupied prior to the Revolution.

These agricultural patterns were one reflection of culturally prescribed behaviour that was manifested in the landscape; the structure and arrangement of settlement forms was another. The combination of 'I' house and forebay barn, characteristic of the Midland hearth, spread relatively unaltered southward into frontier Maryland and Virginia and westward to the Ohio Valley. Despite the elaboration of these forms in the Shenandoah Valley, the forebay barn did not spread farther throughout the upper South but was replaced by the structurally more flexible crib form in Kentucky and Tennessee. The four-crib barn became a characteristic feature of the trans-Appalachian South. Thus, greater differences existed in barn types than in house types on either side of the Ohio River.[35] Fences also varied considerably from place to place west of the Appalachians, but they were not always useful cultural indicators. Thus, in the Kentucky Bluegrass, where limestone outcroppings were frequent, stone walls were often built adjacent to post-and-rail or worm fences; in southern Ohio post-and-rail fences appear to have been most prevalent. Throuthout the early trans-Appalachian west the single-family farm continued to dominate rural settlement patterns, and the courthouse town, in a variety of forms and with a range of names from folk to classical (especially in Ohio), formed the initial basis of frontier urbanism.[36]

Such landscape artifacts provide invaluable clues to early patterns of cultural diffusion, but they are only partial indicators of culturally prescribed behaviour

34 Two more regionally proscribed specializations were wheat with sheep in the eastern Ohio hill lands and dairying in the Western Reserve; see *ibid.*, 234-8.

35 Henry Glassie, 'The Pennsylvania Barn in the South,' *Pennsylvania Folklife* 15 (Winter 1965-6): 8-19 and (Summer 1966), 12-25; Glassie, *Pattern in the Material Folk Culture of the Eastern United States* (Philadelphia 1968), 74-101; Martin Wright, 'The Antecedents of the Double-Pen House Type,' *Annals of the Association of American Geographers* 48 (1958): 109-17; Hubert G.H. Wilhelm, 'The Pennsylvania-Dutch Barn in Southeastern Ohio,' *Geoscience and Man* 5 (1974): 155-62

36 Edward T. Price, 'The Central Courthouse Square in the American County Seat,' *Geographical Review* 58 (1968): 29-60; Wilbur Zelinsky, 'Classical Town Names in the United States,' *Geographical Review* 57 (1967): 463-95

west of the Appalachians. Other sets of cultural complexes are less obvious but no less important. Unfortunately, evidence of early patterns of speech, diet, dress, folk customs, and craft practices is both scanty and subject to considerable change over time.[37] This makes it difficult to use these complexes as significant cultural indicators and to map their changing distributions.

Continuity and regional variation were more clearly defined in social structures and patterns of social organization. The presence of slavery south of the Ohio River (and its virtual absence farther north) provided the basis for contrasting social morphologies and political orientations. From Kentucky southward the continuity of Southern cultural traditions from the seaboard to the interior, and especially the institution of slavery, provided a different framework for social evolution than that farther north. Although slavery and slaveholding were less widespread in central Kentucky than in central Tennessee or the lower South, society was nevertheless more class-structured than in southern Ohio. A landholding élite of larger planters and ambitious yeomen about to enter the planter ranks provided a traditional leadership structure for the conduct of political and civic affairs.[38] Life was more oligarchic than egalitarian; liberal individualism was an ideology less widely shared by the smaller yeoman, the poor white, and, most obviously, the slave. With strong rural traditions and a relatively slow pace of urbanization, the county (and especially the seat of the courthouse) was a more important focus for social life than north of the Ohio River, where numerous small towns set the tone for the location and functioning of local governmental, commercial, and social affairs. These Ohio towns tended to contain more professional people, craftsmen, churches, and schools than similar kinds of settlements in Kentucky. Indeed, New England cultural influences were often able to penetrate well into the Ohio Valley because many of the most influential settlers were Yankee professional people (merchants, teachers, and ministers) who inhabited the bustling small towns of the region.[39]

37 Much information on these topics remains to be gleaned from contemporary travel accounts, personal writings, and public records. For useful general commentaries, see Caroline F. Ware, ed., *The Cultural Approach to History* (New York 1940); James G. Leyburn, *Frontier Folkways* (New Haven 1935); Power, *Planting Corn Belt Culture*; and Glassie, *Pattern in Material Folk Culture*.

38 Stanley M. Elkins and Eric McKitrick, 'A Meaning for Turner's Frontier Part II: The Southwest Frontier and New England,' *Political Science Quarterly* 69 (1954): 565-602

39 Elkins and McKitrick, 'A Meaning for Turner's Frontier Part I: Democracy in the Old Northwest,' *ibid.*, 321-53; Wayne Jordan, 'The People of Ohio's First County,' *Ohio State Archaeological and Historical Quarterly* 49 (1942): 1-40; William N. Parker, 'From Northwest to Midwest: Social Bases of a Regional History,' in David C. Klingaman and Richard K. Vedder, eds., *Essays in Nineteenth Century Economic History: The Old Northwest* (Athens, Ohio 1975), 3-34

There is no more obvious expression of the persistence of hearth culture traits than in the debates that ensued over the ratification of state constitutions and bills of rights. In Ohio, despite the strong influence of Jeffersonian Republicans from the upper South and the high regard expressed for the constitutions of Kentucky and Tennessee, it was the Federalist principles derived from New England and Midland traditions that moulded the legal and governmental institutions of the state.[40] A decade earlier in Kentucky the most burning issue in the state convention had been slavery. The anti-slavery movement, led by non-slaveholding yeomen, failed to dislodge the traditional power élite of larger planters and wealthier yeomen, thus leaving the institution intact until the Civil War.[41]

EMERGING NATIONAL INFLUENCES

All state conventions convened after 1791 had to accommodate to the federal constitution and its amendments, which contained the basic ideological principles of the new nation. Other institutional influences of the early republican era were also at work in creating the configuration of trans-Appalachian societies. Thus, the Northwest Ordinance of 1789 was designed not only to provide an orderly transition in the territorial status of a newly settled area but also to restrict the expansion of plantation slavery north of the Ohio River. The egalitarian basis of Midwestern societies was to be ensured by excluding the two elements that created the greatest differences in wealth distribution throughout the nation: the ownership of large acreages of land and the ownership of slaves. Although the Midland and Yankee source origins of a majority of early settlers in the Old Northwest were a more immediate and direct factor restricting the expansion of Southern traditions, the commercial viability of such labour-demanding crops as tobacco and hemp was compromised in southern Ohio.

Another legislative act, the Land Ordinance of 1785, which established a national survey system for the disposal of public lands, was first applied in southeastern Ohio. This new cadastral system was to delineate a new American landscape of relative order and symmetry that departed radically from colonial patterns and reduced the morphological variety of nineteenth-century settlement

---

40 Power, *Planting Corn Belt Culture*, 9-12, 83-4, 121, 139; Barnhart, 'The Southern Influence,' 28-42; Beverley W. Bond, Jr., 'Some Political Ideals of the Colonial Period as They Were Realized in the Old Northwest,' in *Essays in Colonial History Presented to Charles McLean Andrews by his Students* (New Haven 1931), 299-325
41 Barnhart, 'Frontiersmen and Planters,' 19-36; Byrd, 'The Kentucky Frontier,' 181-203, 286-94

landscapes.[42] Variation in the shape of land grants, especially the quarter section, continued to exist but the location of farmsteads and roads had to accommodate to the basic angularity of the township and range system. Urban settlements acquired an unconsciously planned and more standardized appearance while retaining internal variety in house forms and construction materials.

Socio-cultural variations among populations on early trans-Appalachian frontiers were reduced in more subtle ways. The ethnic variety of the late colonial period was not sustained during the early republican era. The absence of large-scale immigration from Europe between 1770 and 1820 created a void in the continuity of European and American populations that made it more difficult for ethnically conscious groups in the new nation to retain traditional identities into the early nineteenth century. Not only were there few numerical and cultural reinforcements from the Old World, but the socio-religious upheavals of the late colonial period and the emergence of symbols of national consciousness further eroded traditional allegiances.

The cultural effects of the Great Awakening from the 1760s, for example, transcended ethnic and economic divisions. The resultant modifications in religious affiliation did produce a proliferation of denominations but the divergence that occurred in the interior was still contained within the rubric of Protestantism, both in its evangelical and more traditional forms. The Great Awakening created a process of subsequent fragmentation that has characterized American Protestantism ever since.[43] The Baptists and Methodists achieved the largest numerical gains from the revivals, in part at the expense of the Presbyterians, Episcopalians, Lutherans, and some German sectarian groups. It was these two denominations that gave special character to religious behaviour in the upper South and, in occasional fusions with older denominations (such as the Methodist Episcopal church), in early Ohio. Midland and Yankee traditions, however, encouraged the survival of Presbyterian and sectarian denominations north of the Ohio to a degree that might not otherwise have occurred. On the other hand, the evangelical movement revealed not only a more fundamentalist

---

42 See, especially, William D. Pattison, *Beginnings of the American Rectangular Land Survey System, 1784-1800* (Chicago 1957); Norman J.W. Thrower, *Original Survey and Land Subdivision* (Chicago 1966); H.B. Johnson, 'The United States Land Survey as a Principle of Order,' in Ralph E. Ehrenberg, ed., *Pattern and Process: Research in Historical Geography* (Washington, DC 1975), 114-30; and W.D. Pattison, 'Reflections on the American Rectangular Land Survey System,' in *ibid.*, 131-8.

43 Cedric B. Cowing, *The Great Awakening and the American Revolution: Colonial Thought in the 18th Century* (Chicago 1971); William W. Sweet, *Religion on the American Frontier*, 4 vols. (New York and Chicago 1931-46), and *Religion in the Development of American Culture, 1765-1840* (New York 1952)

aspect of American religion after 1776 but also a more secularizing trend that emphasized the relationships between religious principles and everyday moral conduct rather than between an abstract God and real human beings.

This principle was written into the Constitution in the form of separation of church and state, a distinctive institutional change in the new nation with far-reaching cultural consequences. State responsibility for public education during the nineteenth century produced powerful forces of trans-regional assimilation through the medium of the English language and an emphasis on citizenship. On the other hand, the principle of religious freedom dictated that distinctive religious groups had the option of establishing private educational institutions more attuned to the maintenance of traditional cultural values. Diversity within national unity remained a viable proposition. From this perspective one could argue that the religious changes of the early national period contributed more to cultural stability than to change, and yet more to cultural convergence than to divergence. The values and motivations of the pioneer settlers before and after the Revolution remained virtually unchanged and quite possibly intensified. The socially defined goals of land ownership, profitable enterprise, and wealth accumulation for immediate consumption and for the next generation, expressed within an emerging national system of liberal democracy, continued to dominate American ways of life.[44]

CONCLUSION

The study of cultural diffusion and change in the early American past is an exceedingly difficult task. An overemphasis on material cultural relicts contributes to the self-fulfilling prophecy that the function of material culture is primarily economic, that solutions to the practical problems of living are achieved through the economic system. But in early American society, as in no other, the coincidence of ideology, place, and material culture was so remarkably close that economically motivated modes of behaviour provide critical clues to the American cultural ethos both then and now. At the same time, mapping a culture or subculture in an area still undergoing settlement is an impossible task. If we accept the premise that the behavioural and material aspects of culture accumulate and are manifested over a considerable period of

44 See, for example, Hans Kohn, *American Nationalism: An Interpretive Essay* (New York 1961); Seymour M. Lipset, *The First New Nation: The United States in Historical and Comparative Perspective* (New York 1963); Howard Mumford Jones, *O Strange New World* (New York 1964), chaps. 9 and 10; and James A. Henretta, *The Evolution of American Society, 1700-1815: An Interdisciplinary Analysis* (Lexington, Mass. 1973), chap. 6.

time, we cannot begin to delineate major cultural regions and their subdivisions in the trans-Appalachian west much before the 1840s. On the other hand, if we accept the premise that cultures are larger than the sum of their parts, no set of mappable trait distributions will ever be sufficient to define major American cultural regions.

It has been argued in this paper that the transformation of colonial cultural and regional variety in the trans-Appalachian west during the early national period was not simply one of linear reduction from seaboard to interior. The revised cultural order of the post-colonial world was derived to a considerable degree from the cultural traditions of the preceding colonial world. What gave them continuity in space were the practical experiences of settlers occupying new areas armed with the values of liberalism, capitalism, and material conquest. The transposition occurred not only at the regional level but throughout the new republic, so that both trans-Appalachian and cis-Appalachian landscapes were changed in fashions often accommodating to antecedent forms and structures.

The complexity and dynamism of the late colonial and early republican worlds do not lend themselves to any one form of analysis. Frontier societies were the product of both local and national circumstances. A culture area approach must be sensitive to both the universal and the distinctive character-istics of the culture bearers, their movements, and their acculturative experi-ences. The diffusion of culture traits did not spread out from hearth regions in any uniform manner but was subject to transmission, modification, and fusion as migrants moved westward beyond the Appalachians. The basic structure was founded upon an almost universal adherence to the materialistic ideology of the new nation. Regional differences not only of degree but of kind were the result particularly of fusion and reconfiguration of traits and institutions in certain key areas of the interior. Cultural accretions were there created, and they spread westward to combine with the institutional modifications of the early republican era to produce the more extensive but still broadly distinctive cultural regions of the early nineteenth century.

SAM B. HILLIARD

Antebellum tidewater rice culture in South Carolina and Georgia

The last twenty years have been a period of remarkable vigour in American and Canadian historical geography. The emergence of several dozen books and articles dealing specifically with 'geographies of the past' represents the collective work of a significant group of relatively young scholars who are asking fundamental questions about the nature of North American development that, to their minds at least, have been ignored or only partially answered previously. Although interests have been varied and coverage uneven, progress over the past two decades has been impressive. As a result of their efforts we now have a reasonably clear view of the details of the establishment and subsequent development of European settlement along a broad front from Newfoundland to Florida. Major themes in much of the work have been the struggle to establish viable colonial economies, especially agriculture, and the adjustment of activities to fit changes in population, migration, industrialization, and markets. The latter was particularly encouraged by Andrew Clark, for he saw temporal modification in the arrangement and functioning of occupied space ('changing geographies') as a legitimate and essential element in historical geography.

This paper cuts across these themes in that it outlines the emergence of a system of cash-crop farming in a particular area and analyses its role in the region's agriculture. Furthermore, it deals specifically with the natural environment within which the crop was grown and adjustments of the system to exploit that particular environment.

Of the agricultural specialty regions that evolved in the United States prior to the twentieth century, one of the first occurred along the Georgia-South Carolina coast. Virginia and Maryland discovered rather early in the colonial period that their commercial agricultural future lay in the cultivation of tobacco, while the Caribbean colonies were busily engaged in becoming sugar suppliers to the world. Both crops were tried in South Carolina and Georgia and both were produced in a few localities, but the real fortunes of the coastal area lay in the culture of two commodities that were to flourish for a time and then vanish – rice and indigo.

Indigo was the first to disappear. The West Indies had produced the dye for some time, and according to tradition its culture was introduced into South Carolina by a West Indian lady, Eliza Lucas.[1] The first significant crop was harvested in 1745, and within three years exports from Charleston amounted to some 183,000 pounds. Despite considerable annual fluctuations, production increased through subsequent decades and the industry remained a viable one until the Revolution, when the market collapsed under intense competition from the West Indies and a lack of crown subsidy. Although the plant continued to be grown and dye produced locally as late as the Civil War, the commercial industry barely survived the eighteenth century, with Charleston's exports dwindling to a paltry 3400 pounds in the year 1800-1.[2]

While indigo had a relatively short tenure as a major commercial crop, rice was grown in quantity throughout the colonial and antebellum periods, and it was rice that gave the area its identity. Of all the agricultural regions that developed prior to the Civil War, none surpassed that of the Georgia-Carolina Rice Coast in intensity of production, dependence upon a single crop, and ingenious accommodation to the environment. From about 1750 until around 1900 it was never seriously challenged as *the* cash crop of the coastal lands of South Carolina and Georgia, and on many operations it was the only cash crop

1 Harriott Horry Ravenel, *Eliza Pinckney* (New York 1896), 102-7. It is correct to say that indigo was 'introduced' into South Carolina, for that is precisely what happened. However, strains of indigo grew wild in Carolina and Georgia at the time.

2 Early references to indigo culture may be found in James Glen, 'A Description of South Carolina,' in Chapman J. Milling, ed., *Colonial South Carolina: Two Contemporary Descriptions* (Columbia 1951), 9-10; Alexander Hewat, *An Historical Account of the Rise and Progress of the Colonies of South Carolina and Georgia* (London 1779), 2: 138-45; *South Carolina Gazette,* 22 and 29 Oct. 1744, [unpaged]; and *South Carolina Chronicle*, May 1755, 201-3, and June 1755, 256-9. For details on the culture and manufacture of indigo by twentieth-century investigators, see J.E. Copenhaver, 'Culture of Indigo in the Provinces of South Carolina and Georgia,' *Industrial and Engineering Chemistry* 22 (Aug. 1930): 894-6, and Dwight J. Huneycutt, 'The Economics of the Indigo Industry in South Carolina,' unpublished MS thesis, University of South Carolina, 1949. The best and most recent study of the reintroduction and marketing of indigo is David L. Coon's 'Eliza Lucas Pinckney and the Reintroduction of Indigo Culture in South Carolina,' *Journal of Southern History* 42 (Feb. 1976): 61-76.

grown. Rarely has a single crop ever dominated so completely the energies of a group of agriculturalists as did rice during its heyday along the South's Atlantic coast.

According to legend, the introduction of rice into South Carolina was accidental. A brig from Madagascar was forced to enter Charleston harbour in 1693 or 1694, and its captain gave a bag of rice to Landgrave Thomas Smith, who planted it in his garden; from this bag of rice the entire South Carolina rice complex presumably sprang. Curiously, the story is thoroughly discredited by Alexander S. Salley and Lewis C. Gray but is repeated in a number of secondary sources and provides the title to Duncan C. Heyward's volume on rice planting.[3]

However, there seems little doubt that Charleston was the point of introduction and that the decades 1690-1720 marked the period of introduction and early experimentation. From Charleston rice culture spread along the coast in both directions. During the 1730s it was known along most of the South Carolina coast and by mid-century was in Georgia.

The rapid spread of rice cultivation was stimulated by high profits and a ready market. Except when crops failed or prices sagged (due to world market conditions), the amount of land under rice and total production increased steadily. Not until the end of the antebellum period did rice production along the Atlantic coast show any signs of faltering, although it suffered a precipitous decline after the Civil War.[4]

The total rice crop of 1839 amounted to some 80 million pounds, of which almost exactly three-fourths was grown in South Carolina. Georgia produced another 12 million pounds, and most of the remainder was scattered among the states of Louisiana, North Carolina, Mississippi, and Alabama. The uncontested leader in rice production was South Carolina, with Georgetown being the leading district. Attracted to the low-lying lands along the rivers that flowed into Winyah Bay, settlers moved in during the early 1700s, and by 1730 or 1740 the Georgetown district was producing a substantial part of South Carolina's rice. It is not known just when Georgetown County became the leading Carolina producer, but it must have been early, for the sixth census (1840) revealed it producing over 36 of the total national production of 80 million pounds, or

3 Salley, Jr., 'The Introduction of Rice Culture into South Carolina,' *Historical Commission of South Carolina Bulletin* 6 (1919): 3-23; Gray, *History of Agriculture in the Southern United States to 1860* (New York 1941), 1: 277-90; Heyward, *Seed from Madagascar* (Chapel Hill 1937)

4 The westward shift in rice growing has been as spectacular as the shift in wheat growing. The centres are now Louisiana, Arkansas, Texas, and California. For details on the shift, see A.H. Cole, 'American Rice Growing Industry: A Study in Comparative Advantage,' *Quarterly Journal of Economics* 41 (Aug. 1927): 595-643.

about 45 per cent. The crop of 1849, the largest rice crop for which we have detailed records, totalled 215 million pounds, of which 47 million pounds (still more than 20 per cent) were accounted for by Georgetown County. In 1859 the figures were 187 and 56 millions (roughly 30 per cent), respectively (Table 1).[5]

The core of rice production was along the coast from Georgetown, South Carolina, to Savannah, Georgia. Some indication of the high concentration can be seen in the data for the eleven coastal counties, and Table 1 shows both production and 'percentiles' of rice production by county, starting at the North Carolina boundary and working southward. For example, Horry and Georgetown produced 45 per cent of the nation's total in 1840; if Charleston is added, the figure rises to 60 per cent; Colleton's production adds another 7 per cent; and so on. Table 1 indicates the clear dominance of the eleven coastal counties, the relative importance of each county, and the declining importance of the South Carolina counties during the two decades.

South Carolina's production declined from 74 per cent of the total in 1840 to 72 in 1850 and 62 in 1860. It remained the leading rice producer throughout the period, but its dominance diminished somewhat as Georgia's production increased.

Several varieties of rice were introduced and considerable experimentation with different planting systems resulted in more than one kind of rice culture. It is certain that the first Carolina rice was unirrigated, although most likely it was grown in moist soil. Gradually rice growers gravitated to the low-lying floodplains, but the reasons almost surely related as much to soil fertility as to moisture availability. Irrigation (flooding of the fields) was a later innovation probably introduced during the early 1700s, but the objective was weed and grass control rather than moisture supplementation. The floodplains were extremely fertile, having been veneered by alluvium from upstream and augmented by an accumulation of fertile organic material developed *in situ* by decayed swamp vegetation. These inland floodplain swamps soon came to be the preferred rice habitat, and it was to such sites that planters were attracted. They offered the best medium for rice growing because flooding was relatively simple, and the soils were slower to dry out during the summer.

Knowledge of the inland swamp rice plantation is meagre compared with that of the tidewater rice plantation, but enough documentary evidence is available to permit comment on its usual location and character.[6] Once field flooding

5 Agricultural data were reported in the decennial censuses for even years (1840, 1850, and 1860), but the figures actually refer to the preceding year's crop.
6 Harry J. Carman, ed., *American Husbandry* (New York 1939), 275-8; Gray, *History of Agriculture* 1: 279; and Heyward, *Seed from Madagascar*, 11-16

TABLE 1
Rice production in the eleven coastal counties, South Carolina and Georgia

Production:	1840		1850		1860	
	Thousands of pounds	Cumulative per cent	Thousands of pounds	Cumulative per cent	Thousands of pounds	Cumulative per cent
South Carolina						
Horry	80	–	485	–	238	–
Georgetown	36,360	45	46,765	22	55,805	30
Charleston	11,939	60	15,701	29	18,890	40
Colleton	5484	67	45,309	50	22,839	52
Beaufort	5629	74	47,230	72	18,791	62
Georgia						
Chatham	6159	81	19,454	81	25,934	76
Bryan	no data	–	2409	82	1610	77
Liberty	223	82	1892	83	2548	78
McIntosh	2826	85	3123	85	6421	82
Glynn	1937	87	3830	86	4843	84
Camden	1006	89	6401	89	10,330	90
Total for South Carolina and Georgia	73,076	90	198,864	92	171,609	92
Total for nation	80,841	100	215,313	100	187,167	100

Source: US censuses of 1840, 1850, and 1860. Counties are listed in order from north to south.

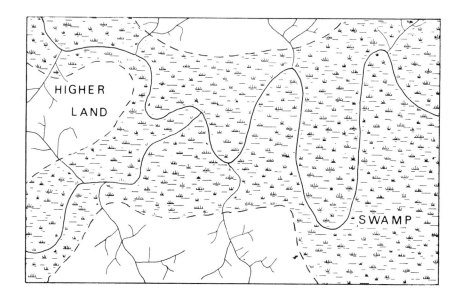

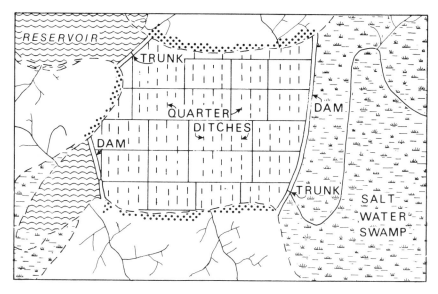

Figure 1 Hypothetical development of rice fields in an inland swamp. Based upon a reconstruction by William A. Noble, 'Sequent Occupance of Hopeton-Altamaha, 1816-1956,' MA thesis, University of Georgia, 1956, p. 14

came to be commonly practised, it became necessary to devise means of impounding and controlling the swamp water supply; this meant not only field clearing but draining, ditching, and banking. In its simplest form an inland swamp rice field involved two dams and associated ditches, one downstream to contain the field floodwater and another upstream from the rice fields to impound the freshwater stream. Depending upon the size of the swamp, additional dams and canals were constructed to impound or drain fields as desired (Figure 1). Fields were flooded or drained by simply controlling the gates upstream and downstream from the fields. Face ditches and quarter ditches functioned as 'arteries' and 'veins' to facilitate the movement of water onto the fields during flooding and off the fields during drainage.

One wonders how the inland swamp field evolved and what its relationship was to the development of the South's Atlantic rice culture area. Most likely it was an intermediate stage between the experimental plots of the early eighteenth century and the rather sophisticated tidewater system prevalent by the mid-nineteenth century. It was the first large-scale system of rice production, and we can speculate that upon such fields experiments with flooding were first tried. The initial attractiveness of the floodplain was its inherent fertility and the fact that it was less subject to desiccation during dry summers, but as irrigation became more widely practised it proved to be an ideal location. Ditches and drains were logical outgrowths of the swamp-draining process. Later, as fields became larger, the upper dam was erected to control excess floodwater. From this stage the progression of innovations that led to field flooding is not hard to imagine. Periodic natural inundations probably convinced growers that the plant did well under water, while pesky weeds and grasses were stunted or killed. Harm from periodic summer droughts was minimized by the impounded fresh water, although the reservoir often proved insufficient during prolonged dry spells. The technical problems of field levelling and embanking were worked out according to the dictates of terrain and necessity. However, the role of local innovation must not be exaggerated. Undoubtedly, the astute planter tested new ideas as they emerged, but the practice of field flooding is ancient, having been employed for centuries in Europe and Asia, and it should be recognized that many planters were well educated and almost surely cognizant of rice culture practised elsewhere.

It is next to impossible to determine the areal extent and comparative importance of inland swamp rice culture. A number of sources refer to the practice but usually as a prelude to a much more detailed discussion of the tidewater rice culture. Furthermore, one gets the distinct impression that many observers simply did not know the difference.[7] Despite the lack of detailed knowledge, it is clear that rice was planted extensively on inland swamps. During the early colonial period it was limited to areas near the coast simply because that was the only settled area, but by the nineteenth century rice was grown in small quantities throughout the coastal plain from North Carolina to Louisiana. Even as late as 1860 small quantities were reported hundreds of miles from the coast, and this writer knows of abandoned rice fields near Augusta, Georgia (immediately below the Fall Line). Admittedly, such rice production was but a pittance compared with that produced in the tidewater counties by the mid-nineteenth century, but the early production must have been swamp-grown, and much of the rice produced later in the tidewater area may have been produced on land *not* inundated by tidal flow.

The major difficulty in growing rice in inland swamps was the ineffective control of freshwater streams. Prolonged drought limited the floodwater available, and torrential rains upstream broke dams and washed out fields. Thus it became a problem of too much or too little water, depending upon conditions at a given time. Duncan Heyward cites this as the principal reason for the shift from inland swamp to tidewater locations, and there is evidence to support his observation.[8] Population increase in the interior South during the early 1800s with its associated land clearing and ploughing made significant inroads into the natural vegetation cover, and the tendency to favour clean-cultivated crops, such as cotton and corn, increased surface water runoff. The effects downstream were marked and, in time, came to be disastrous. Without the damping effect of a rich vegetation cover fluctuations in stream flow became more marked, and the 'freshet,' a periodic problem during the colonial period, came to be a frequent hazard in the nineteenth century. In fact, tidewater rice fields were not immune from this effect, as we find increasing complaints of swollen streams damaging fields throughout the nineteenth century.[9]

The shift from the inland swamp to tidewater sites has not been documented adequately. The advantages of tidewater field flooding were recognized but the change was not abrupt, and both types existed simultaneously. Early nineteenth-

7 The most puzzling aspect of the entire Carolina rice complex is the apparent confusion between tidewater and inland swamp rice. Early sources rarely go into detail, and most secondary sources gloss over the early period and jump quickly into long descriptions of tidewater rice, which has received the greatest attention. Recognizing this discrepancy, Converse D. Clowse has an admirable treatment of early rice culture that draws on con-temporary documents. *Economic Beginnings in Colonial South Carolina, 1670-1730* (Columbia 1971), 123-30
8 *Seed from Madagascar*, 14
9 *Ibid.*, 214

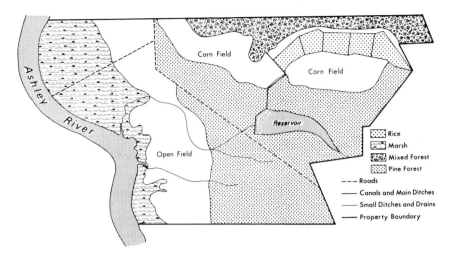

Figure 2 Early plantation complex in the Charleston district belonging to
Ralph Izard, and estates of Whitmarsh Fuller and a Mr Perkins. Plat surveyed
in 1789.

century plats of several plantations suggest that freshwater reservoirs were
common even on plantations situated within or near the tidal zone. One located
on the Ashley River shows no rice fields adjacent to the river but a complex of
canals leading from a reservoir, suggesting swamp rice culture (Figure 2). Another
plantation, 'Clay Field' in Christchurch Parish, shows an arrangement of
reservoirs and rice fields that leaves no doubt as to the source of irrigation water
(Figure 3). One plat of a single plantation shows two types of fields: the
tidewater pattern with access canals, roads, buildings, and rice fields located in a
bend of the Cooper River, and some distance away a pond and a clearing labelled
'old rice fields,' attesting to earlier swamp rice culture (Figure 4).[10] In many
cases there must have been a blending of the two types of irrigation, for Solon
Robinson observed a tidewater planter on the Cooper River who had '... ponds
of fresh water covering 100 acres of upland, which are held in reserve to water
the rice fields when the river is too salt.'[11]

10 Originals for Figures 2, 3, and 4 are labelled 'the McCrady Plats' and are in the Charleston Museum. This writer used microfilm copies in the State Department of Archives, Columbia, SC.
11 Herbert A. Kellar, *Solon Robinson: Pioneer and Agriculturalist* (Indianapolis 1936), 2: 355

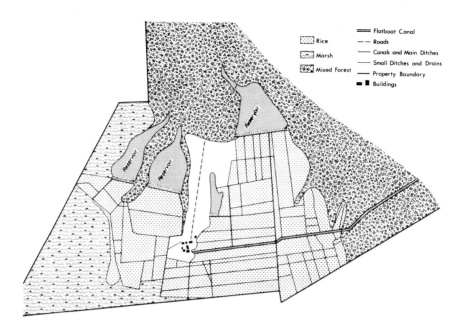

Figure 3 Survey of 1816 of Clay Field Plantation in Christchurch Parish, South Carolina. The relationship of the reservoirs to the rice fields is quite clear.

Despite the continued use of impounded fresh water for flooding, the advantages of tidewater rice culture led to its adoption by many planters, and it soon emerged as the system of rice culture most characteristic of the area. The dominance of the tidewater counties as rice producers is clear, yet only a fraction of this area was devoted to rice. The critical demands of tidewater flooding limited rice to a few areas specifically suited for its growth. Its habitat was the narrow zone between the tidal salt flats and the freshwater swamps above the tidal zone. The arrangement and function of the rice fields were similar to those of the inland swamp plantation, but they were located adjacent to estuaries so as to facilitate irrigation. The tidewater planter depended upon the diurnal variation in sea level and its accompanying effects on freshwater level within estuaries to flood or drain the rice fields. In order to flood his fields the planter simply waited until the tide raised the fresh water in the stream above the field level, then he opened trunks to allow water onto his fields. By utilizing successive high tides he could flood the fields to the desired height. Field drainage was accomplished simply by reversing the process and allowing water to run off the fields at low tide.

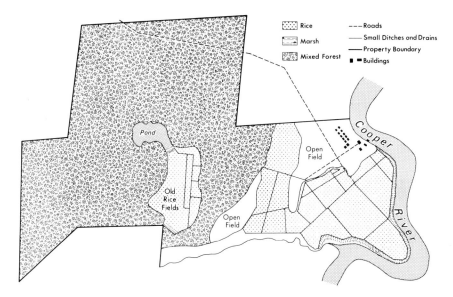

Figure 4 Plat of Bluff Plantation of 1200 acres on the Cooper River. Date is uncertain – either 1811 or 1817. Two types of rice fields are shown: one labelled 'old rice fields' and another adjacent to the river, presumably tidewater fields.

To the casual observer tidewater rice fields appeared to be simply tidal flats or cleared swamps. Yet the necessity of field flooding with *fresh* water severely limited the number of suitable sites. A location too close to the ocean was disastrous because of periodic saltwater encroachment, and one too far upstream was unsuitable simply because the tidal range diminished rapidly as distance from the sea increased.

Fortunately, the rice grower has left us with more than written documents for studying his work. Much of the coast has been modified only superficially in the fifty to one hundred years since rice fields were abandoned, and air photographs as well as large-scale topographic maps reveal a great deal about tidewater rice fields.[12] Many are easily visible on photographs, maps, and the landscape itself; thus, the outstanding producing areas can be identified (Figure 5). In viewing these relict rice fields one is struck by their spotty distribution. It

12 A pioneer effort is that of Douglas C. Wilms, 'The Development of Rice Culture in 18th Century Georgia,' *Southeastern Geographer* 12 (May 1972): 45-57.

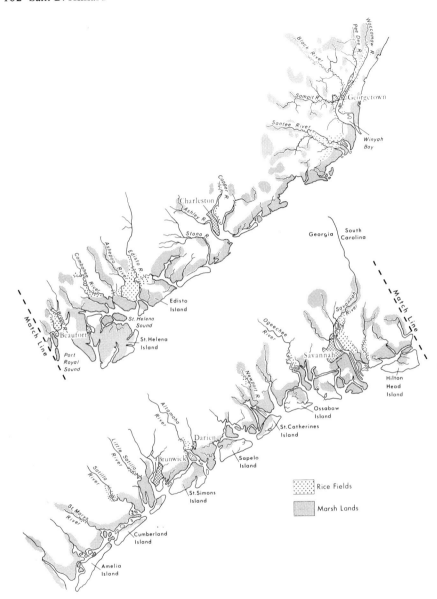

Figure 5 Map of the Georgia-South Carolina tidewater rice area

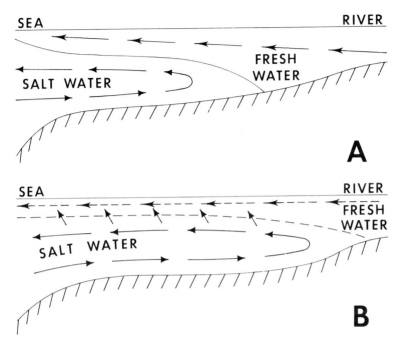

Figure 6 Longitudinal profile of two types of estuaries. Type A represents a salt wedge estuary with freshwater layering, ideal for tidewater rice. Type B is poorly suited because mixing of salt and fresh water is relatively thorough.

is obvious that the tidewater plantation was not simply a product of the tidewater environment; it occurred only where precisely matched sets of conditions existed, and these were met in only a few areas. Examination of relict rice fields and their relationship to hydrographic variables indicates the importance of fresh water availability and estuary size and shape. The marked variation among estuaries has led some observers to classify them according to type, varying from the strong-flowing freshwater river channel to the saline lagoon.[13] Although a detailed classification is of no concern here, it is clear that estuary size and shape affect the degree of water mixing and, ultimately, water salinity. Some estuaries develop pronounced 'layering' of fresh water atop the salt water, whereas in others there is significant mixing (Figure 6). Those fed by

13 K.F. Bowden, 'Circulation and Diffusion,' in George H. Lauff, ed., *Estuaries* (Washington, DC 1967), 15-36

small streams have little or no freshwater component and are, quite literally, arms of the sea. Ideal rice-growing conditions were met when freshwater stream flow dominated the estuary. This permitted the greatest buildup of the freshwater layer, forcing a sharp discontinuity between fresh and salt water, in some cases so sharp that a vertical distance of only twelve to eighteen inches separated the two (Figure 6A). Furthermore, with a strong stream flow this discontinuity is a horizontal one traceable for miles upstream.

At the opposite end of the scale is the vertically homogeneous estuary. It is dominated by tidal currents rather than stream flow, and mixing is relatively thorough. In such estuaries the vertical change in salinity is scarcely discernible; consequently, no freshwater layer is available for diversion onto rice fields (Figure 6B). This fact partially explains the puzzling distribution along the South Carolina coast, where one finds abandoned rice fields within five miles of open sea at the mouth of the Santee but has to look some fifteen miles up the Combahee from St Helena Sound to find similar features. Another factor is the indented and cross-channelled nature of St Helena Sound, unlike the mouth of the Santee (Figure 5). Obviously the former would be much more affected by cross currents, resulting in greater mixing and poorer conditions for rice growing.

A simple way of visualizing the conditions necessary for tidewater rice growing is to think of the encroaching saltwater wedge as a 'dam' of denser material plugging up the flow of the stream. It results in an impoundment of fresh water that is then 'tapped' for flooding the rice fields. Obviously the effectiveness of this impoundment depended upon: (1) a substantial tidal range; (2) a significant flow of fresh water periodically stronger than tidal currents; and (3) a channel shape that permitted impoundment and reduced lateral currents. When any one of the conditions was poorly developed or absent, rice production was difficult; lacking more than one, it was impossible.

Although the rigid physical requirements go a long way towards explaining the spotty distribution, they do not imply that rice was foregone at other sites. A great deal of land was available upon which *small* fields could be managed successfully, and we must not forget the inland swamp rice producer who depended not upon tidal flooding but upon impoundment and diversion of fresh water for field flooding. However, it seems safe to say that the areas outlined in Figure 5 accounted for much of the rice produced, and virtually all of that produced by tidewater plantations, within South Carolina and Georgia. The major areas were Winyah Bay, the Santee, the Ashley-Cooper near Charleston, the Edisto-Ashepoo, the Combahee, the Savannah, the Ogeechee, and the Altamaha. Of these, the Winyah Bay and Santee River areas were by far the most important producers.

By the mid-1800s tidal swamp reclamation had been underway for over half a century, and some accounts had appeared that described in detail the process of swamp clearing and rice growing. These descriptions and a number of unpublished diaries and daybooks of the more literate planters provide a clear view of the development and functioning of the rice-growing system. Reclamation of the huge areas necessary to sustain the tidewater rice industry was almost a superhuman effort and, given our perspective of eighteenth- and early nineteenth-century technology, it seems all but impossible. In some cases rice fields were two or more miles across and extended sixteen to eighteen miles upriver. Entire islands were enclosed by dams and planted to rice. The quantity of earth moved, the amount of labour used, and the ingenuity required in the process were enormous. Relatively small fields required months to reclaim, and on most plantations the improvement process took years, with additional fields being added as time and labour permitted.

The techniques of clearing and preparing tidewater swamps for rice culture deserve special attention, since the functioning of the hydraulics is the key to tidewater rice culture. Considerable variation in clearing techniques existed among planters but the process became somewhat routine, permitting us to describe it with some confidence.[14] Figure 7 illustrates a model of the development of typical rice fields, starting with the digging of a temporary embankment (Step 1) and ending with the addition of a field not adjacent to the tidal river, necessitating an access canal whose level rose and fell with the tide (Step 6). Obviously such development was sequential, with new fields being added at the same time that rice was growing on older fields.

Step 1 of Figure 7 depicts the first major step in reclamation. After the site had been selected and the outer bank's location established and cleared of trees, a temporary ditch was dug and the soil deposited so as to provide some protection for the workers from high tidewater. This fact, together with the necessity of providing a firm foundation, clear of stumps and logs, for the permanent embankment, accounts for the temporary ditch (Step 1). Any small sloughs or spring channels were left open during this step to avoid flooding of the intended fields.

14 References to the evolution and function of a tidewater rice plantation are legion. Good examples are: Heyward, *Seed from Madagascar*, 17-44; David Doar, *Rice and Rice Planting in the South Carolina Low Country* (Charleston 1936); George C. Rogers, Jr., *The History of Georgetown County, South Carolina* (Columbia 1970), 324-41; and *DeBow's Review*, 1 (1846): 320-57, 4 (1847): 504-11, and 16 (1854): 604-15. Studies of individual planters and plantations include: J.H. Easterby, ed., *The South Carolina Rice Plantation as Revealed in the Papers of Robert F.W. Allston* (Chicago 1945); Arney R. Childs, ed., *Rice Planter and Sportsman: The Recollection of J. Motte Alston, 1821-1909* (Columbia 1953); and Patience Pennington [Mrs Elizabeth W.A. Pringle], *A Woman Rice Planter*, ed. Cornelius O. Cathey (Cambridge, Mass. 1961).

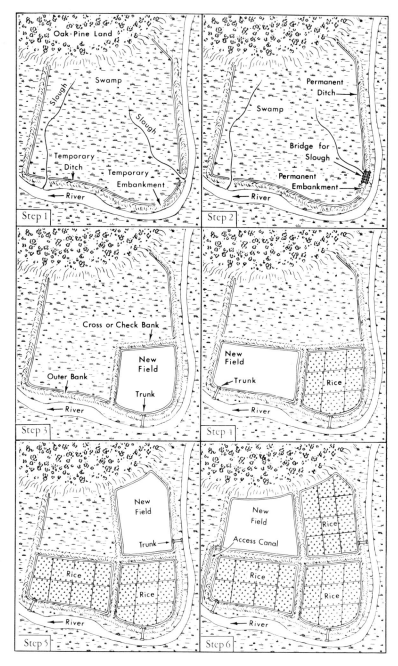

Figure 7 Hypothetical plats of the development of tidewater rice fields

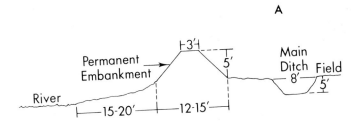

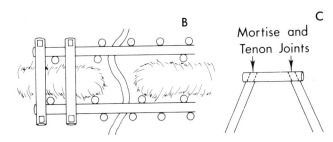

Figure 8 A is a cross-section of an embankment; dimensions are in feet. B and C are views of a 'bridge' built over a slough or break in the embankment. The bridge was filled with earth to dam the slough.

The next step was to erect the permanent embankment, which was located atop the temporary ditch. It was raised to a height of at least five feet (high enough to withstand spring tides) and was three feet wide at the top. Its bottom width varied from twelve to fifteen feet, and care had to be taken to form the embankment with gently sloping sides to avoid slumping by waves (Figure 8A). Earth for the permanent embankment was obtained from a ditch dug inland from the embankment, but additional earth sometimes was carted from nearby uplands. In its finished form the outer margin of the field consisted of a ditch and embankment designed to: (1) keep high tidewater out of the floodwater in the field as desired; (2) provide a channel for water being drained from the field to reach the trunks; and (3) provide an access canal for small boats. Water was controlled by means of a wooden trunk in the embankment that connected the main ditch with the river. The trunk was constructed with its floor at low-tide level (Figure 9). Where small streams flowed through the intended field, special

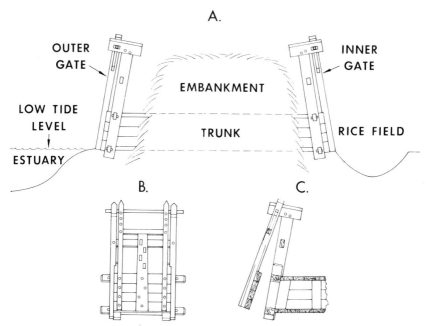

Figure 9 Cross-section of a trunk and detail of gates. Gates could be locked closed, lifted and locked open, or allowed to swing (C) for automatic operation. For flooding the outer gate was lifted and left open, while the inner gate was allowed to swing. During tidal flow water poured into the trunk from the estuary, forcing the inner gate open. As the tide ebbed the reverse flow kept the inner gate closed, retaining water on the fields. Drainage was done by lifting the inner gate and allowing the outer gate to swing.

care was taken to ensure that the embankment was secure. Many planters suggested that a wooden frame or 'bridge' be built over the slough and then filled with solid earth. The same technique was sometimes employed in repairing breaks in the embankment (Figures 8B and 8C).

Once the entire area was surrounded by the permanent embankment and trunks were installed, it could be drained and cleared. Trees were girdled and the underbrush was removed. If possible, trees were then felled and burned and the stumps removed, but in most cases such thorough clearing took years to accomplish. The first object was to plant rice as soon as possible, and this usually meant growing rice among the gaunt skeletons of dead but erect trees. If the initial area was small, it was then planted, but where large areas were banked most operators subdivided into smaller plots (ten to forty acres), thus permitting small fields to be planted before the entire area was cleared. Moreover, subdivision into small fields — each with its own banks and trunks — facilitated more precise water control, since minor differences in elevation always existed. Step 3 shows a small field being developed by the erection of 'cross' or 'check' banks separating it from the uncleared area. The field was then cleared of trees and logs and criss-crossed by drains that led into the channels adjacent to the banks. Each field was fed by its own trunk and was levelled, so that a reduction of water level in the main channel or 'ditch' would remove water from the fields. The small drains (called 'quarter' or 'half' drains, depending upon their size) simply acted as tributaries to the main ditch. Dimensions varied but major drains might be 300 feet apart, with small drains at 150 feet, 75 feet, and, in some cases, 37½ feet. In many fields new drains were added as compaction and oxidation reduced the field level, the object being to flood and drain the field easily and quickly, leaving no mounds or quagmires.

As time permitted, new fields were cleared and drained, with each having its own trunk (or trunks) and check banks. In rare cases field levels varied considerably, but most planters tried to keep adjacent fields within a large unit at the same level, making water control much easier. Furthermore, breaks in check banks between fields were much less disastrous and easier to repair if the adjacent fields were near the same level.

Many variations could be added, depending upon the predilections of individuals and the natural situation, but the above describes a representative plantation. Several conclusions can be drawn: (1) the natural conditions necessary for tidewater rice culture had to be met precisely, thus requiring careful attention to site; (2) the time and labour requirements were substantial, giving a distinct advantage to the planter with abundant labour; (3) reclaiming a tidal swamp for a rice field demanded a high level of technical expertise, since levelling embankments, laying off ditches and fields, and setting trunks and gates required considerable engineering knowledge; and (4) knowing the vagaries of coastal environments with their periodic storms, devastating tides, and occasional freshets from upstream, one can imagine a substantial amount of maintenance to keep the fields in order.

Managing a rice plantation and producing a crop were equally demanding. The system of rice culture that existed by the middle of the nineteenth century was the culmination of years of experimentation and adaptation. Practices that ensured success were passed from neighbour to neighbour and from father to son. A combination of astute management, careful record keeping, and dissemination of ideas served well, for in the 150 years or so following its introduction into South Carolina the system was – to use a term much in vogue around 1850 – 'perfected.' There were, of course, a number of variations from region to region and among planters, but they were minor; one is struck more by the similarities than by the differences.

In a sense one could consider a crop year starting as soon as the previous year's harvest was completed. If possible, land preparation, or 'breaking,' was done during fall and winter. Postbellum records report that ploughing, but more often than not breaking, was done with heavy iron hoes.[15] Even when ploughs were used they were shovel ploughs and did little to turn the stubble or straw under, so it had to be burned. Some planters kept the fields flooded during winter, but much of the winter repair work, such as ditch cleaning, trunk and floodgate repair, and augmenting and shaping embankments, necessitated dry fields, and not all fields remained flooded during winter. Although not universal, harrowing in spring was common, followed by planting. Some planters preferred to plant with the hoe, covering the seed fully. Others preferred open planting, which involved sowing in open trenches with rice seed coated with clay ('claying') to prevent floating.

Immediately after seeding, the first flooding, or 'sprout flow,' was applied to encourage germination. After the rice had sprouted, fields were drained to allow hoeing and then flooded again. Although growing methods varied among producers, the remainder of the growing season involved alternately flooding and draining the fields, the objects being to provide ample moisture, prevent stagnation and rotting, control weeds, encourage strong root and stem growth, and control insect and bird pests (Table 2). Cultivation was done with the hoe, and several hoeings were necessary.

Harvest took place during September. The usual cutting implement was the sickle. After being cut, the stalks were left in the field, resting on the stubble, to cure for a day or so, and then taken to the plantation yard to be stacked. Where fields were small and located adjacent to well-drained upland, rice was carted to the mill, but in most places boats (locally called 'flats') were used. Small boats could be used easily on small ditches, but where long distances and large quantities were involved access canals were constructed to facilitate the removal of rice from the soggy fields. Where such canals traversed several water levels, it was necessary to construct rather elaborate floodgates, large enough to permit

15 This fact is frequently noted by travellers; the astonishment of Solon Robinson is but one example: 'Can you believe me when I tell you that every acre of these crops is put in with hoes – that a plow is never used upon the plantation except to scratch the ground a little between the corn rows?' Kellar, *Solon Robinson*, 2: 350

TABLE 2
Field operations in tidewater rice cultivation

	Depth	Purpose	Duties or cautions	Duration
Sprout flow	cover field	'pip' (sprout) seeds	remove floating trash keep birds away	4 to 14 days or until 'pipped'
Drain		develop root system	keep birds away	let plants grow 1" high
Point flow	cover field	protect from birds soften clods kill grass provide moisture	do not leave too long or plants become weak keep birds away	3 to 7 days or until plants are 3"-4" high
Drain		remove weeds and stir soil	first hoeing second hoeing, 14 to 18 days later	until plants are 6"-8" high
Long or stretch flow	flood above plants to float trash and then gradually lower to show tips of plants	provide moisture keep down weeds	remove floating trash	10 to 20 days at constant height
Drain		remove weeds and stir soil	third hoeing leave dry until plants 'joint,' then fourth hoeing	2 to 3 weeks
Lay-by flow	flood enough to cover field, then after rice 'heads' raise to support stems	provide moisture keep down weeds support stalks	keep at height of long flow until plants 'head,' then raise to support stalk	until harvest

flats to pass, yet strong enough to withstand hydraulic pressures generated by tidal ebb and flow.

On some plantations the rice seed was threshed by treading, but the flail was more common. Except for a few fanning mills that were introduced late in the antebellum period, winnowing was done by hand. Since the rice grain did not emerge 'clean' from the threshing process, it underwent further processing or 'milling.' Originally a laborious hand process, milling was accomplished with the mortar and pestle, and through time the more elaborate mills boasted huge, multiple mortar and pestle units, grinding stones, revolving screens, and elevators. Obviously such mills were expensive to construct, and only large landholdings could justify their cost. According to Robert Allston, perhaps the most literate and best known of the Georgetown planters, those with more than 400 acres of rice usually had their own mill. A number of toll mills also existed and, in time, mills sprang up across the Atlantic, creating a small demand for rough (unmilled) rice.[16]

Within the tidewater zone rice was the dominant cash crop, and on many landholdings was the only crop sold. However, its dominance varied among the eleven rice counties and even more among individual operations. Fortunately, the census manuscripts provide a detailed view of each landholding, listing a number of the most important agricultural items. By extracting data from landholdings in each county the relative importance of certain crops can be illustrated. Table 3, based upon 1850 census manuscripts, shows the proportion of the sampled landholding units that reported a quantity of each commodity as well as the mean figure.[17]

Considering rice production alone, only three counties showed a high production of rice per landholding: Chatham and Glynn in Georgia and Georgetown in South Carolina, all of which averaged around a quarter of a million pounds per landholding. Other counties ranged from the production of 91,640 pounds in Camden County, Georgia, to a low of 805 pounds in Horry (at 45 pounds per bushel this was but 18 bushels; the largest producer in the Horry County sample reported only 7000 pounds). Georgetown, Glynn, and Chatham

---

16 *DeBow's Review*, 1 (1846): 344, 349

17 The sample consisted of the first ten names listed on each page of the county's Schedule IV census returns. Since each full page contained the names of forty-two operators, the sample represents about 24 per cent. The choice of sample names was dictated by a need to obtain some operators from as many parts of the county as possible. It is presumed that the data reported represent the order in which landholdings were visited. See, for example, Michael P. Conzen, 'Spatial Data From Nineteenth Century Manuscript Censuses: A Technique for Rural Settlement and Land Use Analysis,' *Professional Geographer* 21 (Sept. 1969): 337-43.

TABLE 3
Percentage of farms reporting on, and average value per farm of, selected crops in 1850

County	Wheat	Corn	Oats	Rice	Cot-ton	Sweet potatoes	Farms in sample
Horry	7	98	3	37	0	85	
	9	169	42	805	0	183	200
Georgetown	2	59	13	47	0	47	
	11	535	180	258,854	0	699	100
Charleston	1	83	25	47	30	80	
	11	500	264	21,681	21	787	226
Colleton	14	99	27	56	52	95	·
	20	520	106	19,336	14	420	240
Beaufort	10	96	27	52	68	90	
	26	592	106	75,246	25	555	241
Chatham	0	74	0	56	20	69	
	0	509	0	224,054	14	324	39
Bryan	0	100	12	36	23	92	
	0	300	38	86,023	14	256	55
Liberty	1	100	19	62	63	98	
	10	428	62	10,366	10	471	61
McIntosh	0	97	0	51	51	91	
	0	616	0	60,368	14	700	35
Glynn	0	100	3	48	65	100	
	0	1019	20	216,567	17	649	29
Camden	0	94	1	39	50	78	
	0	345	60	91,640	7	344	60

Top figure is the percentage of sampled farms reporting *any* amount of the commodity.
Bottom figure is the average quantity reported per farm; it is calculated for only those farms reporting *any* amount. Rice production was reported in pounds, cotton production in bales; all other crops were reported in bushels.

Source: US census manuscripts for 1850

counties were the domain of the large producers; other major rice-producing counties, such as Colleton and Beaufort in South Carolina, contained a large number of rice growers with but modest rice productions. A handful of very large-scale planters in Georgetown, Chatham, and Glynn counties produced almost all of the rice, but there was a larger group of operators who produced no rice at all. Of the three, Georgetown was most dominated by the large planter. A count of Georgetown rice producers in 1850 showed two reporting over a million pounds, fifty-six reporting over 100,000 pounds, and only thirty-seven reporting fewer than 10,000 pounds. The average production per planter was 258,854 pounds, but only 47 per cent of the sample produced any rice at all. In contrast the typical rice grower in Colleton County produced only 19,336 pounds, but 56 per cent of the sample reported rice. On the other hand, it must be noted that the dominance of the very large planter in some areas was perhaps greater than that shown by the manuscript census data. The census reported each plantation separately, thus obscuring the fact that many planters owned more than one plantation, and it is known from narrative data and secondary studies that multiple-plantation ownership was common. Furthermore, the early establishment of a rather complex planting élite with entire families being rice planters, and frequent intermarriage among planting families, often resulted in their achieving social and economic dominance of a particular community.[18]

The presence of a large number of landholdings that reported no rice and a similar group that produced rice in quantities too small to provide significant income raises an important question about other crops. Were these small-scale semi-subsistent farmers or did they find other cash crops? Cotton was the most likely alternative, and it was a strong secondary cash crop, although its distribution was uneven. Virtually no cotton was produced in Horry and Georgetown counties (the northernmost South Carolina counties), but in a number of counties the producers reporting cotton equalled or exceeded those who reported rice. In most cases cotton was reported by non-rice growers or by those who produced rice in small quantities only. A few large rice planters also grew cotton but rarely in large quantities. It appears that most of the large operators concentrated on either rice or cotton. Considering the environmental requirements of the two crops, such specialization is understandable, since rice was grown almost exclusively on floodplains while cotton, even the Sea Island variety, preferred better-drained soil. On many landholdings both habitats could be found, but on the best tidewater sites the premium land was rice land, not

18 Every centre—Darien, Savannah, Charleston, Georgetown—had its élite but nowhere did the rice barons rule more completely than in Georgetown. See Rogers, *History of Georgetown County*, especially 252-341.

TABLE 4
Percentage of operators reporting rice and cotton by county in
South Carolina and Georgia, 1850

	Rice only	Cotton only	Both	Neither
Georgetown	48.0	0.0	0.0	52.0
Chatham	48.7	12.8	7.7	30.8
Bryan	20.0	7.3	16.4	56.4
Liberty	18.0	19.7	44.3	18.0
McIntosh	28.6	28.6	22.9	20.0
Glynn	24.1	41.4	24.1	10.3
Camden	26.7	36.7	13.3	23.3
Charleston	30.5	14.2	16.8	38.5
Beaufort	19.9	36.1	32.8	11.2
Colleton	30.0	25.8	26.3	17.9
Horry	37.5	0.0	0.0	62.5

Source: US census manuscripts for 1850

cotton land. Another factor favouring specialization was the traditional plantation tendency towards monoculture. The high capital and specialized labour requirements of each crop (rice mills, ditching, diking, cotton gins) discouraged small-scale entry into another cash-crop specialty, and the rather specific expertise needed to produce either rice or cotton (both rather 'temperamental' and 'fussy' plants) forced many planters and overseers to become either 'rice men' or 'cotton men' (Table 4).

It is clear that the tidewater area was the domain of the rice planter and that rice was the principal cash crop, yet a closer look at the census manuscripts indicates some danger of oversimplification if one describes the area as a homogeneous rice-producing area. It was noted earlier that rice growing was a specialized occupation and that only a fraction of the area of the eleven counties was devoted to rice; only about half of those listed as 'agriculturists' actually produced rice, and few of those were large planters. A clear picture emerges from the pages of the census manuscripts: a relatively small group of large-scale rice planters concentrated in Georgetown, Chatham, and Glynn counties, with a scattering in other counties; an even larger group of non-rice producers in all counties, especially Horry and the Georgia counties; and a surprisingly large group of farmers who produced rice but in quantities considerably lower than that necessary to qualify as planting 'giants.'

ARTHUR J. RAY

The Hudson's Bay Company
fur trade in the eighteenth century:
a comparative economic study

Although studies of the North American fur trade abound, few have been approached from a comparative economic point of view. Such an approach would necessarily involve attempts to determine the extent to which the economies and economic behaviour of the Indians and Europeans differed, the kinds of conventions that were established to link the two economies, and the ways in which the patterns of exchange influenced other aspects of Indian cultures. Given the broad-ranging nature of these questions, it is not possible here to deal with all of the issues that they raise. Therefore, attention will be directed towards the first two areas of enquiry. And discussion will be limited to an analysis of the Hudson's Bay Company trade during the period before 1763, drawing upon the records of the most important post, York Factory.

Figure 1 shows the structure of the fur trade. There were three spheres of activity centred in the European markets, at the trading posts, and in the post hinterlands. The Hudson's Bay Company was involved in the first two spheres and faced the problem of dealing in the highly fluid European market, on the one hand, where changing supply-and-demand conditions operated to set prices, and with the Indians, on the other, who had no conception of the market. Transactions in Europe were facilitated by use of the British sterling monetary system. However, the Indians of the subarctic lacked an equivalent system, so that initially the company was forced to conduct its business with them on a barter basis. In order to keep an account of this trade, the Hudson's Bay Company developed the so-called *made beaver* (hereinafter *MB*) as the basic unit of value. The *MB* was originally equivalent to the value of a prime whole beaver skin on the London market. The governor and committee of the company

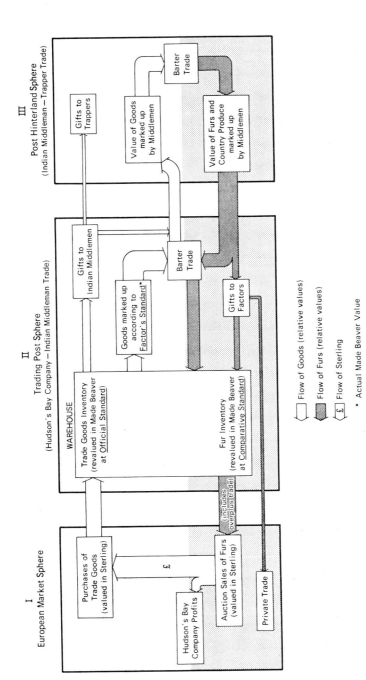

Figure 1 Flows of furs and goods in the Hudson's Bay Company trading system

assigned *MB* values to all European trade goods in what was known as the *standard of trade* and equated all of the Indians' fur and 'country produce' in terms of *MB* in the *comparative standard*. These 'price lists' were sent to the posts each year along with the shipments of goods from London. Significantly, no media of exchange such as scrip or tokens were employed at this time.[1]

By the end of the seventeenth century the *MB* accounting system was well understood by the Indians and Europeans alike, as the subsequent discussion will demonstrate, and trade ceased to be conducted on a purely barter basis. By having a unit of account that was mutually understood by both parties, the Hudson's Bay Company was able to extend credit ('debt') to the Indians. The amount of credit that was extended depended upon the success that the Indians had in hunting and trapping in any given year and upon the intensity of French competition. Generally, if the Indians had a poor year because of famine, the scarcity of fur bearers, or harsh winter conditions, making returns inadequate to meet their demands for goods, the company traders gave them credit that approximated the average annual return an individual Indian might be expected to bring to the post.[2] When competition between the French and English was strong, credit was used more extensively in an effort to obligate the Indians to return year after year. In the eighteenth century credit was used most widely at Moose Factory during the 1750s because this post lay closest to the main line of French expansion and French opposition was strongest during the first half of that decade.[3]

Besides having to devise an accounting system, the Hudson's Bay Company had to make another major adjustment in order to trade with the Indians. It was forced to participate in the traditional Indian pre-trade gift-giving ceremony. These exchanges were a form of balanced reciprocity that served to establish or renew political and social ties between the Indians and the company.[4] If the traders had refused to participate in these exchanges, the Indians would have broken off relations. Thus, at the trading posts furs and trade goods changed hands in two different ways – by reciprocal gift exchanges and by barter trade. In the hinterlands of the posts the same two modes of transaction were employed when Indian groups came together for purposes of exchange.

1 Arthur J. Ray, 'The Early Hudson's Bay Company Account Books as Sources for Historical Research: An Analysis and Assessment,' *Archivaria* 1 (1975-6): 9-10
2 Arthur J. Ray, *Indians in the Fur Trade* (Toronto 1974), 137-8
3 Public Archives of Canada, Hudson's Bay Company Microfilm Collection (hereafter PAC HBC), Correspondence Inward, A 11/43/99-102
4 Arthur J. Ray, 'The Factor and the Trading Captain in the Hudson's Bay Company Fur Trade before 1763,' in Jim Freedman and Jerome H. Barkow, eds., National Museum of Man Mercury Series, *Canadian Ethnology Service Paper no 28* (Ottawa 1975), 2: 587-9; Marshall Sahlins, *Stone Age Economics* (Chicago 1972), 219-20

TABLE 1
York Factory standards, 1720-60

Item[a]	1720 Quantity	1720 Value[b]	1740 Quantity	1740 Value[b]	1760 Quantity	1760 Value[b]
Powder, lbs.	1	1	1	1	1	1
Shot, lbs.	4	1	4	1	4	1
Guns 4 ft.	1	14	1	14	1	14
3½ ft.	1	14	1	14	1	14
Flints, no.	16	1	16	1	16	1
Ice chissels	1	1	1	1	1	1
Hatchets	1	1	1	1	1	1
Broad cloth, yds.	1	3	1	3	1	3
Tobacco, lbs.[c]	1	2	¾	1	¾	1
Brandy, gals.	1	4	1	4	1	4
Knives	4	1	4	1	4	1
Twine, skein	1	1¼	1	1	1	1
Kettles	1	1½	1	1½	1	1½
Wolverine	1	2	1	2	1	2
Wolf	1	2	1	2	1	2
Bear	1	2	1	2	1	2
Grey fox	1	2	1	2	1	2
Red fox	1	1	1	1	1	1
White fox	2	1	2	1	2	1
Black fox	1	3	1	3	1	3
Deer	2	1	1	1[d]	1	1
Moose skins	1	2	1[e]	2	1	2
Lynx	1	1	1	1	1	1
Marten	3	1	3	1	3	1
Fisher	–	–	2	1	2	1

a Selected items only
b All values in *MB*
c Brazil tobacco
d Buck
e Parchment

The structure of the trading system reveals that there were significant differences between the economies of the Indians and Europeans, and certain conventions, such as the *MB* accounting system and the gift exchange, had to be developed and elaborated to facilitate smooth economic intercourse. An examination of the operation of the system under varying economic conditions serves to raise a number of questions about the economic behaviour of the two groups.

Table 1 shows that the official prices for goods and furs remained remarkably stable over a long period of time. The historian E.E. Rich, one of the first scholars to comment on this phenomenon, suggested that two factors were probably primarily responsible. He pointed out that the company directors wanted to maintain central control and ensure that their posts did not compete with each other.[5] Hence, the standards of trade were set in London by the governor and committee. The problem with this suggestion is that although it might explain spatial uniformity in prices, and indeed there were few major discrepancies among the posts, it does not really account for temporal stability. If price changes were in order, the governor and committee could have altered the standards at all of the posts simultaneously.

Rich's other suggestion, that the stability of the official standards of trade was caused by the unwillingness of the native peoples to permit the company to adjust prices in accordance with market conditions in Europe, warrants closer consideration. According to Rich: 'It was impossible, apparently, to make a clean departure from the standard and to demand excess furs for an article such as a gun or a hatchet for which the price was known ... there was no attempt on either side to raise prices in accordance with the laws of supply and demand. The standard, perhaps with some accepted adjustment according to the locality or the personalities involved, was applied whether furs were scarce or plentiful, and whether goods were in supply or not. When the Indians had got used to a convention there was no breaking it with safety.'[6]

The economist Abraham Rotstein, accepting Rich's interpretation, went further to suggest that the 'Indian commitment to a fixed standard of trade was not limited to the region of Hudson Bay.' Rotstein concluded that in the North American fur trade 'competition did not typically take the form of price competition. Differences in the standard proved, in the dynamic and peculiar nature of the fur trade, to be of secondary importance to other forms of competition.' Regarding these other modes of rivalry for the supply of furs, Rotstein posited that most of the competitive energies of the Indians and Europeans were channelled into the political sphere and were expressed in the form of violence, war, and the manipulation of Indian alliance systems.[7]

Although there is little doubt that politics were an integral part of the fur trade, or that the Indians resisted price increases in trade goods, the existence of a fixed set of official standards requires closer scrutiny before it can be assumed that price competition was not a central feature of the trading system.

5 Rich, 'The Indian Traders,' *Beaver* 301 (1970): 12
6 Rich, 'Trade Habits and Economic Motivation among the Indians of North America,' *Canadian Journal of Economics and Political Science* 26 (1960): 44
7 Rotstein, 'Fur Trade and Empire: An Institutional Analysis,' PhD dissertation, University of Toronto, 1967, pp. 66, 72

Granting that political factors and trading conventions may have played a role in stabilizing official prices, practical economic considerations need to be taken into account as well. For instance, soon after contact the Indians developed a strong demand for some consumable luxuries like alcohol and tobacco and an increasing dependence upon other more basic items such as firearms, ammunition, metal wares, and cloth. To obtain these goods many bands travelled long distances, sometimes more than a thousand miles round trip, encountering many hazards along the way. Furthermore, the cargo capacities of their canoes were limited to about 100 *MB* of furs per man.[8] These constraints would have encouraged the Indians to press for stable prices, or at least ones that changed very slowly over time, for two reasons. Unless the Indians had a fairly accurate picture of the prices that they would receive for their furs before they set out for the Bay, they would have had to face the prospect of undertaking long, dangerous voyages without having any certainty that their furs would fetch prices that would allow them to satisfy their own demand for goods.

Also, because of the time that was required to make the trip down and back from the Bay, and the shortness of the canoeing season, trade had to be conducted as expeditiously as possible. The advantage of having a relatively fixed standard of trade was that it could serve as a base of reference for the Europeans and Indians that enabled them to come to terms relatively quickly. Indeed, the governor and committee in London were quick to appreciate this point and hoped that a fixed standard might enable some groups to visit the Bay more than once a year. For example, on 22 May 1682 they sent the following instructions to Governor John Nixon at Fort Albany: 'In all places where we have already traded *you are in your dealing with them to keepe to the Standard* of commerce which was formerly agreed and setled by Mr. Bayley [Nixon's predecessor] which will not only facilitate your Trade when the Indians come downe with their Goods but may give such quick dispatch that some of the neerest Indians may make two returnes in a season.'[9] The governor and committee added that quick treatment of the natives was desirable for the additional reason that it gave the servants of the company less opportunity to engage in illegal private trade. It was for these purely economic and practical reasons that the fixed official standards of trade served the Indians and company alike.

Yet, although the official standards played an important role in the fur trade, other evidence also indicates that some price flexibility was necessary and *de facto* rates of exchange often differed substantially from the official ones.

8 Glyndwr Williams, ed., *Andrew Graham's Observations on Hudson's Bay, 1767-1791* (London 1969), 276
9 E.E. Rich, ed., *Copy Book of Letters Outward* (Toronto 1948), 79

From the outset the *comparative standard* was too rigid because all commodities were valued in terms of prime winter pelts. However, as the factors at the posts pointed out, the Indians brought in significant quantities of summer pelts and badly worn coat beaver. These poorer grades of fur had to be discounted. The amount of the discount would have been settled by higgling and haggling.[10]

Besides having to make allowances for variations in the quality of peltry that they received, the company traders were increasingly pressured by the governor and committee in London to raise their standards in the late seventeenth and early eighteenth centuries, when England and France were at war. Wartime conditions meant that the costs of trade goods rose, as did transportation costs, while at the same time the demand for furs in Europe declined. The company directors hoped to ease these financial pressures by obtaining better prices for their goods, but they did not want their factors to antagonize the natives by taking such a course of action. Hence, the men at the posts faced a dilemma.

It appears that the solution to the problem was one which involved an extension of the number of items over which higgling and haggling regarding the *de facto* rates of exchange took place. Whereas originally this dickering centred around evaluations of the quality of the pelts that the Indians brought to the posts, by the late seventeenth century it had been extended to include bargaining over the unofficial rates at which many of the trade goods would be exchanged. In the case of discrete items like kettles or guns the factors simply demanded more furs than the *standard of trade* specified. In the case of items that were measured at the time of trade like cloth, powder, tobacco, or brandy more subtle means were used to advance prices. In these instances short measures were given, scales were surreptitiously weighted, or water was added prior to exchange, as became customary when dispensing brandy. An examination of Andrew Graham's observations suggests that almost 65 per cent of the gain that was made by unofficially advancing trade good prices came from items that had to be measured at the time of trade.[11]

Although the factors were thereby able to establish an unofficial rate of exchange (the *de facto* rate) that came to be known as the *double standard*[12] or *factors' standard*, they did so with the full knowledge of their Indian trading partners. Contrary to many popular views, the Indians were not easily duped and were fully aware of the fact that the official standards were being contravened.

---

10 PAC HBC, York Factory Account Books, B 239/d/1
11 Williams, *Graham's Observations*, 277-9
12 The term *double standard* is not entirely appropriate in that it was not two times the official rate of exchange; therefore, the term *factors' standard* will be used hereafter.

For this reason much of the substance of the trade speeches that were exchanged between band leaders and the factors centred on discussions of the measures. The Indians customarily asked to see the old measures and to receive 'full measure and a little over,' that is, trade at the standard. The factors typically responded by saying the company's measures were already larger than those of the opposition.[13] Significantly, the measures (the *official standards*) were not questioned in these exchanges; rather, the fullness of the measures received were. In short, it appears that the official standards increasingly served only as a language of trade, or reference point, that enabled the two sides to come to terms quickly regarding the *de facto* price schedules that would be employed in a given year. The Indians' ideal was to be dealt with at the official rate, whereas the *standard of trade* represented the lowest price that the factors would accept.

The degree to which *de facto* prices fluctuated can be measured by analysing the *overplus* and the data on goods traded. The *overplus* represented that portion of the fur returns (valued in *MB*) that had been obtained by applying the *factors' standard.*[14] If one calculates the ratio of *MB* units of goods traded per *MB* units of *overplus* obtained, it is possible to determine the net markup over the *standard of trade* in any given year. A ratio of 1:1 would indicate a markup of 100 per cent, whereas a ratio of 2:1 would be only 50 per cent.

If the *overplus* data and the ratios of the *MB* value of goods traded per unit of *overplus* derived are examined for York Factory, it appears that the strength of French competition had a strong influence on the *de facto* rates of exchange. French opposition in the vicinity of York Factory (Figure 2) was relatively weak until the early 1730s, when Pierre Gaultier de Varennes, Sieur de la Vérendrye, began building a string of posts across the York hinterland. Thereafter rivalries intensified until the late 1750s, when the French were forced to abandon western Canada, leaving the Hudson's Bay Company with a monopoly hold on the trade for a short time.

These changing competitive conditions clearly influenced the amount of *overplus* that the traders gained in the trade, as shown in Figure 3.[15] The volume of the *overplus* taken at York Factory reached a peak in the trading year of 1730-1, when a total of 20,000 *MB* were obtained. An erratic decline then began as French competition intensified and a low point of 4000 *MB* was reached in 1753-4. As the French withdrew the *overplus* began to rebound until the early 1760s. Thereafter *overplus* returns fluctuated, partly reflecting the uneven

13 Conrad E. Heidenreich and Arthur J. Ray, *The Early Fur Trades: A Study in Cultural Interaction* (Toronto 1976), 82-3
14 Ray, 'Early Hudson's Bay Company Account Books,' 13-18
15 The source for information in Figures 3 to 8 is PAC HBC B 239/d/1-72.

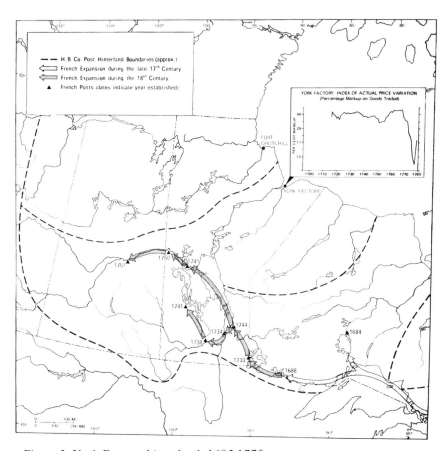

Figure 2 York Factory hinterland, 1695-1770

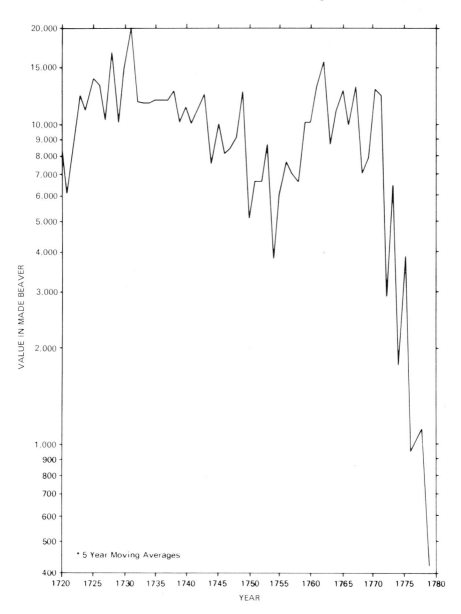

Figure 3 York Factory: *overplus* trade* (plotted on semi-logarithmic scale)

success of the Nor'Westers, who were beginning to establish themselves in the interior in the late 1760s. The pressure that this new group of competitors exerted on the Hudson's Bay Company forced the latter to alter its long-standing policy of 'sleeping by the frozen sea [Hudson Bay]' and move inland to meet the opposition directly. In 1774 Cumberland House was built on the lower Saskatchewan River and much of the inland trade of York Factory ceased as a result. This shift accounts for the abrupt decline in the *overplus* at York Factory after 1774.

Although the *overplus* data give a picture of the net success that the traders achieved by applying the *factors' standard*, they do not offer a clear indication of the variations in *de facto* price levels because the total amount of *overplus* that was taken in a given year was partly dependent upon the volume of trade. Therefore, to obtain an indication of the extent to which exchange rates fluctuated, the ratios of the *MB* value of goods traded per unit of *overplus* gained have been plotted on Figure 4 using a five-year moving average to smooth out the data and better portray long-term trends.

Figure 4 shows that from 1714 to 1725, while the York Factory traders were trying to re-establish trading contacts with the Indians, the terms of trade were continually being improved. During the next decade the company enjoyed a monopoly in the area and took advantage of the situation to advance the unofficial rates of exchange. Thus, between 1725 and 1735 a markup of slightly more than 50 per cent was in effect. Subsequently, as the pressures from the French began to mount, the factors were forced to relax their standards. During the 1750-5 period, when French opposition was strongest, markups of less than one-third were being exacted. With a short-term renewal of monopoly conditions in the late 1750s and early 1760s, a price markup in excess of 50 per cent was again enforced. In the late 1760s and early 1770s the penetration of the Nor'Westers compelled the York Factory traders to lower the *factors' standard*, and by 1770 only a 10 per cent advance was being taken. With a termination of inland trade after the 1774-5 trading year, most of the trade of York Factory came from Indians living in relatively close proximity to the post where the company had a monopoly. So once again the *de facto* price levels for trade goods rose.

Significantly, besides showing that local demand conditions for the Indians' furs did strongly influence exchange rates, the data in Figure 4 also suggest that the Indians resisted markups in excess of 50 per cent even under monopoly conditions. This was the case at other posts also.[16] Undoubtedly part of the

16 Arthur J. Ray, 'The Hudson's Bay Company Account Books as Sources for Comparative Economic Analyses of the Fur Trade: An Examination of Exchange Rate Data,' *Western Canadian Journal of Anthropology* 6 (1976): 44-50

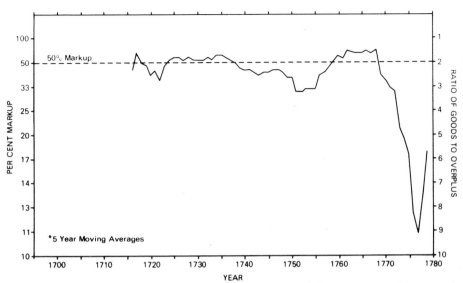

Figure 4 York Factory: index of actual price variation* (percentage markup on goods traded)

reason for this resistance was related to the fact that the cargo capacities of the canoes was limited, so that the Indians could bring in only eighty to one hundred *MB* of furs per man. According to Andrew Graham, three-quarters of these furs, or sixty to seventy-five *MB*, were spent on necessities and the remainder on luxuries.[17] Thus, if the Indians' purchasing power had been effectively devalued by 50 per cent, they would have been able to buy only forty to fifty *MB* of trade goods (valued at the *standard of trade*). In other words, they would not have been able to satisfy all of their basic requirements. Any further devaluations of their furs would have meant that there would have been little point in continuing to trade, considering the hazards and efforts that were required to do so.

Besides influencing the *de facto* rates of exchange, changing competitive conditions affected the relative value of goods that changed hands in the pre-trade gift-giving ceremonies. Although these exchanges had traditionally served primarily as material expressions of good will, this intention was subverted to a considerable extent in the fur trade as the Hudson's Bay Company traders and the French introduced the notion of gift giving for the

17 Williams, *Graham's Observations*, 276-7

purposes of reward and encouragement. For instance, at York Factory trading leaders who brought more than thirty canoes with them were accorded preferential treatment during their stay at the post and offered more lavish gifts at the outset. Furthermore, once trade was concluded additional presents were given to the Indian leaders and their lieutenants. The quantities of goods that were given away were proportional to the number of men who had been brought with them.[18] As English-French competition escalated, the two groups tried to outbid each other in the lavishness of their presents in order to materially demonstrate their greater friendship for the Indians.[19] Consequently, gift giving became an increasingly expensive practice during periods of sharp rivalry.

An indication of the impact that trade rivalries had upon costs of conducting business can be obtained by examining the expenses section of the York Factory account books. Expenses consisted of trade goods that had been given to the Indians as presents and as payment for food brought to the posts, letters that were carried to other posts, etc.[20] It is important to note that expenditures of goods for food and services rendered by the local Indian population tended to be relatively stable. Therefore, most of the temporal variations of expenses reflect the changing cost of gift giving.

Figure 5 shows that expenses at York Factory rose between 1715 and 1720 while the traders attempted to rebuild their partnerships with Indian groups in the interior. Expenses declined during the next five years and then remained relatively steady between 1725 and 1735. Thereafter, as English-French rivalry in the area intensified, expenses increased substantially until a peak was reached in the middle of the 1750s. As the French withdrew, there was a corresponding decline in expenses at York Factory. In short, the data show roughly the same pattern as has been observed for the *overplus* and *de facto* price indices.

It should be stressed that the *factors' standards* and expenses were the two aspects of business over which the traders at the post had control. For this reason the *overplus* and expense data can be used to monitor the performance of the factors under different trading conditions. Indeed, the governor and committee in London used them partly for that purpose.[21] If the expenses are subtracted from the *overplus*, it is possible to derive what might be termed the factor's net profit or loss. This has been done for York Factory; the data, presented in Figure 6, show that from about 1720 to 1730 the factors' profits were on the increase. Thereafter a precipitous decline ensued until a nadir was

18 Ray, 'The Factor and the Trading Captain,' 589
19 Ray, *Indians in the Fur Trade*, 138-40
20 Ray, 'Early Hudson's Bay Company Account Books,' 11-13
21 Ray, 'The Factor and the Trading Captain,' 596-7

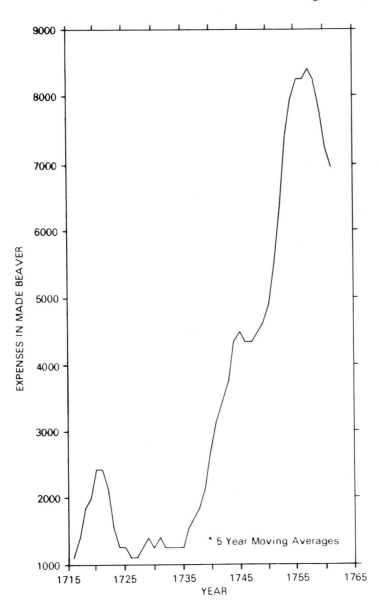

Figure 5 York Factory: expenses*

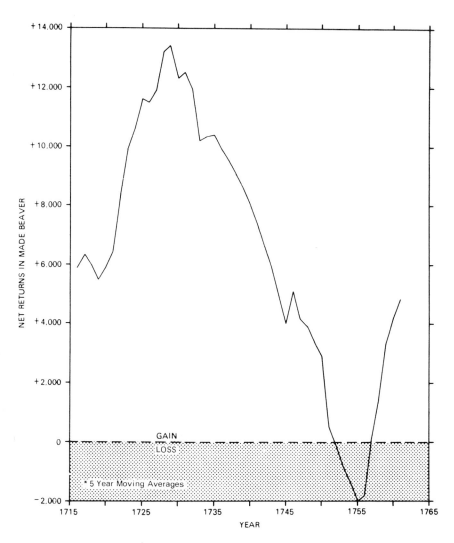

Figure 6 York Factory: factors' net returns in relation to official standards*
(determined by subtracting expenses from *overplus*)

reached in 1755. A recovery began after that date as the French abandoned the region. Significantly, when French competition was at its height in the mid-1750s, expenses exceeded the *overplus* and a net loss was recorded.

The factors' profit and loss figures have to be used cautiously. It cannot be assumed that they represented a true profit or loss to the company until more research is done. First it will be necessary to determine how much of a markup had been built into the original *standard of trade* and how changing economic conditions in Europe influenced it. Thus, the profit and loss figures used here are intended only to indicate how the traders were faring at their posts in terms of their own system of reckoning.

When viewed against the background of the profit and loss graph, it is understandable why alcohol became a popular trade item. Brandy provided a good source of *overplus*. Company records show that at York Factory brandy was diluted by one-third prior to being given away or traded.[22] Figure 7 shows the amount of *overplus* that the York Factory traders would have obtained by applying this ratio to the volumes of brandy that the Indians had bought. It reveals that during the period from 1720 to the late 1750s the brandy *overplus* varied between 220 *MB* and 1110 *MB* or from 3 to 18 per cent of the total *overplus* for York Factory (Figure 8). It is important to note that as competition escalated and with it gift-giving expenses, so too did the volume of brandy traded and therefore the opportunity to apply the *factors' standard*. In this respect the alcohol trade differed from that of other commodities, such as cloth, where strong French competition would have forced a cutback in the *factors' standard* because the measures offered by either party were readily comparable. This would not have been the case with watering ratios, and therefore it is not surprising that it was at the height of French-English rivalry that the brandy *overplus* as a percentage of the total *overplus* reached a peak (Figure 8).

From the point of view of the traders, brandy offered the additional advantage of enabling them to hold down rising expenses somewhat since it figured prominently among the commodities given as gifts to the Indians. By watering the brandy, they dispensed one-third less alcohol every year than would otherwise have been the case, thereby saving a substantial amount.

Finally, the brandy trade offered the Europeans a means of getting around the difficult problem that they faced with respect to Indian consumer behaviour. As noted earlier, the Indians typically bought sixty to eighty *MB* of basic necessities every year and twenty to forty *MB* of luxury items. Therefore the traders had to cope with the fact that Indian consumer demand was relatively inelastic on a short-term basis. This was partly a consequence of the facts that

22 K.G. Davies, ed., *Letters from Hudson Bay, 1703-40* (London 1965), 263

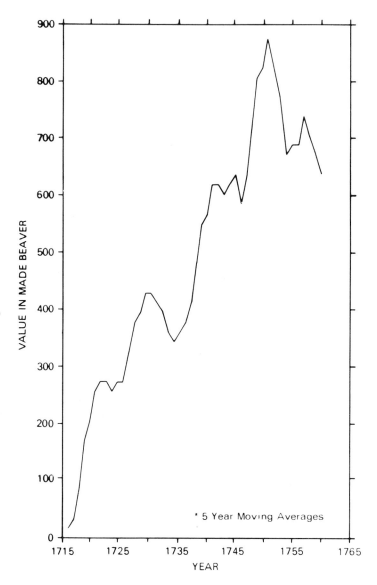

Figure 7 Estimate of York Factory *overplus* derived from the brandy trade*

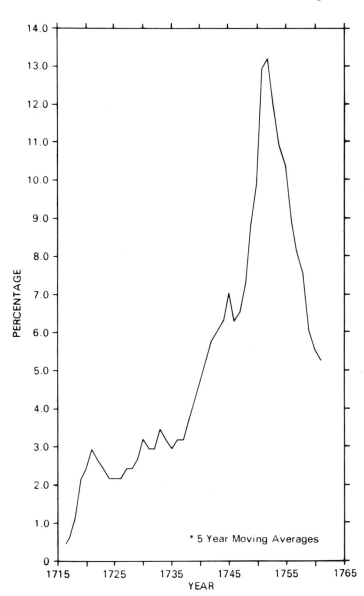

Figure 8 Estimated percentage of total York Factory *overplus* consisting of
brandy *overplus**

the cargo capacities of their canoes were limited and they had a mobile life style. These constraints, and the social taboo against hoarding, meant that the Indians did not acquire goods to accumulate wealth, but rather purchased articles to satisfy only their immediate needs. Thus, when French-English competition intensified, increasing the purchasing power of the Indians, the latter tended to respond by decreasing the per capita supply of furs that they brought to the posts.[23] Being addictive in nature and consumable on the spot, alcohol offered the potential of absorbing some of the excess purchasing power of the Indians during those periods when trade rivalries led to an inflation in the value of their furs.

Given these factors it is easy to understand why alcohol figured so prominently in the fur trade and ultimately had such a disruptive influence on the Indians. That it did not wreak greater havoc before 1763 stemmed partly from the fact that French-English rivalries never reached the levels of intensity that characterized those of the Hudson's Bay Company and North West Company of a later period. Also, before 1763 the Indians travelled great distances to reach the posts, and these lengthy voyages forced them to keep fairly rigid time schedules. Therefore they could not afford to stay at the forts for more than a few days before returning to the interior. And most of the Indian groups only visited the posts once a year, making it virtually impossible to become addicted to the liquor. After 1763, however, the number of posts multiplied and no Indian had to travel any great distance to reach one. The cutthroat nature of competition that characterized the period from 1763 to 1821 led to a dizzying spiral in the relative value of the Indians' furs that far outpaced their demand for most durable goods. Under these circumstances the inherent weakness of the system with respect to alcohol abuse became glaringly obvious.

In conclusion, the structure of the trading network that evolved reflected the need to link two disparate economic systems in a manner that enabled exchange to take place smoothly and regularly. Elements from both economies were incorporated into the system. The pre-trade gift-exchange ceremony was of Indian origin. After accepting it, the European traders began to change it and use it for their own ends. The most significant alteration was the introduction of the idea of giving gifts as rewards for economic services rendered. The Europeans introduced a monetary system in the form of the *made beaver* unit of account and the standards of trade. The Indians quickly learned to cope with this system, and soon trade ceased to be carried on solely on a barter basis. Credit could be extended and by the late eighteenth century *made beaver* tokens and scrip were

23 Williams, *Graham's Observations*, 275

employed. In this way the Indians were gradually introduced into a cash economy.

An examination of the system in operation has shown that price competition was an essential element because the Indians did respond to more favourable terms of trade. However, their response to better terms of trade differed from that which the Europeans expected. Rather than increasing their per capita supplies when prices were more favourable, the Indians brought in fewer furs. In an effort to counteract this problem the Europeans increasingly resorted to the use of alcohol in the trade. Thus, given the manner in which the two economic systems were linked in the fur trade, and the contrasting economic behaviour and motivations of the Europeans and the Indians, the abuse of alcohol was probably inevitable. Only strong monopolistic control by one of the European groups could have prevented it, given the absence of any powerful local government to regulate it.

The author thanks the Hudson's Bay Company for granting him permission to consult and quote the company's archives.

D. AIDAN McQUILLAN

Territory and ethnic identity: some new measures of an old theme in the cultural geography of the United States

One of the most fascinating, most vexed, and most completely unresolved problems in Canadian historiography — which is also a matter of deep interest to cultural geographers — lies in ... the viability of ethnic characteristics as between different ethnic groups whose distinctive settlements have marked so much of the course of the peopling of this country.

ANDREW H. CLARK,
Annual Meeting of the Canadian Association of Geographers,
Winnipeg 1970

Andrew Clark's fascination with the persistence of cultural differences among immigrant groups found expression, for the most part, in his studies on Maritime Canada. In particular, he considered religion and national background as major factors in differentiating the origins of Nova Scotia's population.[1] This interest in ethnicity was deeply rooted in his own family background. He recalled with pride that his grandmother, the descendant of a Selkirk settler in Prince Edward Island, still spoke Gaelic in the 1930s. Religion and language were certainly two of the major elements of ethnic identity that remained operative through the nineteenth and into the twentieth century.

What we understand by ethnicity in the 1970s is a slightly different phenomenon from what it was understood to be in the 1920s, the 1840s, or the 1770s. The component characteristics of ethnicity have continuously taken on

---

1 Andrew H. Clark, 'Old World Origins and Religious Adherence in Nova Scotia,' *Geographical Review* 50 (July 1960): 317-44

new connotations and the relative importance of these components has shifted with changes in the general social climate.[2] While the various manifestations of ethnicity have changed or even faded away, at least five essential elements have been of such importance that they have survived in ethnic identification over a considerable period of time. These characteristics, in addition to religion and language, include race (with allowance for the limited validity of the term to indicate an ambiguous characteristic), folk culture, and a territorial identity.[3] Immigrants to the United States whose mother tongue was not English found that language was a major factor differentiating them from the remainder of society, at least for the first generation.[4] The use of racial characteristics to distinguish ethnic groups became fashionable in the 1930s; the racial homogeneity of a group was preserved through endogamy, and the rate of intermarriage among ethnic groups continued to attract the interest of historians and sociologists.[5] The attributes of folk culture, which are prominent in studies of ethnic groups, are enormously varied; they range from distinctive styles in

2 For example, Roman Catholicism as a factor in the identity of the American Irish was quite different in the 1960s from what it was in the 1860s at the height of the Know-Nothing movement. The latter was one of the overt attacks on Irish immigrants and their slavish obedience to the Catholic hierarchy. Thus in the 1860s Roman Catholicism was a source of contempt for Irish immigrants. In the early 1960s, with a Catholic president and an internationally popular pope, Roman Catholicism was a source of deep pride in the identity of the American Irish.

3 There is a considerable literature in the sociology and anthropology journals on the characteristics that are important in ethnic identity. Milton Gordon has summarized the enduring characteristics: 'First and foremost we note that early man identified himself as a member of a group, his "people," and that this "peoplehood" was roughly coterminous with a given rural land space, political government, no matter how rudimentary, a common culture in which a principal element was a set of religious beliefs and values shared more or less uniformly by all members of the group, and a common racial background ensuring an absence of wide differences in physical type.' *Assimilation in American Life: The Role of Race, Religion and National Origins* (New York 1964), 23

4 J.A. Fishman *et al., Language Loyalty in the United States: The Maintenance and Perpetuation of Non-English Mother Tongues by American Ethnic Groups* (The Hague 1966)

5 There is a large literature on intermarriage patterns, including J. Drachsler, *Intermarriage in New York City* (New York 1921); A.B. Hollingshead, 'Cultural Factors in the Selection of Marriage Mates,' *American Sociological Review* 15 (Oct. 1950): 624; H.B. Johnson, 'Intermarriages between German Pioneers and Other Nationalities in Minnesota in 1860 and 1870,' *American Journal of Sociology* 51 (Jan. 1946): 299-304; R.J.R. Kennedy, 'Single or Triple Melting Pot? Intermarriage Trends in New Haven,' *American Journal of Sociology* 58 (July 1952): 56-9; J.I. Kolehmainen, 'A Study of Marriages in a Finnish Community,' *American Journal of Sociology* 42 (Nov. 1936): 371-82; and L. Nelson, 'Intermarriage among Nationality Groups in a Rural Area of Minnesota,' *American Journal of Sociology* 48 (March 1943): 585-92.

peasant dress, folk festivals, music, preferences in food, and distinctive cuisine to styles of architecture.

One of the components of ethnic identity that is of particular interest to cultural geographers is identity with place. Cultural geographers have been attracted by the folk artifacts and elements of material culture in the landscape that distinguished one immigrant area from other immigrant areas in North America.[6] Studies of the distribution of house types, dairy barns, fences, saunas, and place names bear witness to the immigrant contribution to a varied cultural landscape. In the first part of this essay I would like to review briefly the ways in which 'places' have been associated with ethnic identity not only in the New World but also in the Old World. In the second part of the essay the efforts of three immigrant groups to establish a territorial base for their new communities on the grassland plains of Kansas will be investigated in some detail.

PLACE AND IDENTITY

Geographers and historians have linked the cultural imprint of immigrants on North America's landscapes to the idea that immigrant groups settled in those areas in the New World where the physical landscape resembled their homeland environments. The Finns, for example, settled in wooded locations in western Canada and northern Ontario that closely resembled the physical landscape of their Finnish homeland.[7] Germans, it was claimed, preferred the heavy-textured loam soils of the wooded lowlands in Pennsylvania, whereas the Scotch-Irish selected interior, thin, hilly soils, similar to those which they had known in Ulster.[8] The Germans and Norwegians in Wisconsin also settled on wooded lands, while the English and Yankee settlers from New England farmed in prairie openings.[9] Attempts to establish similarities between the areas settled by immigrant groups in the Midwest and their European homeland often originated in the immigration pamphlets and literature of the nineteenth century. However,

---

6 A good example of this interest is the work of John J. Mannion, who has studied the rate of survival of Irish traits within Irish immigrant communities in Newfoundland, New Brunswick, and southern Ontario. *Irish Settlements in Eastern Canada: A Study of Cultural Transfer and Adaptation* (Toronto 1974)

7 E. van Cleef, 'Finnish Settlements in Canada,' *Geographical Review* 42 (April 1952): 252-66

8 R.H. Shyrock, 'British versus German Traditions in Colonial Agriculture,' *Mississippi Valley Historical Review* 26 (June 1939): 39-54; W.H. Gehrke, 'The Ante-Bellum Agriculture of the Germans in North Carolina,' *Agricultural History* 9 (July 1935): 143-60

9 B.H. Hibbard, *History of Agriculture in Dane County* (Madison 1904)

several studies by historical geographers have discounted the apparent preference of immigrants for an American environment that resembled the 'old country.'[10]

An individual derives his identity not only from the group of which he is a member but also from the places that he identifies with the group.[11] An individual may perceive his own identity in terms of a series of nested concentric circles with self at the centre, followed by family, kin-group, and a series of less and less personal associations extending to membership in the national group at the outer perimeter. The territorial counterparts to this series of circles are the home, the family farm, the township or parish (in cities the equivalents are city block and neighbourhood), the county, the province, and finally the state. The designation 'German' differentiated an immigrant from an 'Italian,' but among German immigrants to have come from Bavaria was, indeed, quite different from having come from the Palatinate. One need only hear the question in a Brooklyn neighbourhood bar, 'Where is he from?' and the answer, 'Mayo, God help us!' to realize the subtleties that exist among subsets of the Irish immigrant population that are designated only with reference to place.

The place assigned to an individual for purposes of identity was usually his birthplace, and this in turn was often used as a surrogate for nationality and citizenship. Since few Europeans were geographically very mobile, at least before emigrating across the Atlantic, there are few problems in using birthplace to identify citizenship; most individuals grew to maturity in the areas where they were born. There may be problems, however, in using birthplace as a surrogate for nationality. It is common today to treat nationality and citizenship as one. The two terms, however, are not synonymous, as any Yugoslav-Croatian, Israeli-Arab, Northern Irish Catholic, or French Canadian would quickly explain. Nationality implies membership in a group that shares a common cultural heritage; citizenship implies only a legal status within the state.

10 These views have been subjected to critical analysis by James T. Lemon in *The Best Poor Man's Country* (Baltimore 1972) and also in his 'Agricultural Practices of National Groups in Eighteenth Century Southeastern Pennsylvania,' *Geographical Review* 56 (Oct. 1966): 467-96. Other examples are by Hildegard B. Johnson: 'Distribution of German Pioneer Population in Minnesota,' *Rural Sociology* 6 (March 1941): 16-34; 'Factors Influencing the Distribution of the German Pioneer Population in Minnesota,' *Agricultural History* 19 (Jan. 1945): 39-57; and 'The Location of German Immigrants in the Middle West,' *Annals of the Association of American Geographers* 41 (March 1951): 1-41.

11 The relationship between place and personal identity has been the subject of research in cultural geography in recent years. See Y.F. Tuan, *Topophilia* (Englewood Cliffs 1974), and E. Relph, *Place and Placelessness* (London 1976).

In the nineteenth century the struggle by national groups to achieve statehood resulted in the close identity between the nation and its territory. In the romantic rhetoric of nineteenth-century nationalism the images of sacrifice, the shedding of martyrs' blood on the soil of the fatherland, emphasized the identity of national groups with the territory for which they fought. Although in some cases nation and state were almost fused into one, there were gradations in the strength of territorial identity. N. Glazer has suggested that differences existed among North American immigrants according to the stage of political evolution in Europe at the time of their emigration.[12] There were those who had achieved a strong national identity but had not yet attained statehood in Europe, such as the Irish and Germans; there were others who had acquired political sovereignty but had not yet developed a strong sense of national identity, such as the Scandinavians (although the inclusion of Norwegians in this category is arguable). The identification of cultural groups with a territorial base was well developed in European nationalist movements of the nineteenth century. Each group sought to establish its independnce, its right to exist and to determine its own future by gaining sovereignty over the territory claimed.

In some instances the national identity of immigrants was reinforced after their arrival in North America. Glazer may have exaggerated this point only slightly when he claimed that 'The Erse revival began in Boston and the nation of Czechoslovakia was launched at a meeting in Pittsburgh.'[13] It is not surprising, therefore, that some groups tried to establish an independent republic within the territory of the United States. The first attempt occurred in 1818, when a request was submitted to the federal government for a tract of land on which to settle impoverished Irish immigrants.[14] The request was rejected. In doing so the government established a principle that it would not assist the formation of ethnic enclaves within the United States. Such settlements on a large scale were considered suspect — an internal threat to the territorial integrity of the American republic. The Germans in particular were suspect; they had settled in large numbers in Winsconsin and in Texas. They were accused of nurturing the ambition of creating a new German state, and in Wisconsin some feared that they might even succeed.[15]

---

12 Glazer, 'Ethnic Groups in America: From National Culture to Ideology,' in M. Berger, T. Abel, and C.H. Page, eds., *Freedom and Control in Modern Society* (New York 1954), 158-73

13 *Ibid.*, 167

14 M.L. Hansen, *The Immigrant in American History* (New York 1940), 132

15 Glazer, 'Ethnic Groups,' 161; F.J. Turner, 'The Significance of the Frontier in American History,' *Annual Report of the American Historical Association* (1893): 15

Whatever political aspirations some of the European immigrants might have entertained at the macro level of settlement, it soon became clear that those aspirations could not be realized. At the micro level, at the level of township and city ward, it is very doubtful that political motivation was a significant factor in the development of homogeneous settlements. The congregation of immigrants from a similar European background was based on communication, convenience, and neighbourly help.[16] Such communities provided a buffer for those immigrants in the transition from tightly knit, stable, rural communities of Europe to the turbulent and atomistic society of the United States. In the cities in particular, immigrant ghettos provided opportunities for employment and shelter alongside people who shared the same language, the same values and religion, and the same cultural heritage as the newly arrived immigrant. Through time the urban ghettos also developed into structured communities in their own right, being the locus for the introduction of immigrants into social ranks and for the creation of social networks. Eventually some immigrant groups sought to exclude outsiders from residing in their well-developed communities. The urban ghetto provided identity, security, stability, and employment for the uprooted European in the bewildering and mobile American society.

Although rural immigrant communities have not been afflicted by the sharp competition and conflict that marked the evolution of some urban ghettos, there are strong functional similarities between urban and rural immigrant communities. G.D. Suttles has identified three functional traits of urban territorial groups that are also applicable to rural groups. Firstly, 'the greatest practical advantage of territorial groups is that they help to designate the range of associations which an individual may consider trustworthy.' Parents could also control the selection of playmates and school mates for their children. The education of children, the religious training, and the development of a new generation in the mores and values of the group were readily achieved through territorial grouping. Secondly, territorial groups encourage a sense of community responsibility. Homogeneous ethnic communities make 'short-run opportunism a dangerous proposition since the opportunist must continue to live with his victims ... Territoriality, then, builds accountability into a society without anyone's having to work at it.'[17] Finally, the exclusive territorial group allows for no gradation in the levels of affiliation to the group; the individual is either a member of the group or he is not.

16 David Ward, 'The Emergence of Central Immigrant Ghettos,' *Annals of the Association of American Geographers* 58 (June 1968): 343-59
17 Suttles, *The Social Construction of Communities* (Chicago 1972), 161, 162

Much of the research on the territorial grouping of European immigrants in the United States has focused on urban examples. The reason may appear simple enough. The United States today is overwhelmingly an urban society and to understand the assimilation of Europeans into American society one should look first at those urban areas, particularly along the Atlantic seaboard, where so many immigrants remained. But there is also a great deal to be learned from the rural immigrant communities. In rural areas daily personal contacts beyond the family circle are much less frequent (and so the potential for conflict is much lower) than in the city. Furthermore, the family farm is a symbol of the continuity and unity of the family to a greater degree than a city tenement or block. An aggregation of family farms, the territorial base of the rural ethnic community, assumes an importance not only in the survival of the ethnic group's distinctive identity but also in its assimilation into American society.

In the remainder of this essay I shall investigate the manner in which three immigrant groups – Swedes, Mennonites, and French Canadians – established and retained a territorial base for their rural communities in central Kansas. Two sample townships are selected for each immigrant group: the first township represents the heart of the ethnic settlement, the second represents the outer fringe of the settlement. The basic premise is that the survival and growth of ethnic territory in the townships reflect the endurance of group loyalty and ethnic identity. But there are factors other than group loyalty which may affect the development of territory. Two important factors in the survival of an ethnic community are the size of the ethnic population and the density of population within the ethnic settlement.

The financial success of each group in managing farms must also be considered before the survival of ethnic territory can be attributed to group loyalty. In the discussion which follows there are four major aims: (1) to examine the value system of each group in order to determine the expected strength of the territorial case; (2) to explain the goals of each group as they established their new communities in Kansas; (3) to account for the influence of population dynamics and financial management in the development of territory; and (4) to analyse the changing patterns of land ownership and to relate these patterns to the process of Americanization and the survival of ethnic identity.

SWEDISH, MENNONITE, AND FRENCH-CANADIAN COMMUNITIES

The survival of immigrant communities is determined by a large number of factors – the persistence of a foreign language, the development of separate or supplementary educational systems for the children, and the influence of the church or a strong shared ideology, not only in defining the mores and values of a group but also in discouraging exogamy. Each of these factors is intricately interwoven in the value system of each group. The significance of a given factor varies from group to group and, although it is difficult to isolate each one, at least two factors are of direct importance for the survival of the territorial base of an ethnic community. These two factors are marriage behaviour and the nature of family ties within the structure of society.

The nature of family ties is very important in the cohesion and stability of a rural community. For example, the stem family was fairly common in Sweden, whereby each son strikes out on his own to establish his own nuclear family, often on a farm at some distance from his parents. In Quebec the extended family was of great importance. The combined effect of strong family ties and a deep attachment to the family farm resulted in excessive farm subdivision in nineteenth-century Quebec. The Mennonites seem to have had a strong patriarchal family system. The paternal desire to have sons established on neighbouring farms was powerful, although not so powerful as to permit excessive farm subdivision that would threaten the economic viability of the old farm. On the basis of the nature of family ties alone it is expected that Swedes would be weakest and either Mennonites or French Canadians strongest in maintaining the territorial base of their communities.

The territorial base of a community could be weakened by the admission of outsiders as marriage partners. Thus, endogamy and the influence of religion in promoting endogamy are important for the preservation of ethnic territory. The Mennonites, because of the distinctiveness of their religion and the severity of strictures against marrying non-Mennonites, were the most endogamous of the three groups. Many of the Swedish immigrants in central Kansas were evangelical Lutherans, and although they too were wary of marrying outsiders it was possible to find Norwegian, Danish, and German Lutherans as marriage partners. Because of the multiplicity of nationalities within the Roman Catholic Church, French Canadians could find many co-religionists to marry — albeit of different linguistic backgrounds — who were not French-Canadian. When religion, endogamy, and family ties are considered together the Mennonites are expected to be the strongest and the Swedes the weakest of the three groups in maintaining the territorial base of their community. However, we must also look at the declared goals of each of these groups as they established their settlements in central Kansas.

FORMATION OF THE IMMIGRANT COMMUNITIES

The first Swedish farmers to settle in central Kansas in large numbers in the late 1860s came from overcrowded settlements in Illinois, particularly around

Galesburg, which in turn had been founded in the 1840s and 1850s. The would-be Kansas settlers formed colonization companies for the expressed purpose of creating homogeneous communities in Kansas where everyone would be Swedish and of the same religious faith.[18] The colonization companies bargained with the Union Pacific and the Kansas Pacific for the odd-numbered sections in townships that had been assigned to the railroad companies.[19] The original communities were located along the Smoky Hill River Valley, and they spread out to cover a large territory in southern Saline and northern McPherson counties. Union Township is located in the central part of this settlement, while Rockville Township in Rice County is an outlier to the southwest of the main settlement (Figure 1). In 1875 there were eighty-four farm operators in Union Township and eleven in Rockville Township; by 1895 the numbers had increased to ninety-seven and fourteen, respectively.

The Mennonite immigrants who decided to settle in central Kansas did so on the understanding that they would be permitted to form homogeneous settlements. Consequently, they too entered into contracts with a railroad company, the Atchison, Topeka, and Santa Fe, to obtain lands in a broad stretch of territory that extended through southern Marion, southern McPherson, Harvey, and eastern Reno counties.[20] They began to arrive in large numbers in 1874. Although they were joined by a few of their co-religionists from Indiana and Pennsylvania, the great majority of them came directly to Kansas from Russia and had no experience of North American life or agriculture. In Menno Township, in the centre of Mennonite settlement, immigrants from the same agricultural villages in Russia attempted to recreate their village communities.[21] Their efforts were short-lived, and most Mennonite farmers in Menno Township soon adopted individual farm holdings, similar to those of the Mennonites in Meridian Township, at the edge of the largest Mennonite settlement in Kansas. The number of Mennonite farmers in Menno Township was fifty-four in 1875 and over one hundred in 1885, whereas in Meridan Township the figures were twelve farm operators in 1875 and twenty-six in 1885.

The French Canadians, unlike the Swedes and the Mennonites, did not organize their migration to Kansas on a large scale, and they did not bargain with

18 Alfred Bergin, 'The Swedish Settlements in Central Kansas,' *Collections of the Kansas State Historical Society* 12 (1909-10): 23

19 E.K. Lindquist, *Smoky Valley People: A History of Lindsborg, Kansas* (Lindsborg 1953)

20 C.B. Schmidt, 'Reminiscences of Foreign Immigration Work for Kansas,' *Collections of the Kansas State Historical Society* 9 (1905-6): 485-97

21 Abraham Albrecht, 'Mennonite Settlements in Kansas,' MA thesis, University of Kansas, 1925

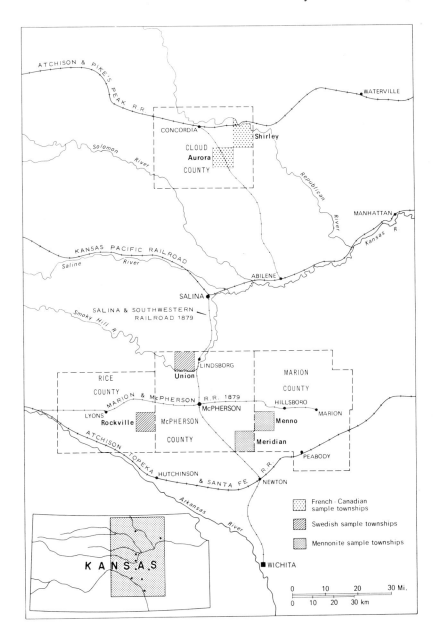

Figure 1 Location of the sample townships in Kansas

one of the railroad companies for land that would allow them to form a homogeneous settlement. There was one similarity between the French-Canadian and the Swedish communities in Kansas: both were established by overflow population from older communities in Illinois. The French Canadians, however, came west in small groups of several families from Kankakee, Illinois, and they took up land in a small area of northern Cloud and western Clay counties. The families who came west had learned of the new communities by word of mouth (there was a second and smaller community in Rooks County, western Kansas), and close contact was maintained with the mother colony in Illinois.[22] Although there was no other large-scale effort to create homogeneous settlements in Kansas, the French Canadians were encouraged to do so by the authorities of the Catholic Church. The local bishop encouraged the formation of unilingual parishes where the people could be served more easily by a priest who spoke their language.[23] For the Swedes and Mennonites who came to Kansas the goal of homogeneous settlements was explicit. The same goal was never explicitly stated by the French Canadians, although it must have had some appeal since many of them settled together in a small area along the Republican River Valley. There were fifty-six French-Canadian farmers in Shirley Township in 1875 and seventy-four in 1884; in Aurora Township the number of French-Canadian farmers was twenty-one in 1875 and fifty-seven in 1885.

DEMOGRAPHIC FACTORS

Although each of the immigrant groups hoped to maintain the homogeneous communities that they had established, there was no guarantee that they would succeed. As each community matured, old farmers died and other farmers left to try their fortunes elsewhere. The survival of the homogeneous community depended upon their places being taken by an adequate supply of young farmers from within the community, from adjacent areas in Kansas, or from parent communities in Illinois, Quebec, and Europe. The process may be summarized as a 'transfusion model' in which the rate of loss or farmer turnover, the regenerative energy within the community, and the infusion of new farmers either from other ethnic communities in the Midwest or from the 'homeland' provide the basic structure.[24] It should be remembered that the three elements in

22 J.B. Carman, 'Foreign Language Units of Kansas,' Kansas State Historical Society, J.N. Carman papers, 212-13
23 P. Beckman, 'The Catholic Church on the Kansas Frontier,' PhD dissertation, Catholic University, Washington, DC, 1943, p. 134
24 Although the concept is suggested by John Rice in *Patterns of Ethnicity in a Minnesota County, 1880-1905* (Umeå 1973), 83-91, I am indebted to Professor George H. Dury for this idea.

the model are not independent of each other; for example, the regenerative energy within the community is a function of the age structure of the population which, in turn, is affected by farmer turnover and the arrival of new immigrants.

The most direct threat to the territorial homogeneity of a community occurred when farms changed hands. The critical event occurred either because farmers decided to leave the community or because old farmers retired or died. On each occasion the determination of the group to preserve its territorial base had to be asserted. If the rate of farm turnover (and this included the transfer of a farm from father to son) was higher for the ethnic group than for neighbouring American-born farmers, then the preservation of the territorial base would be more difficult for the ethnic group. If, on the other hand, the immigrants were less mobile than the American-born, as A.B. Hollingshead has suggested,[25] then it would be easier to preserve the territorial base and even to expand it. Figure 2[26] indicates that in general each ethnic group indeed had a lower rate of farm turnover than its American-born neighbours. The only exceptions were the Swedish cohort of farmers who first appeared in the census of 1905 and the French-Canadian cohorts of 1885, 1895, and 1915. When the turnover curves for each ethnic group are compared it is found that the differences are very small (Figure 3). In so far as a pattern may be discerned the Swedes had a lower drop-out rate in the early years and the Mennonites a lower drop-out rate in later years than the French Canadians. Although the differences in rate of farm turnover among the ethnic groups, and between each ethnic group and its neighbouring American-born group, are not statistically significant, the French Canadians do appear to have been the most restless and therefore more susceptible to loss of territory to outsiders than the Swedes or Mennonites.

The internal regenerative dynamics of a group are an essential element in the survival of any community. If the number of children being born is insufficient to replace the number of adults who are dying or leaving, then the ethnic community faces an uphill struggle to survive, even in the short term. If the number of children per family is high, then the pressure to expand the territory of the community will be great. There are two methods of examining the regenerative power of a community: (1) by comparing the percentage of childless farmers in an ethnic group with the percentage of the neighbouring American-born farmers who were childless; and (2) by comparing the average number of children per family among the ethnic group and the neighbouring non-ethnic group.

25 Hollingshead, 'Changes in Land Ownership as an Index of Succession in Rural Communities,' *American Journal of Sociology* 43 (March 1938): 764-77
26 Data in Figures 2 to 6 are derived from manuscripts of the Kansas state censuses, 1885-1925.

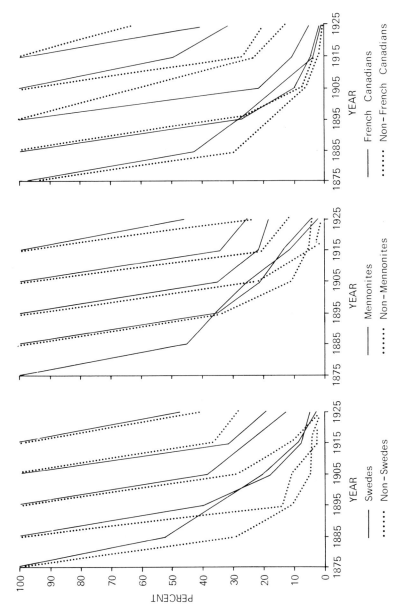

Figure 2 Comparison of drop-out rates among the three ethnic groups and their neighbours, 1875-1925

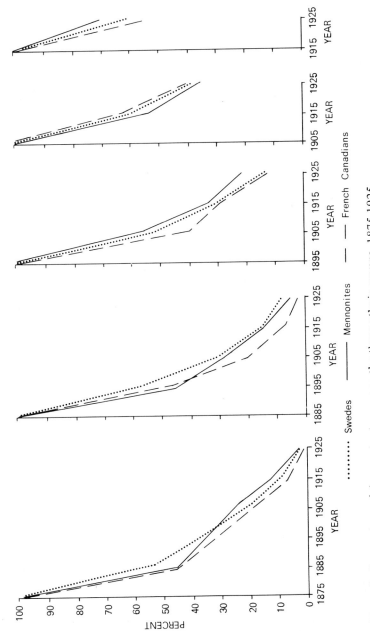

Figure 3 Comparison of drop-out rates among the three ethnic groups, 1875-1925

Figure 4 indicates that the Swedes had a higher percentage of childless farmers than the neighbouring group of American-born farmers, and therefore were susceptible to loss of territory. The French Canadians, on the other hand, had fewer childless farmers than their neighbours and thus were not so susceptible to territorial losses. The Mennonites were in an intermediate position; they were very similar to their neighbours and appeared slightly stronger in 1875, 1895, and 1925 only.

The usual method of measuring the regenerative strength of a community is to examine the average family size.[27] The more children per family, the healthier the demographic future of the community. It should be remembered that when the average family size falls below two, the replacement ability of the community is inadequate. In the discussion that follows the numbers refer to the average number of children, under nineteen years of age, per farm family. The French Canadians appear to have been the most reproductive of the groups; the average size of French-Canadian families was larger than that of other families in Shirley and Aurora townships. The Mennonite and Swedish families were somewhat similar to their neighbours in terms of average family size, although the Mennonites had a few children more than their neighbours. The Swedes were in the weakest position of all, with the average number of children per farm family falling below two by 1915 (Figure 5).

Of the three ethnic groups the French Canadians were the most reproductive and the Swedes the least. The French Canadians not only had the largest average family size but also the smallest percentage of childless farmers. Swedish families were smallest in size on the average, and both the average and the percentage of childless farmers were highest among the Swedes. From these observations alone it would be expected that the French Canadians would be the most likely to expand their farmland and that the Swedes would have the greatest difficulty in maintaining their territory, while the Mennonites would be in an intermediary position capable of at least holding their own.

The third element in the demographic 'transfusion model' is the infusion of newcomers to the community. These replacement farmers were either sons of farmers within the township or else farmers who had come from adjacent communities in Kansas, from the Midwest, or from the old country. It is not easy to obtain detailed information on the origin of replacement farmers; there is no record of the year in which a farmer came to settle in a particular

27 Family size here refers to 'census family size,' which includes the number of children living at home when the enumerator took the census. The accounting of the family did not include those children (usually about sixteen years of age or older) who had left home and were working elsewhere.

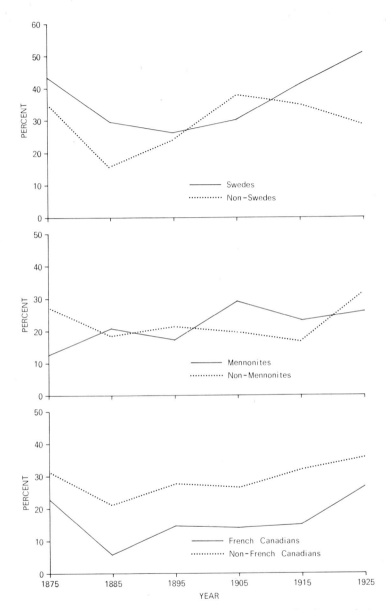

Figure 4 Percentage of farmers without children in the six sample townships, 1875-1925

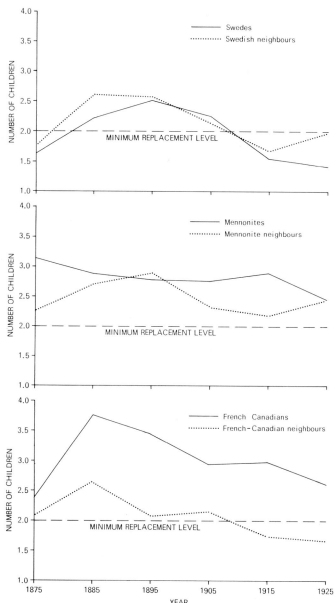

Figure 5 Average number of children under 18 years of age per farm family, 1875-1925

township. However, during the state census enumerators asked farmers two questions that are useful in piecing together information on the origin of the newcomers: these concerned his birthplace and his last place of residence before coming to Kansas. A word of caution is required in interpreting the census data. One should not infer that the replacement farmers actually arrived in Kansas during the decade preceding their appearance in one of the sample townships. Some of them may have been living in nearby townships in Kansas for several decades. Finally, as the decades passed and communities matured one would expect the number of Illinois and foreign replacements to decline and the number of Kansas-born to increase. Variations from this expectation indicate the importance of external links with older communities in the Midwest or abroad in maintaining the territorial homogeneity of the Kansas settlements.

The number of Swedish replacements declined over the period from 1885 to 1925, although there was a slight resurgence in 1925 as young Kansas-born farmers took over their parents' farms (Figure 6). Up to 1905 most of the Swedish replacements were foreign-born, but after 1905 the Kansas-born began to dominate and there were increasingly fewer replacements who came from the Illinois settlements. There was no apparent weakness in the Mennonite communities as far as the number of replacements was concerned. Although there was no major Mennonite immigration from overseas after 1880, a few replacements came from either Nebraska or Indiana. Most of the Mennonite replacements came from neighbouring townships in central Kansas, and by 1925 the Kansas-born accounted for almost 60 per cent of the new farmers. The number of French-Canadian replacements declined in 1905 but increased again in 1915 and 1925. Illinois was always an important source of new farmers in Shirley and Aurora townships, although after 1905 the majority of new farmers was Kansas-born.

When the combined components of the transfusion model are considered together their effect on territorial homogeneity is varied. Although French Canadians were the most restless of the three groups and suffered the highest drop-out rate, they were able to replenish their numbers with a high rate of regeneration within the Kansas communities and a strong supply of replacement farmers from Illinois. The adjacent communities in Kansas were too small to be important for the survival of French-Canadian homogeneity in Shirley and Aurora townships. The Swedes appeared to be in the weakest position from a demographic point of view. The Swedish drop-out rate was greater than that of the Mennonites after 1895, Swedish regenerative power was weak, and the Swedes relied heavily upon the Kansas settlements as a source of replacement. The Mennonites seemed to have been in the strongest position. Their drop-out rate was generally the lowest, their rate of regeneration was moderately strong, and

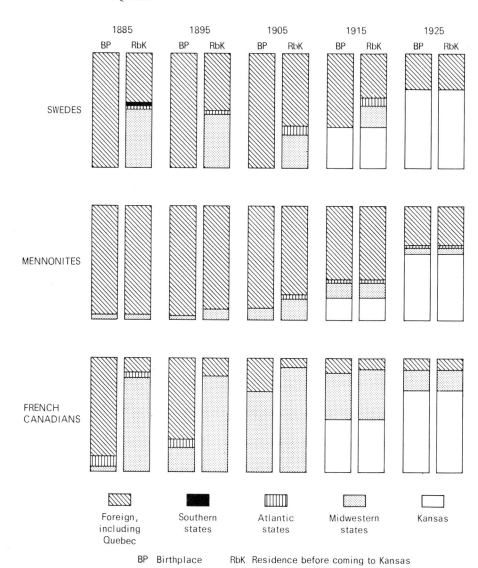

BP Birthplace   RbK Residence before coming to Kansas

Figure 6 Origin of replacement farmers for the three ethnic groups, 1885-1925

they could draw upon large Mennonite settlements in Kansas for replacements. Demographically the Mennonites were strongest and most likely to succeed and the Swedes were weakest and least likely to succeed in maintaining the homogeneity of their communities.

FARM RENTING AND MORTGAGING

In order to maintain the homogeneity of these settlements each ethnic group came into direct competition with native-born American farmers. The immigrants were thought to have been different from the American-born in several respects. In a study of land ownership change and succession in Nebraska Hollingshead has concluded that the native-born American farmers were often displaced by the expansion of immigrant groups for two reasons: during periods of economic recession the American-born farmers, who were financially weaker than the foreign-born, sold their farms and moved elsewhere; and Americans were more mobile, less tied to the soil, than the foreign-born at all times.[28] Another factor that might weaken the territorial base of an ethnic community was the extent to which they rented or mortgaged their farms to outsiders.

The following discussion is based upon data obtained from the Kansas state censuses, which were taken at ten-year intervals between 1875 and 1925. For each of the three ethnic groups there is a control group, most of whom were American farmers – namely, the farmers in the townships studied who were not members of the particular ethnic group.

One of the characteristics of farming in the Midwest was that rented farms increased in number as agricultural communities matured.[29] This trend is believed to have been due partly to young farmers not having sufficient capital to buy land from retiring farmers, and partly to the belief of some farmers that it made better financial sense to invest one's limited capital resources in equipment and livestock rather than in land. This latter point of view was not

28 'Changes in Land Ownership'
29 A.G. Bogue has estimated that in 1850 between 7 and 11 per cent of the farms in Clarion Township, Bureau County, Illinois, were rented, and between 10 and 22 per cent of the farms in Union Township, Davis County, Iowa. By 1900 the rate of farm tenancy in these townships had increased to 50 and even 60 per cent. 'Farming in the Prairie Peninsula, 1830-1870,' *Journal of Economic History* 23 (March 1963): 25-6. M.B. Bogue has also discovered that in other parts of Illinois the rate of farm tenancy was 38 per cent in 1880, 41.5 per cent in 1890, and 45.8 per cent in 1900. *Patterns from the Sod: Land Use and Tenure in the Grand Prairie, 1850-1900* (Springfield, Ill. 1959), 156. Data from federal and state censuses for central Kansas show that rented farms increased from 35 per cent in 1900 to 47 per cent of all farms in 1925.

TABLE 1
Percentage of rented farms among the three ethnics groups in
the six townships, 1885-1925

	1885	1905	1915	1925
Swedes	10	34	48	49
Mennonites	13	27	31	39
French Canadians	15	44	47	49

Source: manuscripts of the Kansas state censuses; data for
1895 are not available

widely shared. The major goal of immigrants was to own their own farms and homes.[30] The Swedes and French Canadians in particular, remembering the uncertainty of overcrowded conditions in Sweden, Quebec, and the Illinois settlements, were anxious to obtain their own farms. Ownership of the farm was an easier goal to attain, because of the Homestead Act, for the first generation of immigrants to Kansas than for the second. When the second generation came of age there was no longer any free land available within the community, so renting became more and more prevalent. Unfortunately the manuscripts of the Kansas state censuses do not record from whom the tenant farmer rented his land. Some farms, however, could be rented from retiring members of the ethnic group, so that farm renting represented only a partial weakening of the territorial base of the community.

The differences in the number of rented farms among the three groups remained fairly constant from 1885 to 1925. In 1885 and 1905 the proportion of rented farms was highest among the the French Canadians and lowest among the Mennonites and Swedes (Table 1). In 1915 and 1925, however, the French Canadians and Swedes were approximately equal, while the Mennonites held the lowest number of rented farms. In the six sample townships renting was always lower among the immigrants than among their American-born neighbours. Of the three immigrant groups, the Mennonites seemed the most determined to establish a strong territorial base for their community.

Another area of potential weakness in the territorial control of a community was farm mortgaging. The foreclosure of a mortgage during economic depression often resulted in the involuntary transfer of land from the ethnic group to outsiders. Again, the Mennonites were the most conscientious of the three

---

30 In a study of immigrant farmers E. de S. Brunner has asserted that 'The primary goal
of the new and old immigrant alike has been and is, land and home ownership . . .'
Immigrant Farmers and Their Children (Garden City 1924), 115

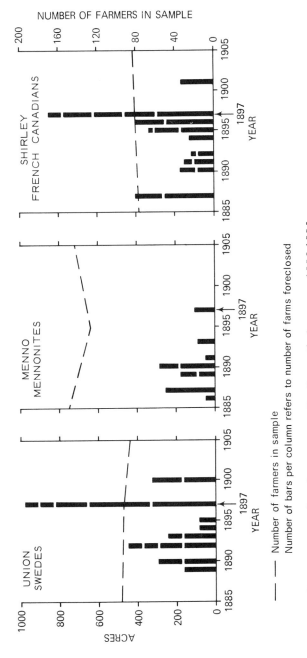

Figure 7 Farm mortgage foreclosure among the three ethnic groups, 1885–1905

groups in protecting their land from transfer to outsiders. Not only were they inclined to obtain their mortgages from fellow Mennonites, they had the lowest frequency of mortgage foreclosure among the three groups (Figure 7).[31] Of the three ethnic groups, the French Canadians suffered the heaviest losses, and the Swedes somewhat fewer, because of mortgage foreclosure during and after the severe economic depression of the 1890s. In terms of the financial management of their lands the Mennonites were the most successful, and this in turn made it possible for them to consolidate their territorial base, whereas French Canadians were in the weakest position to maintain their territorial base.

TERRITORIAL DEVELOPMENT AND AMERICANIZATION

In each of the six townships the patterns of land ownership change were mapped for each decade from 1885 to 1925 using data obtained from the county tax records (Figures 8-13). It was not unexpected that the Mennonites would appear the strongest of the three groups in acquiring ownership of the land in their communities. What is remarkable is the rapidity with which they achieved that goal. Unlike the Swedes and French Canadians, who were able to obtain government-supplied homestead lands in their townships, the Mennonites had to buy all of the land in Menno Township. All of the government land had been sold at a public auction in 1870 before they arrived. With the exception of the decade from 1885 to 1895, the Mennonites never lost much of the land that they had gained from outsiders. After 1905 they bought out every parcel of land in Menno except for section 10, which remained in the hands of the large land-owning Şcully family. In Meridian Township, on the western margin of the Mennonite settlement, Mennonites also expanded their land base steadily over the decades until they owned almost half of the township in 1925.

In view of the preceding discussion of family ties, endogamy, religion, and especially of demographic dynamics, it is somewhat surprising that the Swedes and not the French Canadians were second to the Mennonites in territorial strength (Figures 14 and 15). The Swedes were able to find unalienated government land when they came to Union Township; many of their homesteads were only 80 acres in size rather than the usual 160.[32] Nevertheless, by 1885

31 Data in Figures 7 to 15 are derived from county tax records, 1875-1925.
32 The Swedes obtained most of their homesteads before 1879, and the townships in which they had located were within an area reserved for railroad land grants. 'Until 1879, most persons could homestead only 80 acres in the reserved government sections within the grants made to railroads; thereafter they might increase this to 160 acres.' F.A. Shannon, *The Farmer's Last Frontier: Agriculture, 1860-1897* (New York 1968), 53

Figure 8
Union Township:
land ownership, 1885-1925

Land owned by Swedes

Land owned by others

Land gained by Swedes from others

Land lost by Swedes to others

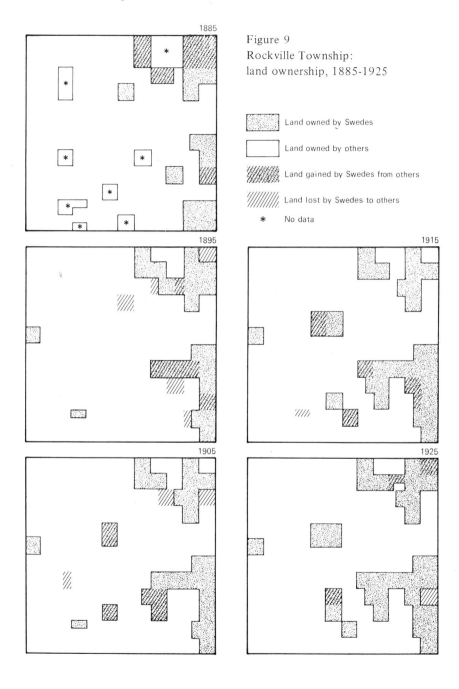

Figure 9
Rockville Township:
land ownership, 1885-1925

Land owned by Swedes

Land owned by others

Land gained by Swedes from others

Land lost by Swedes to others

*   No data

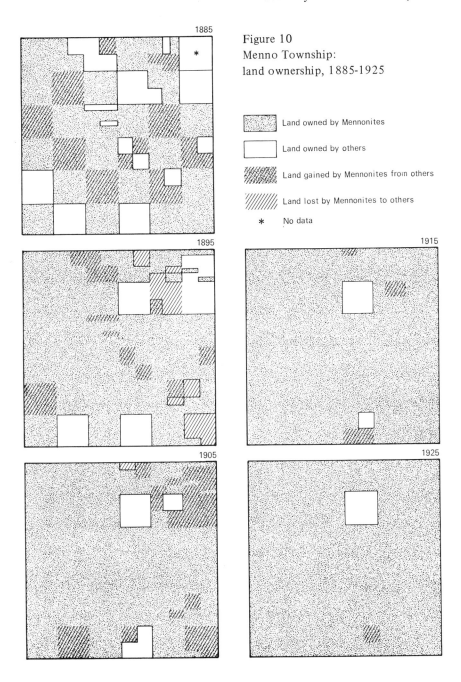

Figure 10
Menno Township:
land ownership, 1885-1925

Land owned by Mennonites

Land owned by others

Land gained by Mennonites from others

Land lost by Mennonites to others

* No data

Figure 11
Meridian Township:
land ownership, 1885-1925

Land owned by Mennonites

Land owned by others

Land gained by Mennonites from others

Land lost by Mennonites to others

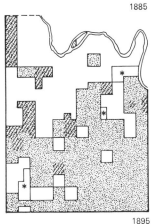

1885

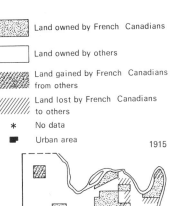

Figure 12
Shirley Township:
land ownership, 1885-1925

Land owned by French Canadians

Land owned by others

Land gained by French Canadians
from others

Land lost by French Canadians
to others

*   No data

■   Urban area

1895

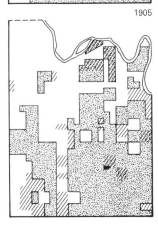

1915

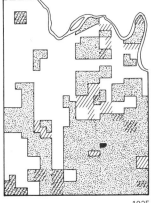

1905

1925

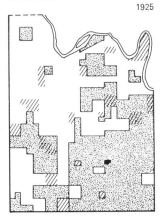

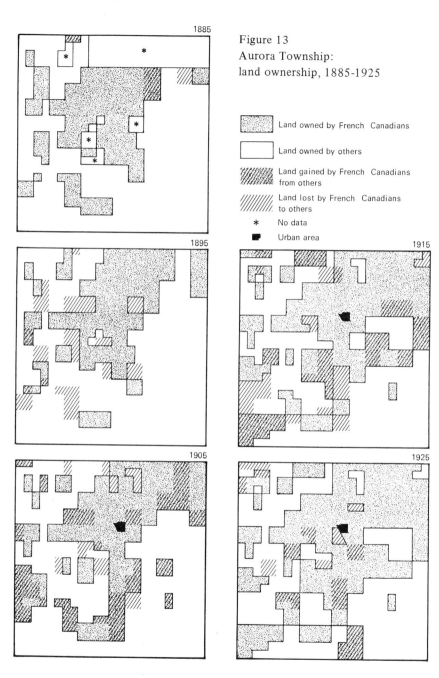

Figure 13
Aurora Township:
land ownership, 1885-1925

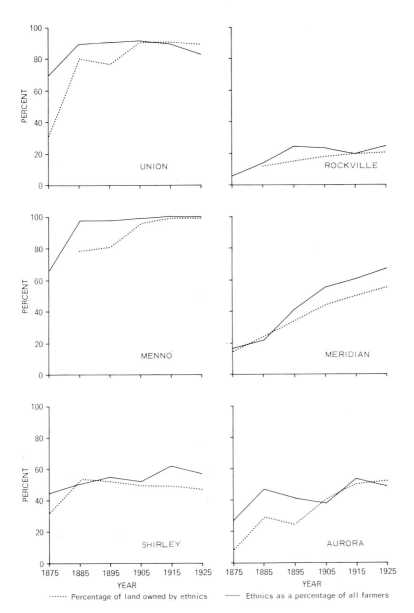

Figure 14 Ethnic-owned land as a percentage of the total land in each township, 1875-1925

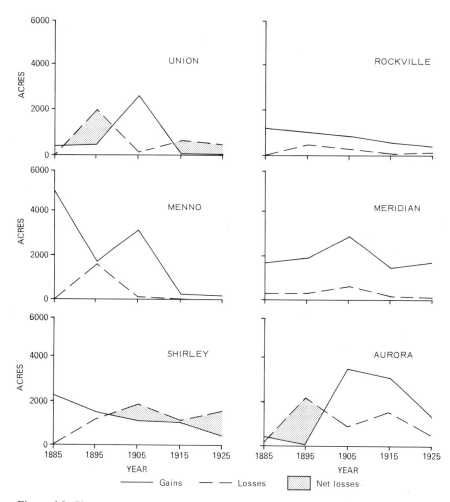

Figure 15 Changes in land ownership for the three ethnic groups in the six townships, 1885-1925

Swedish farmers had acquired over 80 per cent of the land in Union. The decade from 1885 to 1895 was a bad one. The Swedes, like the Mennonites in Menno, suffered their heaviest losses in this decade. Although a good portion of this land was recovered by 1905, especially in the southern part of the township, in the years from 1905 to 1925 the Swedes suffered a net loss of land to non-Swedish farmers. In Rockville Township, the outlier of the Swedish settlement, Swedish farmers were few in number, and although they steadily gained more land than they lost the amount of land accumulated was very small indeed. The Swedes were considerably less successful than the Mennonites in building up a solid land base.

French Canadians were in the strongest position of the three immigrant groups for building a homogeneous community. When they arrived in Shirley Township they were able to obtain a large amount of homestead land, even in the odd-numbered sections that were normally reserved as railroad lands. In 1885 French Canadians owned over half of the land in Shirley Township but after 1895 they steadily lost out to their non-French-Canadian neighbours. In Aurora Township, located on the edge of the French-Canadian settlement, the pattern was slightly different from Shirley Township. Although losses far outweighed the gains from 1885 to 1895, the Aurora farmers regained the lost land by 1905 and continued to expand up to 1915. The French-Canadian record was a much more mixed one than that of the Swedes and Mennonites. The pattern of land ownership was the most fragmented; French Canadians were the least isolationist of the three ethnic groups in their Kansas communities.

CONCLUSION

The assimilation of immigrants into American society may be analysed in different ways. For example, cultural assimilation implies the adoption of English, the breakdown of religious barriers, and the disappearance of folk festivals and customs. Social assimilation, on the other hand, implies the willingness and ability of an ethnic group to extend its circle of friendship, to intermarry with outsiders, to participate in the social life of the host society, and to have outsiders come and live within the formerly exclusive ethnic community. Ethnic territoriality is perhaps a better indicator of the processes of social assimilation than of cultural assimilation. Although the survival of cultural attributes may be facilitated by the spatial concentration of an ethnic group, cultural assimilation nevertheless *may* occur within homogeneous communities. It is most unusual, however, for social assimilation to take place while the territorial base remains ethnically homogeneous. When the territory remains solidly in the control of the ethnic group, it may be inferred that the group must remain apart, either voluntarily or involuntarily, from the host society. As the territory becomes fragmented, then the social assimilation of the ethnic group is advanced.

The patterns of social and cultural assimilation are the outward manifestations of a much deeper adjustment on the part of each ethnic group. A distinctive value system lies at the core of ethnic identity. With assimilation an ethnic group adjusts its value system until a harmonious relationship is established with the values of the host society. Changes in land ownership can be very revealing of these deeper adjustments. The record of land ownership reflects the nature of family ties and family continuity; it reveals something of the economic success of immigrants, particularly in the face of economic adversity; and it informs us of the strength of community ties (both locally and nationally), particularly in financing farm operations.

Family ties appear to have been much stronger in the Mennonite than in either the Swedish or the French-Canadian communities. There is some evidence that the patriarchal family existed in the Mennonite communities of Kansas, with fathers establishing their sons on neighbouring farms within the township. Family ties were also reported to be strong within the French-Canadian communities, although there is little evidence for them in the land ownership records. There is no evidence of the excessive subdivision of family farms that characterized the strong attachment to the family and family farm in early nineteenth-century Quebec. There is also no evidence that the nuclear family was more prevalent among Swedes than among French Canadians, for example; had it been more prevalent the rate of farmer turnover would have been much higher among Swedes than among French Canadians.

The immigrant farmers did not appear to benefit at the expense of the American-born, especially during periods of economic adversity (Figure 15), as Hollingshead has contended. There are, in fact, several problems with Hollingshead's thesis. His basic premise that immigrant pioneers were financially stronger than the American-born is not widely accepted in frontier historiography. Furthermore, one of the most acute economic depressions in the period of this study occurred in the years between 1885 and 1895. It was during this decade that most of the immigrant groups suffered the heaviest losses, or at best achieved the smallest gains for the entire period between 1875 and 1925. Periods of economic depression were usually a time of urban-rural migration in non-frontier areas. In the early 1890s central Kansas was well beyond the pioneer stage of farming, and there were many more American-born than Swedes, Mennonites, and French Canadians living in local towns and cities. In the urban-rural migration the ethnic farmers would have been heavily outnumbered by the American-born.

By 1925 French Canadians were the most Americanized, followed by the Swedes, with the Mennonites the least Americanized of the three immigrant groups. Two important factors in the rapidity with which a group assumed the traits and behaviour of the host society (and divested itself of its own distinctive ethnic characteristics) were the length of time the group had lived in North America and the level of contact maintained with the old country through a continuing supply of new immigrants. The first Swedish and French-Canadian farmers in Kansas had come from Illinois and their numbers were augmented by new arrivals from Illinois in succeeding decades. The Swedish communities did receive some immigrants directly from Sweden, but the number of French Canadians who migrated to Kansas directly from Quebec was very, very small. The Mennonites arrived in Kansas directly from Russia with no previous experience of North American living or farming. They were backed financially by co-religionists in Ontario and Pennsylvania, but few new farmers came to Menno and Meridian townships from those eastern settlements. After 1880, however, direct immigration to the Kansas settlements from southern Russia ceased and the Mennonite communities were not augmented by non-Kansas Mennonites.

In this essay the survival of ethnic territory is introduced as a way of monitoring the persistence of group loyalty and ethnic identity in a few of the homogeneous immigrant communities established throughout the Midwest. Ethnic territory is both cause and effect in explaining the persistence of ethnic traits. The survival of homogeneous settlement facilitates the retention of traditional mores, values, language, religion, and general way of life. Analysis of the ownership of farm land is but one key to an understanding of the survival of ethnic communities.

DAVID WARD

The early Victorian city
in England and America:
on the parallel development of
an urban image

Andrew Clark's most compelling interest was overseas colonization by European peoples. He was fascinated by the complex adaptations and selective modifications of numerous Old World subcultures in unfamiliar and challenging environments. The interplay of cultural inheritance and frontier conditions was a persistent theme in his work and a fertile source of cross-disciplinary dialogues in which he suggested how geographers might directly contribute to broad historiographic issues. In particular, he stimulated geographical considerations of the definition of the new cultural or national identities assumed by Europeans overseas in what Louis Hartz has called 'new societies.'[1] Although varied Old World cultural traits contributed to the distinctiveness of these new identities, striking similarities in the social origins of early immigrants from different parts of Europe also provided a common element in the early development of the new societies of Europeans overseas.[2] Indeed, differences among these societies were often dependent upon varying resource endowments, which in turn affected the vulnerability of the economic relationships of the new settlements to the international economy. While the critical economic role of mercantile cities,

1 Hartz, *The Founding of New Societies* (New York 1964), and 'A Comparative Study of Fragment Cultures,' in Hugh D. Graham and Ted R. Gurr, eds., *The History of Violence in America: Historical and Comparative Perspectives* (New York 1969), 107-26
2 James T. Lemon, *The Best Poor Man's Country: A Geographical Study of Early Southeastern Pennsylvania* (Baltimore 1972), 1-31; R. Cole Harris and Leonard Guelke, 'Land and Society in Early Canada and South Africa,' *Journal of Historical Geography* 3 (1977): 135-53

which linked pioneers to the world economy, has been elaborated,[3] the socio-cultural contributions of these urban populations to the emerging identities of the new societies remain unclear.[4]

Prior to the nineteenth century, colonial mercantile or administrative cities were few in number and housed extremely diminutive proportions of overseas European populations. Although few pioneers were remote from the economic influences of these towns, the contribution of a distinctive and independent urban tradition to the ideologies of the new societies was decidedly modest. By the time that cities became the leading destination of overseas migrants, the identities of new world societies were already based upon the individualistic and opportunistic values associated with the remote pioneering of new resources.[5] Under these circumstances the subsequent acceleration in the urbanization of immigrant societies and the emergence of deplorable living and social conditions in their rapidly growing cities seemed inconsistent with the aspirations and destinies of societies whose ideologies were often based upon the experiences of sturdy, independent pioneers. The experience of pioneering implied emancipation from the social restrictions and material insufficiencies of Old World societies but because many of the rapidly growing cities in areas recently settled by Europeans did not obviously share in this emancipation, conceptions of urban life tended to remain dependent upon European ideas and images. Concern about urban society and especially the deteriorating material conditions of large industrial cities was naturally first articulated in England. By the close of the nineteenth century these reactions had been so forcefully projected that the term 'Victorian city' became a generic concept to describe the discomfort and ugliness of unrestrained urban growth. Recently, some of the extremely negative connotations of this term have been revised but for nineteenth-century cities all over the world the adjective 'Victorian' has long been used to evoke the conditions that had first aroused English concern.[6]

One of several components of this image of the early Victorian city was the growing spatial and social separation of rich and poor and the emergence of a dichotomous, segregated social geography that threatened the influence and

3 James E. Vance, Jr., *The Merchant's World: The Geography of Wholesaling* (Englewood Cliffs 1970), 68-79

4 With the conspicuous exception of Carl Bridenbaugh's two books on colonial American cities – *Cities in the Wilderness: Urban Life in America, 1625-1742* (New York 1964) and *Cities in Revolt: Urban Life in America, 1743-1776* (New York 1964).

5 Lemon, *Best Poor Man's Country,* 218-28; Sam B. Warner, Jr., *The Urban Wilderness: A History of the American City* (New York 1972), 55-86, 198-229

6 Asa Briggs, *Victorian Cities* (Harmondsworth 1968), 11-87

control of the socially prominent and affluent over the less affluent remainder of society.[7] In general, the assumed amplification of social segregation within cities was explained as an unavoidable consequence of the divisive social consequences of industrial capitalism. Curiously, however, this social geographic image of early Victorian English cities was prevalent in less industrialized overseas societies, which also forthrightly expressed their differences and exemptions from those obstacles to social advancement that contributed to segregated social geographic patterns. The residents of cities that remained within the English imperial system might have been expected to replicate or adapt the urban images of their compatriots, but the prevalence of this urban image in the United States during the same period is more surprising, for the new nation firmly celebrated the differences between societies of the old and the new worlds.

Throughout the early nineteenth century the peculiarities of American society attracted the attention of a succession of adulatory and critical visitors who contrasted the new nation and its mother country. Although these differences were fully illuminated in descriptions of the newly settled west, the American city, like the institution of slavery, presented interpretative difficulties to most observers.[8] Their confusion was shared by native observers who hoped that the congested living conditions and unruly mobs of European cities might be avoided in the United States. The city, in short, might threaten the progressive destiny of an egalitarian society.[9] Unlike most other English possessions, however, the New England and Middle Atlantic colonies had supported several urban settlements of considerable size whose residents might have contributed to the emergence of a distinctive 'American' image of eighteenth- and early nineteenth-century cities. There were indeed distinctive American manifestations of antipathies to cities but efforts to conceptualize the threatening form of their cities were extremely close to those of English cities by English observers. Asa Briggs succinctly revealed the most emphatic illustration of this convergence of urban images when he emphasized the concurrent

7 David Ward, 'Victorian Cities: How Modern?' *Journal of Historical Geography* 1 (1975): 135-51, and 'The Victorian Slum: An Enduring Myth?' *Annals of the Association of American Geographers* 66 (1976): 323-36

8 Eugene P. Moehring, *Urban America and the Foreign Traveler, 1815-1855, with Selected Documents of Nineteenth Century American Cities* (New York 1974), 1-5; Charles L. Sanford, *The Quest for Paradise: Europe and the American Moral Indignation* (Urbana 1961), 178

9 Morton and Lucia White, *The Intellectual versus the City* (Cambridge, Mass. 1962), 18-31; Morton White, 'The Two Stages in the Critique of the American City,' in Oscar Handlin and John Burchard, eds., *The Historian and the City* (Cambridge, Mass. 1963), 84-94

conception of urban society as 'two nations' in the works of Disraeli and Channing.[10] In view of the well-publicized contrasts that were drawn between English and American societies, this prevalence of strikingly similar urban images in the new republic and the former mother country is certainly perplexing.

Indeed, throughout the nineteenth century the chronology of the intensity of popular fascination with urban problems exhibited broadly similar amplitudes in England and the United States. During periods when an urban crisis dominated public debates, especially in the 1840s and 1890s, the transatlantic sharing of ideas about cities was greatest. During the nineties this communication of ideas about urban slums and poverty was not surprising, since industrialization and urban growth had created broadly similar urban problems in both countries.[11] The confrontation with housing reform and the social problems of poverty were issues common to both countries. Common issues did not, however, result in similar strategies of reform in the twentieth century, for in England there was eventually a much deeper commitment to public intervention. In the 1840s, when the level of urbanization and the number of large cities were markedly different in the two countries, not only were ideas about urban problems freely shared but also broadly similar public policies were adopted.[12] During this period most American cities were both smaller and less industrialized than their English counterparts, as well as set in a society that extolled political egalitarianism and the abundance of opportunities.

This essay attempts to explore the contradictions implied by this convergence of urban images in England and America at a time when there were presumed to be major differences in economic development and national cultures. Since many well-publicized commentaries on early Victorian cities and societies have been carefully scrutinized by textual authorities, the judgements and inferences of these seminal commentaries are often of greater historiographic interest than

---

10 *Victorian Cities*, 64

11 Allen F. Davis, *Spearheads for Reform: The Social Settlements and the Progressive Movement, 1890-1914* (New York 1967), 3-22; Roy Lubove, *The Professional Altruist: The Emergence of Social Work as a Career, 1880-1930* (New York 1969), 2-6

12 Charles I. Foster, *An Errand of Mercy: The Evangelical United Front, 1790-1837* (Chapel Hill 1960), vii-viii; Raymond A. Mohl, *Poverty in New York, 1783-1825* (New York 1971), 166-7; Walter Lewis, *From Newgate to Dannemora: The Rise of the Penitentiary in New York, 1796-1848* (Ithaca 1964), 1-20; David B. Davis, 'The Emergence of Immediatism in British and American Antislavery Thought,' *Mississippi Valley Historical Review* 49 (1962): 209-30; Charles E. and Carroll S. Rosenberg, 'Pietism and the Origins of the American Public Health Movement: A Note on John H. Griscom and Robert M. Hartley,' *Journal of the History of Medicine and Allied Sciences* 23 (1968): 16-35

the original works.[13] Indeed, only rarely have either the original observers or subsequent commentators confronted the contradictions raised by a comparative viewpoint. This essay, then, will concentrate on those commentaries which have directly or indirectly confronted the relationships between social geographic images of cities and changes and conditions in the two societies at large. Ultimately the contradictions raised by an examination of commentaries on this relationship will be resolved only by careful empirical investigations of the social geography of early Victorian cities. Certainly recent examinations of these cities suggest that descriptions which emphasized a dichotomous segregated residential pattern were misleading in defining the timing and complexity of increased social segregation.[14] The rich had moved to exclusive suburbs long before the Industrial Revolution, and the most dramatic change in the social geography of nineteenth-century cities was the increased residential separation of the various strata of the poor. In the early Victorian city the petite bourgeoisie, shopkeepers, craftsmen, journeymen, and factory hands were often interspersed and although the very wealthy were segregated from the remainder of society, the various segments of the less affluent majority were far less segregated from each other than they were at the turn of the twentieth century. Social geographic images of English cities were oversimplified, but at least the concurrent process of rapid industrialization offered a dramatic and immediate explanation of the presumed increased social segregation. In the United States, however, industrialization was too limited to support this explanation. Consequently, the development of similar urban images in England and the United States is perplexing both because this image was inappropriate to a presumably mercantile society without the divisive class consciousness of industrial England and because it was a highly simplified and somewhat misleading representation of English cities too.

The convergence of urban images may, however, have been possible precisely because the image itself was not firmly based upon actual conditions in either country. If two countries — with declared differences in national culture and at different levels of economic development — shared similar urban images, then explanations must be sought in those aspects of Victorian values and beliefs that they held in common. English images of rapidly growing industrialized cities were often designed to mobilize public opinion in the interests of specific reforms, and it was because many American reformers had similar objectives that they had little difficulty in adapting English images to describe their own

13 A useful compilation of abridged British sources is B.K. Coleman, ed., *The Idea of the City in Nineteenth Century Britain* (London 1973).
14 Ward, 'Victorian Slum,' 323-36

cities.[15] This broad transatlantic sharing of ideas of humanitarian reform has been well documented but the derivation of common social geographic images of mid-nineteenth-century cities from these reform ideologies has been less clear. The parallel development of similar urban images in the United States and England, at a time of well-publicized national differences both in social and political arrangements and in economic development, records the impressive independent role of a reform ideology in creating our images of Victorian cities. This ideology was based upon the moralist precepts of evangelical philanthropy, and the social geography of the city was manipulated into an image that was appropriate to publicize the objectives of reformers. To be sure, evangelical moralists did not monopolize reform movements but their image of the early Victorian city, if not their reforms, proved to be appropriate to rationalist, utilitarian, socialist, and other conceptions of social change and public policy.

DE TOCQUEVILLE'S COMPARISONS OF ENGLAND AND THE UNITED STATES

The parallel development of this concern with the social consequences of rapid urban growth occurred at a time when most observers were impressed by deep differences between English and American societies. Seymour Drescher has pointed out that the most prominent publicist of these national differences, Alexis de Tocqueville, did not confront these issues in his classic work on the new republic but rather in his less well-known works on England.[16] De Tocqueville initially described English society after at least one generation of large-scale industrialization but at about the time of the first major effort to reform parliament and local government. During the same decade his more celebrated account of democracy in the United States was of a society only modestly affected by large-scale industrialization but regarded as the most advanced experiment in political democracy. De Tocqueville's first account of English society, prior to his visit to the United States, was quite different from later descriptions, which were strongly influenced by his knowledge of American society. His initial description was based upon his limited experiences in London and in the countryside of the landed gentry of the home counties. Consequently,

15 Carroll S. Rosenberg, *Religion and the Rise of the American City: The New York City Mission Movement, 1812-1870* (Ithaca 1971), 31-7, 172-83; Charles I. Foster, 'The Urban Missionary Movement 1814-1837,' *Pennsylvania Magazine of History and Biography* 75 (1951): 47-64; Foster, *Errand of Mercy*, 157-60
16 Drescher, *Dilemmas of Democracy: Tocqueville and Modernization* (Pittsburgh 1968), 51-5, and *Tocqueville in England* (Cambridge, Mass. 1964), 35-53

he contrasted the strength of local governments and the social and economic independence of American farmers with the landed estates, tied labourers, and considerable legislative and judicial power of the English gentry and aristocracy. Under these circumstances he relegated the place of the city in American society to a frequently cited footnote that applauded the absence of a dominant, populous capital city, like Paris or London, with their threatening mobs and extravagant wealth.[17] Nevertheless, he sensed in the growing northeastern seaports the presence of a rabble of the lowest classes who were potentially more dangerous than those of European towns. In particular, he was convinced that freed blacks and unskilled foreign immigrants would disrupt urban life and that only an independent militia capable of controlling the populations of large cities would remove this threat to the experiment in democracy. Large cities, whether or not they were centres of new industry, were apparently not conducive to experiments in political equality.

De Tocqueville thus reiterated Jefferson's concern for protecting the political experiment from the potentially anarchic social conditions of large cities. Political democracy was appropriate only to a society of small farms and modest workshops where the ownership of the means of production was widespread. Tenancy and labouring relationships were inconsistent with political equality and, to the degree that these dependent relationships were prevalent in large cities, they represented a threat to the progressive reform of political institutions. Notwithstanding the compounding effects of large-scale industrialization, large capital cities and great seaports had long been viewed as very difficult social settings in which to establish political democracy. Certainly the increasing exclusivity of the residential quarters of the affluent in the large cities of Europe and, to a more limited degree, in the northeastern seaports of the United States suggests that the segregated patterns, often attributed to the Industrial Revolution, were established during the great growth of international trade in the seventeenth and more particularly in the eighteenth century. Residential exclusivity had been a common strategy of the wealthy for avoiding the discomfort and disorderliness of the eighteenth-century city, but eventually this separation became a matter of concern as a threat to social stability or political democracy. To De Tocqueville, and to many native observers, American cities, long before they attained great size or were transformed by large-scale industrialization, presented serious problems of government. The problems were in part based upon the potential insurgency of the lower classes, who were increasingly remote from, and independent of, their social superiors.

17 Drescher, *Dilemmas of Democracy*, 51; White, *Intellectual versus the City*, 34-5; Moehring, *Urban America*, 1-5

These implications of social isolation were, however, most frequently explored in relation to the effects of industrialization that in England were presumed to have compounded if not created the problem. De Tocqueville revealed, if incidentally, not only that the problem antedated large-scale industrialization in the United States but also that one large English industrial city, namely Birmingham, exhibited many of the progressive attributes of American society. On his second visit to England, after his extensive travels in the United States, De Tocqueville made more explicit references to the interrelationships of urban life, industrialization, and political democracy.[18] He was intrigued by the rapidly growing provincial cities of Birmingham and Manchester and especially by the 'new' societies that he encountered there. Indeed, in Birmingham there was 'as much good will as in London, but there is hardly any likenesses between the two societies. These folk never have a minute to themselves. They work as if they must get rich by the evening and die the next day. They are generally very intelligent people, but intelligent in the American way.'[19]

On his first visit De Tocqueville had viewed English society and its institutions as more aristocratic and less reformed than those of France under Louis-Philippe. His earlier conclusions were revised, for in the workshops of Birmingham he identified economic circumstances that were as conducive to political equality as those which he had discovered in the United States. He suggested further that England and the United States were drawing together in their institutions, morals, and values. He no longer assumed that the American political experiment was founded solely upon indigenous developments, for American society could also be conceived as an extension of the values and preferred institutions of the English middle class.[20] Birmingham, England, a large industrial city, was thus described as an American society, or conversely American society was a manifestation of the political aspirations of the English middle class. De Tocqueville's collaborator, Beaumont, was most amused by their conclusions: 'Birmingham had no eloquence, but was good natured, polite, sometimes indiscreet. Embarrassingly obliging — it is absolutely American. They are far from suspecting the comparison I make, for they have not stopped laughing at the Americans.'[21]

These new insights were, however, put to a severe test when they visited Manchester and sensed a more adversarial relationship and social isolation of

18 Drescher, *ibid.*, 72-9, and *Tocqueville in England*, 18-34
19 *Tocqueville in England*, 62-4
20 *Ibid.*, 193-216
21 *Ibid.*, 64

employer and employed. They observed first-hand the appalling urban housing conditions set amidst the smoke and accumulated filth of a city that had grown so rapidly in the preceding decades. De Tocqueville wrote: 'Everything in the exterior appearance of the city attests to the individual powers of man; nothing to the directing power of society. At every turn, human liberty shows its capricious creative force. There is no trace of the slow continuous action of government.'[22] De Tocqueville described the society of Manchester as industrial feudalism, as a regression to older, unfree social relationships rather than as a new capitalistic social order.[23] Unlike Engels, who described the city about a decade later as a prototype of future urban society of antagonistic classes, De Tocqueville found Manchester to be atypical of the destiny of English cities.[24] To be sure, he was disturbed by a new aristocracy of wealth that was less attentive to social obligations than the older landed aristocracy, but his confidence in the growth of political equality prompted him to assume that this new aristocracy would be displaced along with the remnants of the old. These troubled impressions of Manchester remained with him, and later he conceded that as a price of general prosperity there would always be a minority of indigents created by the insecurities of the market economy. These circumstances were clearly inconsistent with his concept of democracy and, in spite of his perceptive and original comments on Birmingham, De Tocqueville apologetically concluded that it was unjust and absurd to judge a people by its cities.[25]

INDUSTRIALIZATION AND URBAN IMAGES

De Tocqueville's comparative commentaries about English and American societies clearly revealed the difficulties involved in defining the place of cities in old and new societies. For most observers of English life Manchester was the symbol of the new or American society. He inadvertently provided a perceptive and rare insight into the complexity of social change that could only have emerged from the comparative perspective of his experience in the United States. The rewards of this perspective were eventually to be reaped by Asa Briggs, who captured the divergent experiences of Victorian cities, which only

22 *Ibid.*, 64-6
23 *Dilemmas of Democracy*, 72-9
24 Frederick Engels, *The Condition of the Working Class in England in 1844*, ed. and trans. W.O. Henderson and W.M. Chaloner (Stanford 1958), 30-87; Steven Marcus, *Engels, Manchester and the Working Class* (New York 1974), 1-66; Drescher, *Tocqueville in England*, 64-73
25 Drescher, *ibid.*, 66-74

towards the close of the nineteenth century exhibited striking similarities.[26] The vast majority of European visitors to the United States, and for that matter most Americans who travelled in Europe, viewed the class society of Manchester as the inevitable and tragic cost of industrialization. Consequently, the evils of Manchester had to be avoided by other societies, and especially by the United States, if industrialization were not to threaten political democracy and growing equality. The growth of factories in the United States thus became a major moral issue, for in a nation already apprehensive about large cities factories represented a new and more menacing threat to the institutions of the new republic.[27] If industrialization in the United States could avoid the class antagonisms and environmental degradation of Manchester, then the United States would unambiguously demonstrate the virtues of political democracy. Consequently, the establishment of large-scale industry in the United States was accompanied by elaborate moral justifications. This was especially true in New England, where the corporate scale and integration of textile manufacturing quickly exceeded that of Britain. Factories and industry were justified on the basis of not only a reduction in dependence upon English imports but also the promise of an alternative American industrial society. The paternalism of the Boston Associates in their provision of supervised boarding houses was applauded as an alternative to the slums of English cities. The development of factory settlements on water power sites in rural settings was viewed as an answer to congested industrial cities. Lowell, Massachusetts, because of its commitment to cotton production, was identified as an American 'Manchester' but without the social and material distress of the English city.[28]

This comparison of a large commercial and industrial centre with a relatively small factory settlement was certainly contrived. Dickens, for example, reserved judgement on the Lowell experiment, and he was no apologist for the conditions in Manchester.[29] Chevalier, who was familiar with English industrial cities, recognized that American working conditions were superior to those of England; nevertheless, he interpreted the New England factories as an 'industrial feudalism' identical to that of English cities.[30] The new manufacturers did,

26 *Victorian Cities*, 11-87
27 Sanford, *Quest for Paradise*, 155-75; John E. Sawyer, 'The Social Basis of the American System of Manufacturing,' *Journal of Economic History* 14 (1954): 361-79
28 Thomas Bender, *Toward an Urban Vision: Ideas and Institutions in Nineteenth Century America* (Lexington 1975), 98; Marvin Fisher, *Workshops in the Wilderness: The European Response to American Industrialization, 1830-1860* (New York 1967), 1-4, 91-6; Douglas T. Miller, *The Birth of Modern America, 1820-1850* (New York 1970), 67-90
29 Moehring, *Urban America*, 103-6
30 Drescher, *Dilemmas of Democracy*, 53-4

however, obtain a moral sanction for their investments. This moral justification of the profit motive and economic growth endured long after the material and social conditions of Lowell had deteriorated to levels which resembled those of English cities. By this time the southern planter and the institution of slavery were viewed as a greater threat than factories to the American social and political experiment.[31] American industry was recognized and celebrated for its mechanical ingenuity in reducing labour demands, and the new growing forces of industrialization were increasingly considered without reference to their urban setting. Similarly, the poverty and discomfort that were observed in association with new industries were thought to be ephemeral, since it was assumed that there was greater upward social mobility and more abundant opportunities in the United States than in England.[32] Those who were somewhat sceptical of the political experiment of the new republic were also convinced that living conditions and employment opportunities were far superior to those in Europe. This optimism was, however, most evident in the imagery, metaphor, and rhetoric that were called upon to articulate the national identity of a new nation.[33]

These positive attitudes to early industrialization in the United States were reinforced as the century proceeded. The political corruption and monopolistic practices of the 'gilded age' were contrasted with the authentic political equality and open access to opportunities of an idealized antebellum society. De Tocqueville's description of American society thus became a nostalgic image for later generations, and although the 'gilded age' was celebrated as a period of economic growth it was clearly recognized as a source of unavoidable and irreversible changes in the nature of American society and especially in the scale of the problems of urban life.[34] Indeed, responses to the more rapid industrialization in the United States after the Civil War were strongly influenced by idealized memories of the egalitarianism and social solidarities of small communities. These memories have been interpreted as cultural continuities similar to those identified among the English working class, whose responses to industrialization were also based upon remembered or idealized views of a more

31 Sanford, *Quest for Paradise*, 178; Henry May, *Protestant Churches in Industrial America* (New York 1949), 24
32 Rowland Berthoff, *An Unsettled People; Social Order and Disorder in American History* (New York 1971), 175-203; Bender, *Toward an Urban Vision*, 109-14; Fisher, *Workshops in the Wilderness*, 124
33 Fisher, *ibid.*, 149
34 Robert H. Wiebe, *The Search for Order, 1877-1920* (New York 1967), 44-75; Michael H. Frisch, *Town into City: Springfield, Massachusetts and the Meaning of Community* (Cambridge, Mass. 1972), 242-9

humane society.[35] English reactions to large cities were, however, intimately related to the presumed ravages of large-scale industrialization. Contemporary American concerns with urban problems not only antedated large-scale industrialization but also occurred during the idealized antebellum period, when economic opportunities and political equality were presumed to have improved. The problems of the American city could thus be viewed as exceptions to social conditions at large. This disassociation of industrialization and the deterioration of urban environments, and a confidence that poverty would be ameliorated by upward social mobility, obscured underlying structural causes of urban problems.[36] Wolfram Fischer has contrasted attitudes to social problems in Western Europe and the United States and concluded that 'in the United States social problems were not treated as historical phenomena caused by industrialization but as the pathology of society as it exists as a disorganization either of individuals or of families or of larger social groups.'[37]

'TWO NATIONS' IN THE NEW REPUBLIC

Many perceptive American observers did, however, recognize in their own cities the problems that dominated discussions of English cities. Specifically, complaints about the congested quarters of newly arrived immigrants and the increased social isolation of the poor from the rich closely resembled contemporary English dialogues.[38] Channing anticipated Disraeli's 'two nations' when he suggested that in cities 'ranks are so widely separated indeed as to form different communities. In most large cities, there may be said to be two nations understanding as little of one another, having as little intercourse as if they live in different lands. This estrangement of man from man, of class from class, is one of the saddest features of a great city.'[39] Channing subscribed to many of the optimistic evaluations of American society but was apprehensive of the

---

35 Herbert G. Gutman, 'Work, Culture and Society in Industrializing America 1815-1919,' *American Historical Review* 78 (1973): 531-88; Edward Pessen, *Most Uncommon Jacksonians: The Radical Leaders of the Early Labor Movement* (Albany 1967), 155-72; Roger Lane, 'Crime and the Industrial Revolution: British and American Views,' *Journal of Social History* 7 (1973-4): 287-303

36 Bender, *Toward an Urban Vision*, 126-8; Fisher, *Workshops in the Wilderness*, 124

37 Fischer, 'Social Tensions at Early Stages of Industrialization,' *Comparative Studies in Society and History* 9 (1966): 64-77

38 Moehring, *Urban America*, 12-46; Rosenberg, *Religion and the Rise of the American City*, 31-7, 164-85; Richard M. Brown, 'Historical Patterns of Violence in America,' in Graham and Gurr, *History of Violence*, 45-84

39 Briggs, *Victorian Cities*, 64

social destiny of large cities. His view of the social geographic patterns of large cities was shared by many of his contemporaries. Phillip Hone, for example, concluded that 'American cities had arrived at a state of society to be found in the large cities of Europe in which the two extremes of costly luxury in living, expensive establishments, and improvident waste are presented daily and hourly contrast with squalid misery and hopeless destitution.'[40] The term 'slum' was used increasingly to describe the resorts of the depraved poor, and these quarters were a source of fascination and an integral part of the emerging dichotomous classification of urban society. Particular districts of cities became symbolic or generic representations of slums, and vivid and detailed descriptions of these well-publicized districts aroused public alarm. Five Points in Manhattan early assumed this critical symbolic role in conceptions of American slums.[41]

These conceptions of urban society not only contradicted De Tocqueville's picture of American society but also his analysis of Birmingham and the provincial English middle class as an 'American' society. The affection for the United States of many prominent English middle-class radicals, who represented the economic interests of manufacturers, certainly illustrated De Tocqueville's proposition.[42] Large cities were apparently not conducive to democracy, but in England the spokesmen of reform were drawn from large industrial cities or 'American' societies set in a partly reformed polity. Consequently, American cities set in a reformed polity should have had more emphatically displayed 'American' traits than did the English cities. De Tocqueville never reviewed his apprehension about large American cities in the light of his analysis of Birmingham, and the paradox of the 'American' societies of English cities was never resolved. Indeed, most observers rejected De Tocqueville's optimistic view of the place of new industrial cities in English society. English industrial cities were not viewed as 'islands' of American society in England but rather American cities as 'islands' of English society in the United States. American cities were increasingly viewed as partial replicas of English cities and it might be presumed, therefore, that broadly similar structural changes had occurred in English and American cities and that the differences in their respective political arrangements were most prevalent in small settlements and in the agricultural sector.

Certainly the egalitarianism and social mobility of Jacksonian and antebellum American society have increasingly been questioned. In particular, improved transportation and enlarged markets altered the status and independence of

---

40 Edward Pessen, *Riches, Class, and Power before the Civil War* (Lexington 1973), 33
41 Moehring, *Urban America*, 100-10
42 Frank Thistlethwaite, *The Anglo American Connection in the Early Nineteenth Century* (Philadelphia 1959), 165-72

American artisans as merchant capitalists began to control small-scale manu-facturing and to substitute unskilled and semi-skilled operatives in some segments of the manufacturing process. Consequently, long before large-scale industrial enterprises altered social and economic relationships of employment, small masters as well as journeymen complained of reduced opportunities and a deterioration in their access to markets.[43] In England, too, complaints about industrialization were as vocal in towns where production remained in small workshops as in those dominated by factories. Among some American craftsmen discontent was far closer in content to the more corporate notions of English Chartists than to the individualism of many Jacksonians who hoped to limit government intervention. To Edward Pessen, 'The political and social landscape that these American observers drew bears a remarkable resemblance to the dismal English landscape painted by William Cobbett and their radical contemporaries in old England.'[44] De Tocqueville's description of American society and later idealizations of antebellum society require careful scrutiny.

Contemporary American observers thus regarded the increasing social segregation in large cities as exceptions to the egalitarian and opportunistic conceptions of American society. Increased segregation was, however, quite consistent with those views of American society that attributed inequalities of wealth and limitations on mobility to the growth of mercantile capitalism in the antebellum period long before the large-scale industrialization of the 'gilded age.' In short, the presumed increase in social segregation in antebellum American cities, closely resembling that of contemporary English cities, might be related to the effects of mercantile rather than industrial capitalism. The well-publicized national differences in polity and an overemphasis on large-scale industrialization may have obscured underlying similarities in the effects of economic changes on both English and American societies, similarities that were most graphically revealed in common urban problems.[45]

Unfortunately, this argument, however plausible, raises more problems than it solves. Contemporary descriptions of the segregated social geographic patterns of both British and American cities were somewhat exaggerated or at least highly simplified. Social segregation aroused apprehension about the control of the potentially volatile, less affluent segments of society who were usually grouped as 'the poor.' Articulate leaders of these less well-to-do urban residents rarely

43 Pessen, *Riches, Class, and Power,* 42-3; Miller, *Birth of Modern America,* 21; Walter Hugins, *Jacksonian Democracy and the Working Class* (Stanford 1960), 1-20
44 *Most Uncommon Jacksonians,* 128
45 Pessen, 'The Social Configuration of the Antebellum City: An Historical and Theo-retical Inquiry,' *Journal of Urban History* 2 (1976): 267-306

complained of social isolation from the wealthy and did not relate their dissatisfactions to the segregated social geography of the city. Indeed, the riots and popular disturbances that were quite frequent in antebellum cities are no longer interpreted as manifestations of purposeless anarchy but rather as organized political activities.[46] Most disturbances served a political role in generating broadly based support for specific objectives or grievances. In short, many disturbances revealed the growing political participation of a broad spectrum of less affluent people in local or national affairs. Broadly based disturbances were also aroused by tensions derived from differing religious and ethnic loyalties, but during the antebellum period a wider spectrum of the poor probably participated in more broadly based responses to economic changes than in later decades.[47] The almost continuous arrival of new and diverse foreign immigrants and the greater internal stratification of the poor greatly diminished broad community-wide reactions to political or economic issues.

Prior to the Civil War, however, the broadly based participation of a wide range of occupational groups, ranging from the lesser bourgeoisie to journeymen, in common political activity suggests that residential differentiation was either relatively weak or of little social consequence among the vast majority of less affluent urban residents. Although a dichotomous social geographic pattern well describes the increased spatial isolation of the wealthy, it yields a misleading impression of the remainder of society as a homogenous group deprived of the elevating example of social leaders. If English ideas of a dichotomous social geographic pattern, and especially of the dangerous isolation of the poor in slums, was an incomplete and misleading picture of English urban life, why was this geopolitical concept also prevalent in the United States? The concept had at least some credibility in a country in the midst of the divisive effects of large-scale industrialization and a tradition of aristocratic leadership and patronage, but its adoption by American observers, who concurrently celebrated the opportunities and mobility of American society, is a curious paradox. Merchant capitalism well may have provided far more limited opportunities than

46 David Grimsted, 'Rioting in Its Jacksonian Setting,' *American Historical Review* 77 (1972): 361-97; Michael Feldberg, 'The Crowd in Philadelphia History: A Comparative Perspective,' *Labor History* 15 (1974): 323-36

47 Gutman, 'Work, Culture and Society,' 531-88; Hugins, *Jacksonian Democracy*, 221; David Montgomery, 'The Shuttle and the Cross: Weavers and Artisans in the Kensington Riots of 1844,' *Journal of Social History* 5 (1972): 411-46; Bruce Laurie, ' "Nothing on Impulse": Life Styles of Philadelphia Artisans, 1820-1850,' *Labor History* 15 (1974): 337-66; John T. Cumbler, 'Labor, Capital and Community: The Struggle for Power,' *Labor History* 15 (1974): 395-415

contemporary observers were prepared to admit, but there is no reason to suppose that antebellum cities were therefore characterized by a segregated social geographic pattern in which the poor or less affluent were dangerously isolated.

EVANGELICAL PHILANTHROPY AND SOCIAL GEOGRAPHIC PATTERNS

If contemporary impressions of early Victorian cities were only partly grounded in the real world of the city, an explanation of the urban images of early Victorians must be sought in the history of ideas and ideologies. Of the numerous ideological shifts in the early nineteenth century, none was more influential upon thinking about cities than new attitudes towards poverty.[48] These new attitudes were, moreover, embraced as part of a desire to uplift and reform society by evangelical philanthropists, whose ideas and aspirations exhibited striking parallels on both sides of the Atlantic.[49] These similarities in attitudes towards poverty and measures to reduce its dimensions provided a common set of assumptions and aims that were shared by evangelical reformers in England and the United States. Their common socio-geographic visions of the city were thus derived not from their detailed knowledge of cities or from their sensitivity to similarities in economic transformations but rather from their shared ideology of reform. Evangelical moralists stressed specific goals, such as temperance, education, the abolition of slavery, and the mass distribution of Bibles, but since they viewed the social isolation of rich and poor as a major cause of the infidelity and depravity of society, social geographic images were central to their publicity.[50] Poverty was no longer viewed as an endemic social problem but a freely chosen deviant pattern of life that was reinforced by isolation from the elevating example of the socially prominent and by the facility with which outdoor relief could be obtained. The removal of contributory factors to poverty, such as alcohol, and the provision of means of

48 Reinhard Bendix, *Work and Authority in Industry: Ideologies of Management in the Course of Industrialization* (New York 1956), 60-86; Foster, *Errand of Mercy*, 46-54; Nathan I. Huggins, *Protestants against Poverty: Boston's Charities, 1870-1900* (Westport 1971), 15-56; David J. Rothman, *The Discovery of the Asylum: Social Order and Disorder in the New Republic* (Boston 1971), 155-79; Mohl, *Poverty in New York,* 159-62

49 Rosenberg, *Religion and the Rise of the City,* 45-50, 262-73; Mohl, *Poverty in New York,* 166-7, 253; Foster, *Errand of Mercy,* 155-38; Thistlethwaite, *Anglo American Connection,* 76-102

50 Rosenberg, *Religion and the Rise of the City,* 153-57; Mohl, *Poverty in New York,* 159-62.

social improvement, such as Bible societies and later schools, would, it was hoped, make it possible for the poor to escape their poverty by their own initiative. An image of the city segregated into two separate moral 'worlds' energized philanthropic reforms, and many secular reformers, who envisaged more ambitious kinds of intervention, found the geopolitical ideas of the evangelical philanthropists conducive to their own objectives. Indeed, social and moral issues were so inextricably connected in the minds of Victorian reformers that their moral and social images of the city were fused. Although in England 'humanitarian' philanthropy and 'rationalist' utilitarianism have been viewed as antithetical positions, recent evaluations have stressed the difficulty of separating the two ideologies in the actions and objectives of reform movements.[51] In the United States 'individualistic' rationalism was more prevalent than Benthamism but reform movements, to an even greater degree than in England, were founded on socio-moral concepts.[52] The antebellum mission was sustained by evangelical pietism, but to identify this religious commitment as a mere rationale for social control would distort the unity of the early Victorian reformers' mind.[53]

The assumption that the problem of poverty was altered and compounded by apparently recent changes in the social geography of the city was thus shared by diverse reformers on both sides of the Atlantic. Humanitarian causes were dominated by evangelical moralists whose efforts were directed at the reform of the poor by education, the provision of Bibles, temperance, and urban missions. All of these measures were accompanied by exhortations to improve contact with the poor. Visitation was regarded as an essential part of reform measures, for traditional outdoor relief rarely confronted the poor with their faults and failed to provide them with model examples of responsible behaviour. Once visitation schemes and missions in the slums proved inadequate, efforts were made to relocate the poor, and especially the children of the poor, in foster homes where they would escape the depravity of their own environs.[54]

51 Jenifer Hart, 'Nineteenth Century Social Reform: A Tory Interpretation of History,' *Past and Present* 31 (1965): 39-61; Brian Harrison, 'State Intervention and Moral Reform,' in Patricia Hollis, ed., *Pressure from Without in Early Victorian England* (London 1974), 289-322

52 Paul Palmer, 'Benthamism in England and America,' *American Political Science Review* 35 (1941): 855-71; Gutman, 'Work, Culture and Society,' 531-88; Foster, *Errand of Mercy*, 177-89

53 Rosenburg, *Religion and the Rise of the City*, 7-9; Henry May, *Protestant Churches in Industrial America* (New York 1949), 23-31; Timothy L. Smith, *Revivalism and Social Reform in Mid-Nineteenth Century America* (New York 1957), 149-57; David B. Davis, ed., *Ante-Bellum Reform* (New York 1967), i-x

54 Rosenburg, *Religion and the Rise of the City*, 236-8; Bender, *Toward an Urban Vision*, 131-57; Huggins, *Protestants against Poverty*, 15-56

Reformers were convinced of the need to provide the poor with moral example by visitation and by the removal of the young poor from their environs, and both measures presumed a dichotomous division of urban society into a moral and immoral world. Accordingly, the arousal of public concern was based upon graphic elaborations of the social isolation and presumed depravity of the poor. Later in the nineteenth century, when the mediating or compounding effects of environmental and economic causes were accepted as contributing factors to poverty, housing and welfare measures were still assumed to be of questionable benefit if the isolation of the poor allowed them to maintain their deviant behaviour.[55]

The emergence of these values and attitudes in the early nineteenth century followed a remarkably similar course on both sides of the Atlantic. The debates on the English Poor Law were closely paralleled by the discussions of relief in several of the states of the new nation.[56] The greatest cross-fertilization of ideas was, however, among pioneering evangelical moralists who had visited and maintained close personal links with their English counterparts. American institutional arrangements designed to reach the poor with Bibles, missions, and moral example were firmly based upon English experience.[57] It was not, therefore, surprising that an image of the city appropriate to these common aims was shared on both sides of the Atlantic. The establishment of missions among the poor and of experimental ministers at large, who fostered the moral links of the entire community rather than of a circumscribed congregation, presumed a city segregated on the basis of religious fidelity and economic dependency. Chalmer's efforts to organize relief in Glasgow on the basis of self-sufficient precincts influenced Tuckerman's ministry at large in Boston.[58] Although visitation, relocation, and the strict control of relief captured the imagination of contemporary observers, these practices were rarely successfully sustained in any one city for any length of time.

The social geographic assumptions of evangelical moralists were, however, appropriate to less religiously founded indictments of social change, and the simplistic image of a dichotomous social geographic pattern developed a vigorous

55 Huggins, *ibid.*, 15-56, 177-80

56 Mohl, *Poverty in New York*, 166; Paul Faler, 'Cultural Aspects of the Industrial Revolution: Lynn, Massachusetts, Shoemakers and Industrial Morality, 1826-1860,' *Labor History* 15 (1974): 367-94

57 Rosenburg, *Religion and the Rise of the City*, 45-60; Mohl, *Poverty in New York*, 253; Foster, *Errand of Mercy*, 115-38

58 David Owen, *English Philanthropy, 1660-1960* (Cambridge, Mass. 1964), 224-29; Huggins, *Protestants against Poverty*, 15-56; Rothman, *Discovery of the Asylum*, 155-79

independent life of its own. This versatility was possible because segregated residential patterns presumably recorded both a loss of a more organic or synthetic community of mutually dependent classes and the dehumanizing and atomizing effects of large-scale industrialization. Thus, Engels relied upon a segregated social geographic pattern to emphasize his description of Manchester in 1844 as an adversarial and volatile class society.[59] Although Engels related segregation to the workings of the market economy, he, too, may have been influenced by the pioneering efforts in Elberfeld to organize poor relief on the basis of small districts and to ensure the moral eligibility and elevation of the poor by direct contact with the donors.[60]

In the interests of projecting an image of an isolated, depraved, and threatening culture of poverty, a social geographic image of 'two nations' compressed the variability and vitality of the less affluent segment of urban society and defamed the majority of urban residents who overcame discomfort and starvation with dignity. The only empirical geographic examination of the relationship between ideology and residential patterns is John Radford's recent examination of Charleston, South Carolina, in the mid-nineteenth century.[61] Residential patterns in which slaves occupied rear lots and the use of contrived redevelopment to displace and disperse presumably dangerous concentrations of free blacks are interpreted as manifestations of a planter ideology of social control in contrast to the competitive market processes that presumably determined land use in northern cities. Although it was more difficult for northern cities to assemble the unanimity of ideology that prevailed in Charleston, descriptions of the urban poor elsewhere were almost racist, for conceptions of all Victorian cities were deeply influenced by exaggerations of the threatening implications of the social isolation of the poor. These urban images of evangelical moralists and secular rationalists strongly influenced public policies and reform strategies, but because so many of these policies and strategies were spasmodic and had unintended results the relationship between ideology and social geographic patterns was almost certainly indirect. A more direct relationship existed between ideologies of reform and the misleading social geographic image upon which they were based.

A resolution of the degree of residential differentiation of early Victorian cities requires further empirical investigations, but the scale and extent of this differentiation among the less affluent was clearly quite different from the now

59 *Condition of the Working Class*, 30-87
60 Owen, *English Philanthropy*, 224-9; Lubove, *Professional Altruist*, 1-5
61 Radford, 'Race, Residence and Ideology: Charleston, South Carolina in the Mid-nineteenth Century,' *Journal of Historical Geography* 2 (1976): 329-46

classic descriptions of segregation in London by Booth in the late nineteenth century and in Chicago by Burgess early in the present century.[62] Descriptions of the social geography of early Victorian cities might then be viewed as geopolitical images designed to justify reform and derived from new concepts of poverty.[63] This discussion of the striking similarities in social geographic images of American and English cities strongly suggests that these images have an ideological rather than an empirical basis. In spite of profound differences in national ideologies, similar urban images prevailed in England and the United States. The parallel development of English urban images in the United States is a remarkable example of ideological convergence at a time when there was ideological divergence in matters of national identity. The creation of new societies certainly involved the emergence of ideologies founded upon notions of pioneering and egalitarianism, but in the United States, at least, social geographic images of cities were paradoxically quite derivative and certainly unoriginal. These images were not only profoundly affected by the well-publicized anti-urban bias of American political and literary thought but also by the adoption of urban images that were derived in part from English precedents. This apparent inconsistency of urban images and national ideology in the antebellum period remains a persisting problem that continues to confuse the place of urban life in American society.

62 Harold W. Pfautz, ed., *Charles Booth on the City: Physical Pattern and Social Structure* (Chicago 1967), 90-1; Ernst W. Burgess, 'The Growth of the City,' in Robert E. Park, ed., *The City* (Chicago 1925), 47-62
63 Ward, 'Victorian Slum,' 323-36

JAMES T. LEMON

The weakness of place and community in early Pennsylvania

The real horror of our present condition is not merely the absence of community or the isolation of the self — those, after all, have been part of the American condition for a long time. It is the loss of the ability to remember what is missing, the diminishment of our vision of what is humanly possible or desirable.

PETER MARIN, 'The New Narcissism'
Harper's 251 (October 1975), 48

The study of place must have as its content the social realities of community. Today in geography there is a move afoot to recover the concept of place, just as in several spheres much discussion is going on about community. These two notions have to be connected; community is grounded in place, just as place can hardly be substantial without a shared awareness of living together. To understand place and community we need to look at distinctive and unique places and communities, and, of course, the opposite is true — concrete places and communities make sense only if we can conceptualize the structure and processes in place and community. As historical geographers we have been responsible in large measure for keeping regions and the region in the discipline of geography by dealing with economies and material cultures at the regional scale. Now we can extend the work of Andrew Clark, and of others among us, by considering life together at the lower or local scale.

A community in place refers to a group of people with a common purpose of co-operative action. Reciprocity rather than competition, to use Karl Polanyi's terms,[1] found in market exchange or bureaucratic control in redistributive systems, is the dominant style of action in work and play. Therefore, in such a social system little interest is expressed in material growth for surplus accumulation by any one person or the group itself beyond hedging for lean years. Members engage in both physical and mental work because manual work on the land and in shops is respected as much as intellectual work, as was envisioned by Peter Kropotkin.[2] Politically, the leaders draw others into decision-making so as to sustain one another, rather than to divide and conquer and so foster their own aggrandizement. Education encourages the young to enjoy others and the environment rather than dominate them. Members of communities are confident of their future – secure without the need to overwhelm neighbours or nature. Religiously speaking, life in a community rids us of the anxiety of a lonely privatized death. People work not for their own ends but for the sake of the community, achieving self-fulfilment rather than the self-denial needed for an individualistic society. The place is a shaped landscape in which the built forms reflect these social realities, a landscape focused for work, play, and rest, all adding up to enjoyment, not alienation. The place is found among other places within regions where the people share a consciousness of one another as a people. Therefore, although community must be local, the reality of community goes beyond the bounds of local face-to-face contacts. Yet, just as the household cannot be equated with full communities, the region or the country cannot exist without strength at the local level.

If we are to believe Peter Marin, we can today say little about place or community. One is tempted to agree with him; not only have North Americans uprooted themselves but their birthplace is no longer recollected, otherwise individual achievement would be impeded. The memory is so elusive, if not gone, that we have trouble expressing what we mean. Even though we may be searching for community, we are so overwhelmed by the rhetoric of liberalism that any other language strikes us as idealistic romanticism (witness Clark's description of his childhood in Prince Edward Island[3]). Contrast the supposed tough-mindedness of spatial analysis based upon classical literal economic assumptions with the apparently soft aestheticism of the geographers of place

---

1 Polanyi, *The Great Transformation* (New York 1944), especially 67-76
2 Kropotkin, *Fields, Factories and Workshops: or, Industry Combined with Agriculture and Brain Work with Manual Work* (London 1898). Co-operative theory is rather little developed. See A.E. Dreyfuss, *City Villages: The Cooperative Quest* (Toronto 1973), and Murray Bookchin, *The Limits of the City* (New York 1974).
3 *Three Centuries and the Island* (Toronto 1959), vii. Also see Robert Nisbet, *The Social Philosopher: Community and Conflict in Western Thought* (New York 1973).

and landscape.[4] And now Marxist language, although speaking in a collectivist vein, is often hard and abrasive, partly as a result of a generally narrow and centralizing economic concern.[5]

The history of the United States has devastated our memory of community. It has also devastated what communities there have been. History as told by historians has been dominated by individualism on the frontier, mainly the agricultural frontier. The limitless frontier provided the opportunity for the individual to pursue success. And the very success of the Turnerian model, in captivating uncritically a generation or more of American scholars, points clearly to the tenuous hold of place and community on our awareness. The frontier view wiped out the romanticism of those nineteenth-century scholars seeking the basis of New England community deep in the recesses of the Teutonic forest (and mind).[6] But the frontier model arose itself as a romantic reaction to the enormous visible reality of corporations as they shifted their factories to the edges of cities, built their skyscraper offices in the centres, and accepted the flood of foreign workers.

The frontier model ignored places and communities, and consequently served so well as a lightning rod for the fears of that great bulk of middle American individualists — whether living in city, town, or country — in the face of the new structural realities. Possibly the weakness of geography as a school and university subject is a reflection of the continued deflection from these realities. No matter how much English geographers may complain about 'capes and bays' geography, it has been embedded in place, and it is in the curriculum along with the glories and horrors of the Industrial Revolution. Americans by and large just did not learn these facts of the landscape because the learning of places is simply a

4 Edward Relph, *Place and Placelessness* (London 1976), provides a useful discussion but treats community directly on only three pages.

5 For example, David Harvey, *Social Justice and the City* (London 1973), although this is a very important work.

6 Even more recent writing romanticizes the New England village. We are all familiar with Glenn Trewartha, 'Types of Rural Settlements in Colonial America,' *Geographical Review* 36 (1946): 568-96. But a new work has shown that the village was a rarity and that many greens came late. Martyn J. Bowden and Joseph S. Wood, 'The Fabled Village Green: The Myth and Reality of the New England Landscape in the Early Republic,' paper delivered at a meeting of the Eastern Historical Geography Association, Newark, Delaware, Oct. 1976. Even some of the new social historians are predisposed to finding community in early Massachusetts, especially Michael Zuckerman, 'The Social Context of Democracy in Massachusetts,' *William and Mary Quarterly*, 3rd Series, 25 (1968): 523-44; also see Jack P. Greene, 'Autonomy and Stability: New England and the British Colonial Experience in Early Modern America,' *Journal of Social History* 7 (1974): 171-94.

pragmatic matter to be looked up when needed and not as an expression of community. Not surprisingly, American regional geographers, like Clark, were not taken seriously — without even a struggle. Even today historians harbour a quaint notion of geographers as a rather peripheral group interested in how mountains have diverted movements of people — a really unimportant question when compared with the real issue, namely, the conquering of a featureless plain by land-hungry settlers.[7]

Yet today, just as all visible differences of place seem to be wiped out by the culture of television, expressways, and unfocused suburbs, community and place are being recalled and even redeveloped, particularly in the older parts of overgrown cities. Political action in neighbourhoods and co-operative self-help groups are apparent, although nowhere dominant in politics and the economy. Many are pursuing community through a bewildering array of therapy and spiritual groups. Not least, urban, community, and family studies have expanded in the academic scene over the past decade. Just as Melvin Webber announced the placeless city, everyone started studying cities in the past.[8] Indeed, smaller communities sapped of their vitality, however weak and unimportant they may have been, could be strengthened, so that a future Stephen Leacock would not feel compelled to poke fun at them.[9] This may beg comparison with Turner's turning to the frontier in the 1890s; but this time around economic realities may be more clearly on the side of localism than they were with William Jennings Bryan populists in revolt against the city. Energy shortages and capital shortages for ever-increasing complex technologies may force us back to smaller-scale living.[10] But if Marin is correct, then we will have to create communities and

7 Donald W. Meinig, 'Commentary' on Walter Prescott Webb's 'Geographical Historical Concepts in American History,' *Annals of the Association of American Geographers* 50 (1960): 95-6

8 Webber, 'The Urban Place and the Nonplace Urban Realm,' in Melvin M. Webber *et al., Explorations into Urban Structure* (Philadelphia 1964), 79-153

9 Leacock, *Sunshine Sketches of a Little Town* (London 1912). It is interesting that even by then Leacock could see the city overwhelming smaller towns and, despite the humour, was not sympathetic. For a partial analysis of the sapping of small-town culture by automobile-induced pressures, see Norman T. Moline, *Mobility and the Small Town, 1900-1930* (Chicago 1971), although it does not go far enough to see social costs. As a native of a small town I saw during my teen years in the 1940s the remaining culture being emasculated by television and the car. Baseball, church choirs, and school plays virtually disappeared.

10 See Barry Commoner, *The Poverty of Power: Energy and the Economic Crisis* (New York 1976), from a Marxist viewpoint, and E.F. Schumacher, *Small Is Beautiful: Economics As If People Mattered* (London 1973), from a rather petty capitalist but small-scale view.

places in a deliberate self-conscious process of planning but with a good deal more mutual criticism and support than that to which we are accustomed.[11]

Also, if Marin is right, seeking roots in community and place from the American past is a futile exercise. But probably it is no more futile, in a sense, than to look backward to the medieval village, which we will surely want to applaud or, on the contrary, to denigrate. To deliberately plan communities in places today demands a look at our past without the pious crutches of antiquarian niceties. What we are forced to uncover for the sake of future generations are the pressures that dominated our ancestors and still control us.

It is in early Pennsylvania that we can see most unambiguously the beginnings of possessive individualism that overwhelmed previous forms of community found in Europe. It was here that the slate was, as it were, wiped clean. A hard look provides us not with comfort but with expectation that we must find new communities, and a new sense of place. Eighteenth-century realities remain with us, however much they have been transformed. This essay reflects on those realities and on our present condition. Much of the material presented here is already known to many readers from my book.[12] But the cast is more explicitly on the weakness of place and community as expressed on the landscape and in the fabric of society, notably government, tenure, wealth distribution, religious orientation, and religious pluralism. These are considered in the light of certain basic conditions: attitudes to land and resources, the supply of land, the market, and not least the ideology of the people. To sharpen what is said, I will deal with Quakers and Mennonites, and finally present a brief statement based upon Polanyi's model, gathering together the strands.

The visible landscape is where I shall begin, the settlement pattern, the configuration of farmsteads, fields, roads, and towns – in short, land-use patterns. These patterns are set in place for order and community. William Penn recognized this when he advocated agricultural villages set in the centre of townships of small size. Twenty, even ten families to start with on 10,000-acre

11 The recent debate in Toronto on deconcentration of activities from the central area is a step towards trying to give outlying suburbs some strength and focus. But inertia and suburban resistance is hard to overcome. Of course, none of us would like to see enforced movement from cities, as has happened in Phnom Penh and Ho Chi Minh City.

12 J.T. Lemon, *The Best Poor Man's Country: A Geographical Study of Early Southeastern Pennsylvania* (Baltimore 1972; New York 1976), 101. Unfootnoted material is taken from this study. A recent study of one village is in line with much of what I say: Stephanie Grauman Wolf, *Urban Village: Population, Community, and Family Structure in Germantown, Pennsylvania, 1683-1800* (Princeton 1976).

or 5000-acre townships, eventually growing to five times as many families, he thought would be ideal. He proposed a number of specific schemes, including that for Plymouth Township with farm lots radiating out in neat geometric fashion from home lots. All this, he said, 'for the more convenient bringing up of youth, so that neighbours may help one another, and that they may accustom their children to do the same.'[13] Properly considered, physical layout would enhance social life.

But few villages materialized. Only the small townships laid out in the earlier years of the colony were regularly surveyed. What did emerge immediately was a dispersed pattern of settlement with farmsteads set in the midst of fields. Given that many holdings initially were of 500 acres and generally blocky rather than long and narrow (as along the St Lawrence), families lived a great distance from one another. Even with farms of 100 acres (more standard later) and assuming a rectangular shape of 80 rods by 200 rods farmsteads would have been a quarter of a mile apart. But after the first twenty years they were not rectangular; the metes and bounds of irregular plots of diverse shapes and sizes appeared. The scattering and irregularity were not lost on Penn, who, partly because of this, died disappointed. From the outset individualism on the landscape had triumphed over the modest proposals of Penn.

Other visible elements were scattered, without focus, and therefore tended towards placelessness. Whereas in Penn's scheme the Quaker meeting house would have been central within townships, those built were not necessarily so, nor were the meeting houses of other denominations in mixed denominational and national areas. Manufacturing and other services were by and large not clustered, although not surprisingly mills were constrained by streams. Education of youth was not public. Begun on the initiative of a few people, probably the most stable citizens, school buildings were located at the foot of someone's land, or just as often, it seems, adjacent to meeting houses.

Some services were, however, assembled in some towns. Courts, government offices, merchants' offices, and warehouses were gathered in Philadelphia and the county towns that emerged. With the exception of Lancaster, the pre-revolutionary county seats were planned by William Penn's sons. All were located with access within the county and to Philadelphia in mind. They were seated on rivers or streams, in most cases central within counties, at pre-existing crossroads. Lower-scale towns started by individuals speculating in urban subdivisions showed an erratic pattern, clustered in some areas and absent in

13 Daniel Pastorius, 'Positive Information from America,' in Albert C. Myers, ed., *Narratives of Early Pennsylvania, West New Jersey and Delaware, 1630-1707* (New York 1913), 407

others. Few of these urban places were of great economic consequence, and so of little importance to community.

The regional system of county towns and roads tied farmers and others into a system of trade, government, and cultural influence that raised their expectations beyond the local level. The local landscape, particularly the rural patterns within which most people lived, even though bountiful and at least today seemingly picturesque, did not provide a sense of strong community concern. In other words, the centralizing of activities at higher scales, so obvious nowadays, began then. Yet because appearances can be deceiving we must look at other less visible characteristics, starting with the structure and role of government.

The power of government was weak at all levels – provincial, county, and township. In the latter, our chief concern, little structure was provided as the glue of community. At the provincial level Penn contributed to the confusion and uncertainty by not directly engaging in the running of government, except unsuccessfully, for short periods. The land office broke down because he failed to act, while James Logan, the provincial secretary, and other officials lacked sufficient authority to pull together proprietary executive powers. Also, executive members were concerned with their own business, chiefly, it seems, land speculation, although they too had trouble controlling settlement on their lands. The assembly, composed of affluent farmers, and speculators and merchants, at odds with the executive through much of the period,[14] gradually gained power. As a result, a populist landscape was paralleled by a democratization of government but one in which leaders were strongly oriented to the commercialization of land and goods.

At the next scale, the county, a structure emerged chiefly through the action of the assembly. In 1696 the assembly called for the election of assessors by freeholders; in 1711 it appointed commissioners, and in 1722 made the three commissioners elective. The chief role of the county was to raise taxes and keep order, although all were done in a rather low key. The strengthening of counties led to a demand from the back country for the creation of new counties and Penn's sons responded by founding new county towns. Court functions such as registry offices located in these places drew farmers and merchants. The county in Pennsylvania became relatively more important faster than in New England, although the mid-eighteenth century saw its strengthening in the latter as the town weakened.[15]

---

14 Joseph Illick, *Colonial Pennsylvania: A History* (New York 1976), xiv. See also Gary
     B. Nash, *Quakers and Politics: Pennsylvania, 1681-1726* (Princeton 1968).
15 John Murrin, 'Review Essay,' *History and Theory: Studies in the Philosophy of History*
     11 (1972): 256-68

Assembly power lessened executive interest in local government and increased regional or county government, and so the governments of the local townships and urban places were feeble. Rural townships, if named by settlers after their native places for sentimental reasons, were without powers, with the exception of the minor role of justices of the peace and assessors who worked for the county. Assessment rolls were compiled within each township, and for the convenience of the county on an alphabetical basis. No attempt was made to define the location of holdings within townships (so that, incidentally, reconstruction of holdings is a difficult task). This signifies that county officials had little interest in the finer grain of local living. Collecting taxes, even if low, was the crucial job. Unlike New England, where settlers made a valiant attempt to make local government work, despite considerable social cost, Pennsylvanians did not pursue Penn's early advocacy of relatively strong local power. Townships were a convenience for higher-scale jurisdictions.

A second key sign is that of tenure. William Penn sold land; that is the fundamental consideration. Although the Penn family and other large holders acted to a degree as if they were English landed gentry (to the point of calling their vast chunks of land 'manors'), their abiding interest lay in speculation and resale. The leaders were major speculators; the merchant Isaac Norris, for example, by 1713 held over 14,000 acres, and David Lloyd, a major advocate of assembly power, seemed mostly bent on making money on land.[16] And every man's goal was to hold property. Small holders had to look after themselves and their families. Besides, there is no indication that the early Quakers had any intention of holding land communally. Only the Moravians did, and then many members of that group lost their collectivist enthusiasm quickly.

In fact, the legal structure that eventually emerged lost its feudal complications, as fee simple became the clearest and dominant type of holding. Primogeniture, sometimes modified, was used only when a man died intestate. Usually each child received one share, except the eldest son, who inherited two shares. Although tenancy was common – one-third of all rural households in Lancaster and Chester counties and one-third of farming households on the best land of the Lancaster Plain – the goal for most was ownership. Farmers could better accumulate capital for buying good land via tenancy of superior soils than ownership of poorer soils at the time of settlement. Whether owner or tenant,

16 Illick, *Colonial Pennsylvania*, 111; Roy N. Lokken, *David Lloyd: Colonial Lawmaker* (Seattle 1959), 90, 118, 119, 203. Lloyd held perhaps 7000 acres. Also see Robert D. Mitchell, *Commercialism and Frontier: Perspectives on the Early Shenandoah Valley* (Charlottesville 1977). The region is an extension of Pennsylvania in many respects.

the modern system of land holding became the norm, a system in which virtually absolute possessive rights were taken by, and then conferred on, the holder.

The distribution of wealth is the third characteristic suggesting weakness in community ties. According to taxes assessed, differentiation increased throughout the century, at least in Chester County.[17] Whereas in 1693 the upper 10 per cent held 24 per cent of the wealth, by 1800 they had increased their share to 38 per cent. The lower 30 per cent dropped from 17 to 4 per cent. Since taxation generally favours the affluent, these figures likely underestimate the degree to which the rich became richer. Probably the bottom 30 per cent did not lose very much in absolute terms, although that is hard to show since few of the poor left wills or other evidence. Some poor begged on Philadelphia streets,[18] and in Lancaster many worked only at harvest time. Estate inventory valuations indicated that the middle ranks improved their material condition.

The regional patterns show increased differentiation. Assessors perceived variation in soil quality and productivity when determining wealth. The reality of today's Appalachia probably had its origin in some of the few eastern Pennsylvania mountain lands where the poor were left stranded. A society intent upon equalization would not have tolerated the extremes of wealth and poverty that have gradually emerged (except that these extremes were embedded in the social fabric at the outset, when a few received large speculative holdings and many received nothing).

Religion, as seen in denominational pluralism, the difficulties of church leaders, and the individualistic evangelical quality of piety, is another sign of weakness. In many areas denominations overlapped, so that neighbours of English-speaking Anglicans and Presbyterians were German-speaking Lutherans, Reformed, or Mennonites. Although many attitudes towards land and economic activities were shared, traditional theological differences kept people apart, confused those with a long history of regional religious unity, notably in Germany, and made the fixing of parishes impossible. Equally important in this sphere was the problem of leadership. Apart from sectarian groups that

---

17 More recent detailed studies on this matter are Allan Tulley, 'Economic Opportunity in Mid-Eighteenth Century Rural Pennsylvania,' *Histoire sociale/Social History* 9 (1976): 11-28 (and his forthcoming book), and Duane E. Ball, 'Dynamics of Population and Wealth in Eighteenth-Century Chester County, Pennsylvania,' in Jack P. Greene and Pauline Maier, eds., *Interdisciplinary Studies of the American Revolution* (Beverly Hills and London 1976), 85-108. These by and large expand on the view that I present.

18 Gary B. Nash, 'Urban Wealth and Poverty in Pre-Revolutionary America,' in Greene and Maier, *ibid.*, 9-48, deals with Philadelphia.

generated their own leaders, the more conventional churches had trouble. Clergymen sent over from Britain and Germany, expecting deference, found the opposite. The people would not listen to their rules and discipline. Anglican clergy left for Virginia and Maryland, which they imagined to be more amiable. Henry M. Muhlenberg and Michael Schlatter, the 'patriarchs' of the Lutherans and Reformed respectively, found when they arrived in the early 1740s that their members advocated majority rule rather than abide by their authority. In short, Pennsylvania may have been a 'heaven for farmers' and a 'paradise for artisans,' but it was a 'hell' for preachers.[19] Communities, like wider societies, cannot survive without leaders. Pennsylvania society obviously has had trouble with those who did not clearly fit the role of economic success. Church leaders did not.

Much of religion in the United States has stressed individual piety and individual salvation leading to individual immortality. The failure of the church to hold to a view of the 'final day' as collective and earthbound undoubtedly opened the way to privatized religion.[20] The Great Awakening arose in part because George Whitfield came over from England, yet the United States was then and is still particularly fertile ground for enthusiastic individualistic religion providing the comfort of immortality, especially to economically less successful and guilt-ridden businessmen. The emphasis on voluntaristic individual salvation and a weakening of the doctrinal and the organizational could not help but loosen the ties of community. The contradiction within Massachusetts society shows even more clearly than Pennsylvania how the lack of a dialectical relationship among doctrine, organization, and person can result in rigidities without resolution.[21] Preoccupation with salvation paradoxically becomes fixed when it is supposed to be spontaneous. The separation of religious concerns from community parallels the separation of neighbours from one another spatially on their isolated farmsteads.

19 Gottlieb Mittelberger, *Journey to Pennsylvania*, ed. and trans. Oscar Handlin and John L. Clive (Cambridge, Mass. 1960), 48
20 Gregory Baum, *Religion and Alienation: A Theological Reading of Sociology* (New York and Toronto 1975), especially 268-69, argues that the fourteenth-century church and its popes abandoned the vision of an 'entire people' entering 'grace and glory,' a vision held for over a millennium, in favour of the separation of soul and body and the wafting of the former up to heaven upon death. Baum sees this as a change to privatism from collectivism and a powerful impulse towards the modern era.
21 Murrin, 'Review Essay,' 236. Michael Zuckerman, 'The Fabrication of Identity in Early America,' *William and Mary Quarterly*, 3rd Series, 34 (1977): 183-214, in a similar vein to my discussion, although in different terms, argues for a dichotomous society espousing freedom yet conforming.

All the above signs reflect the forces operative in the wider society. A closer look at some of the fundamental conditions giving rise to these characteristics, namely, land, market, and possessive liberalism, will allow us to penetrate the issue more deeply. First, however, we should consider briefly traditional explanations of geographers for visible settlement patterns. Three basic ideas have been put forward: ethnic, topographic, and strategic. Under the first, popular in the late nineteenth century, it was alleged that Celtic peoples lived in dispersed patterns but Teutons inclined towards villages with open fields. Whatever merits such a dichotomy may have had for Europe, and this is questioned by today's scholars,[22] for Pennsylvania the distinction is not relevant. Everyone lived in a dispersed pattern, whether English, German, or Scotch-Irish. According to the landform argument, dispersed patterns occurred in hilly areas and with livestock raising, whereas one was more likely to find clustered villages on plains. Although this view holds some historical truth for Europe, the plains of Pennsylvania (and almost universally in the United States) did not give rise to villages and open fields. Defensive strategy as a factor has also not been particularly relevant. Rather than looking to the Indian uprisings of the 1750s and 1764, as Henry Muhlenberg did to explain the development of new urban places, we should resort chiefly to economic forces.[23] This brief overview suggests that we can reject what were at one time the venerated explanations of geographers.

The land, and how people viewed the land, are key variables. Put more precisely, two interconnected aspects have a bearing: what value people attributed to the land, for use and as a commodity for exchange, and the supply of land, or stated subjectively, how much land people thought was available for them to appropriate.

Today the controllers of resources have reached – some would say over-reached – the limits of environment. Corporate enterprises have generated the priorities that press consumers to use increasingly more of what costs in capital and energy per unit relatively more each year. Resources have come to have exchange value only for producers who are under the compulsion to invent new commodities to raise profits. Plastics from petrochemicals present the clearest examples; the force to create new products means the displacement of goods

---

22 See, for example, Glanville Jones, 'Early Territorial Organization in England and Wales,' *Geografiska Annaler* 43 (1961): 174-81. John B. Frantz, 'The Awakening of Religion among the German Settlers in the Middle Colonies,' *William and Mary Quarterly*, 3rd Series, 33 (1976): 266-8, argues that personal piety actually strengthened German ethnic ties, which in the last analysis would have also weakened community.

23 Muhlenberg, *Journals of Henry M. Muhlenberg* (Philadelphia 1942-58), 2: 391

produced through more labour-intensive work. In agriculture the productive process is so abstracted from nature through chemical fertilizers and machines that land is simply a physical support and an article of exchange. In short, we have come to dominate nature rather than co-operate with it.[24]

The roots of our present difficulties have arisen from attitudes, elucidated by intellectuals,[25] that were generated during the era of Pennsylvania's settlement. In early modern Britain and even in New England attitudes to land were also loosening, as shown in the latter by the almost immediate dispersal of farmsteads.[26] In Pennsylvania land was sought for use, certainly, but the leaders of society were speculators. In this open environment the successful achieved status through land or commerce. To North Americans this may not seem like anything startling, but now when agricultural land has become scarce through larger returns to farmers by means of speculation in urban development, we can see the consequences of our long history of buying and selling land, a game abetted by William Penn and his proprietary colleagues.

The process was aided by the failure of the land office (a consequence of Penn's contradictoriness and inability to act definitively) and of an emerging Quaker élite who often opposed Penn and his executive. The result was the throwing of settlers onto their own resources, so that land was staked out on a first come, first served basis. Everyone was forced to act individualistically, thus reinforcing the view that land was a commodity for exchange. Time and again initial surveys in an area show the perceptiveness of the first to enclose within their survey the best land, even if the cadastre was irregular. The system and then its breakdown fostered a sense of individualism, or, better yet, possessive individualism, a narrow interpretation of ownership. Defined another way, fee simple became freehold, under which tenure was not seen as a set of rights but as absolute control. The development of the idea that property became 'the justification for one's labour' and selling one's labour as a commodity[27] followed from this, although in the United States the latter aspect probably rose to consciousness much later than in Western Europe. Here the presence of new land dominated rather than population pressure, so that few thought of themselves as wage earners. Rather, most saw the land speculator, the pristine entrepreneur, as

24 Commoner, *Poverty of Power*
25 William Leiss, *The Limits to Satisfaction: An Essay on the Problem of Needs and Commodities* (Toronto 1976), 38 (for example, Hobbes and Locke)
26 Bowden and Wood, 'The Fabled Village Green'
27 C.B. MacPherson has used the phrase 'possessive individualism' with considerable power. See, for example, his *Democratic Theory: Essays in Retrieval* (Oxford 1973), especially 199. Also important is the discussion in Polanyi, *Great Transformation*, 72.

the paradigm. Probably, therefore, I should have begun my book with a speculator rather than my rather ordinary farmer, Frederick Brown. My populist feelings were strong then, and like most North Americans I wanted to see the dominant persons as simple and not particularly eager to control man and environment. Probably David Lloyd would have been better as the pace-setter whom Brown and others looked up to, whether conscious of their feelings or not.

The supply of land itself undoubtedly contributed to the depth of feeling. Psychologically, as shown in the engaging movie *The Emigrants* (concerning a Swedish tenant family finding two feet of topsoil in Minnesota), there was enough for every man. Despite the rigours of pioneer life, expectations for improvement were high as people moved on to find ever more fulfilment, or what seemed to be fulfilment. Imagine with Western Europeans, tied into archaic feudal customs or at least rapacious landlords, the powerful feeling of opportunity for absolute control. This psychology is still strongly echoed today in the defence of free enterprise, as if land were still free. Today, of course, the costs are mounting rapidly as corporations attempt to defend the individualism of the early United States in vast conglomerates. Farming itself has become a corporate activity. But earlier the openness of the environment, the supply, was a powerful reinforcing condition for the newly released drives for power that worked against community co-operation, and reduced the consciousness of those who controlled society.

In the eighteenth century land speculation may not have been as potent as in the following century, and the same was true with the control of the market over production. Yet there is little doubt that the penetration of the market into the economy, both local and overseas, contributed to the widening of horizons of farmers and thus increasing dependence upon outside economic forces. Active pursuit of trade by Philadelphia's merchants opened Pennsylvania's produce to the West Indies from the 1690s onward, and throughout the century led to a stress on wheat production. Fortunately for the province it did not quite achieve the dubious distinction of a staple-dependent colony. Livestock slaughtered for ship stores and West Indians encouraged a mixed agriculture. Production for trade was of the same commodities as those needed for domestic use. Dealing in conventional goods rather than the exotic weed, tobacco, undoubtedly prevented Pennsylvania from the social costs of slavery found in Virginia. Yet the prosperity of Pennsylvania did increase dependence upon the outside as imports rose steadily to improve the standard of living — especially for the middlemen of Philadelphia, many of them Quakers. Open commerce reduced community ties by increasing the income gap, by fostering specialization in wheat, and by creating increased dependency upon imports.

The ideology and emotional make-up of the Pennsylvanians and the European context from which they came were crucial. Europe, especially Britain, had been witnessing the quickening of commercialization, as shown in enclosures, the displacement of workers, and the rise of manufacturing in rural areas. From this pattern of change come the migrants – in a sense, self-selected[28] people who exemplified the rising bourgeois spirit, and with a set of mind to think of themselves more strongly as individuals (although certainly religious views and the need for structures, if minimal, balanced this concern somewhat). The arrival of Ben Franklin from more confusing Massachusetts signifies the selection as well as anyone; he was the epitome of the style: secular, pragmatic, analytical, and free enterprising.[29]

The frontier ethos was, as it were, transported across the Atlantic to Pennsylvania rather than being made there, although sustained by a previously unheard-of resource base. The 'new man' of Crevecoeur was individualistic, independent, and self-sufficient, resulting in the illusion of little kingdoms of absolute ownership. Neighbours were cut off from one another, so that distrust and paranoia became marks of these isolated people prone to demagoguery and conformity, and full of self-deception about choices. This was particularly true about religion. In theory the right to choose 'Christ' was a voluntaristic act. In practice, as I can testify from my own experience, it was coerced by demagogues promising only hell if not accepted. The decision was an isolated alienating act leading to cynicism and fatalism. It is the fatalism that we now feel when having to 'choose' a hamburger from McDonald's or Burger King – the fatalism paradoxically reinforced by the constant purveying of the myth of freedom and choice. This is put sharply in the powerful movie *Nashville* through the song 'I ain't free but it don't worry me.' The openness everyone supposedly felt on the frontier has turned into its opposite, an oppressiveness. The lack of care for the environment and for one another in earlier days now has its twisted consequences.

Some may argue that I have ignored Quakers, Mennonites, and other communitarian-minded groups who made up a large share of Pennsylvania's

---

28 Lloyd de Mause, 'The Formation of the American Personality through Psychospecia-tion,' *Journal of Psychohistory* 4 (1976): 7, argues for selection. But Tulley, 'Economic Opportunity,' 117, criticizes my view on this admittedly elusive problem.

29 Illick, *Pennsylvania*, contrasts Penn and Franklin as the model élite persons in early Pennsylvania. Maybe David Lloyd was more clearly the model of practice than Franklin, who rationalized and justified the times.

population. Were they not strong community groups? I have to answer yes and no. As is well known, mutual aid and support within these groups were and are cardinal virtues, as is pacifism. A collectivity of concern was built in from the beginning of Pennsylvania, and in the long run more conservative Mennonite and Amish groups have been able to maintain these qualities. It might be said that they have kept alive, as have other denominations to a degree, the concept of community in the midst of a hostile world.

Yet there is a negative side forcing us to question their representativeness. Basically, members of these groups viewed the rest of society as hostile, and this hostility towards the individualistic society could not help but have bad effects. Within these groups many have found the rigidity and patriarchalism intolerable. Mutual aid and support extract high emotional costs. As John A. Hostetler has pointed out, young Amishmen today find leaving their group an enormous psychological wrench, so much so that suicides are frequent.[30] Then, too, the Quakers' shift to birthright, an accommodation for the children of members, created such an inflexible exclusiveness that others could not penetrate it. This is expressed in the novel *The Story of Kennett*, written by Bayard Taylor in the 1860s about the 1790s, concerning a non-Quaker, fatherless young man wishing to marry a Quaker girl. Despite his high moral character (obviously a necessary virtue), he lacked the proper birth until, as the story inexorably unfolds, his father is established as having been born a Quaker. Even more, not only did he unexpectedly achieve the right birth but he inherited wealth, wealth accumulated through land speculation – another sign of providence. A Quaker, then, had to possess moral character, birthright, and money.

To outsiders the preoccupation with wealth among sectarians has been well noted. Even if rural Quakers worried about the ostentatiousness of Philadelphia's merchants (whose success was partially achieved through slaving), they too, as we have just seen, fell into the same trap of possessiveness. Today Pennsylvanians remark on the frequency with which Amish buggies tie up in front of the banks at Intercourse, New Holland, or wherever in Lancaster County. And while they have admittedly never moved entirely away from the use value of land, their speculative exploits are well known. Indeed, from the outset Quakers were deeply concerned with the exchange value of land. Even today Quakers are considered to drive a hard bargain.

The Mennonite eighteenth-century custom of specifying in wills the precise quantities of wheat, fruit, pasture, and the like to be supplied by sons to widows, while useful for dietary analysis, as I have found, indicates a basic mistrust within the community and a calculating, even commercializing, attitude

---

30 Hostetler, *Amish Society*, rev. ed. (Baltimore and London 1968), 296-300

towards family members. Contracts are used in a market society to compensate for the lack of mutual support. It is curious indeed that the most communal group would resort to such precise calculations. We might expect quite the opposite, with much less worry than in society at large. The fear of neglect of the old – a mark of a society intent on youthful success – must have been a constant fear for Mennonite elders.

The experience of the Moravians of Liitz in Lancaster County is also instructive. Initially, as in Bethlehem, persons lived communally, yet within a generation the community resembled those of the other sectarians. They had dispersed to isolated farms. In Herrenhutt in Germany this did not occur because Count Zinzendorf kept a tight rein on the group.[31] In the midst of a populist United States a clear compromise had to be made for the sake of survival – a compromise that moved them to the buying and selling of land and the family farm as the exclusive basic economic unit. Place and community were thereby weakened.

So, like territorially protective suburbs of today, the sectarians in their places became the bastion of rigid exclusiveness, the contradictory consequence of an open liberal society. Because the underlying processes in individualism permeated the whole of society, these groups became a caricature of community and of place, a distortion, seen particularly in their most conservative expressions: government is totally suspect, others are totally excluded, and the world becomes simply an arena for exploitation. Other people are lost; they are the enemy rather than 'the children of God.'

We might want to say that Massachusetts presented the ideal. Much has been written to show that consensus communitarianism not only did not survive but, while it continued, created extreme tensions within families and many communities, aggressiveness towards those outside the fold, and a repressed hostility to those within.[32] In this negative sense the sectarians achieved in a curious way the clearest expression of what inevitably is the result of a society based on the principle of the free market.

By reference to the concepts of reciprocity, redistribution, and market exchange, described by Karl Polanyi as the dominant modes of social

---

31 Gillian L. Gollin, *Moravians in Two Worlds: A Study of Changing Communities* (New York and London 1967)
32 Kai Erikson, *Wayward Puritans: A Study in the Sociology of Deviance* (New York 1966)

integration,[33] I can sum up. Polanyi argues that over the course of history each concrete situation has stressed one of the three, although sequentially signs of the others have been present. In our case the market exchange was just emerging to reach its purest expression in the England of the 1830s and, of course, in the United States. The seventeenth and eighteenth centuries were the time of the emergence of petty capitalism, of small farmers, merchants, and speculators. It was a time when land became a commodity (if, as Polanyi says, a fictional one). It was not yet the time when labour had clearly become so, although slaves in the United States without rights were a sure harbinger.[34]

The redistributive element in early Pennsylvania society was weak. Needless to say, it was far removed from the ancient kingdoms of Egypt and Mesopotamia, where the redistributive mode probably reached the most pristine form, where a tight hierarchy of kings and/or priests intimidated peasants into giving up their surplus for the glory of the gods. Pennsylvania also did not resemble the clearest present-day expression of a redistributive society, the Soviet Union, with its emphasis on planning by a centralized bureaucracy. Indeed, the province was already removed from redistributive feudalism and even the Toryism of the English gentry. Little redistribution took place in Pennsylvania; taxes were low, the poor were not very visible, and central government was not strong.

It is not primarily the redistributive that I have been discussing in this paper but the weakness of the reciprocal. Local government was minimal, parishes were absent. Voluntary association or Turner's frontier co-operation was present but only minimally sustaining. A purely reciprocal society of which we have very few examples left today is one in which 'as many positions of prestige exist as there are persons available to fill them'[35] and property is held communally. Instead, the family is pretty much on its own land. Place is reduced to isolated farmsteads. Already class contempt was appearing with the categorizing of people into 'better,' 'middling,' or 'poorer sorts,' the 'better' sort referring to those successful in land speculation and mercantile activity, the 'middling' to the solid farmer like Frederick Brown of my book, and the 'poorer' to the sharecroppers, poor craftsmen, and drifters.

The 'hidden hand' of the free market laid its blessing on Pennsylvania. Indeed, then it was a blessing, a release from the oppressiveness of many parts of Europe. Yet now the system has run its course and that hand is laying a curse:

33 *Great Transformation*, especially 67-76
34 See Zuckerman, 'Fabrication,' 201, for the sharp distinction along colour lines.
35 Morton H. Fried, *The Evolution of Political Society: An Essay in Political Anthropology* (New York 1967), 33

the multinationals instead of free homesteaders, limitless consumption instead of work, resource shortages instead of opulence.[36] If the social costs then were greatest where community was forced, then today the situation is reversed. Even so the countervailing forces are present. These seem stronger on the redistributive level apparent in the massive degree of centralization in the multinationals and the federal government. But because the market lives on as the ideal, redistribution of income is negative, biased towards those who have much while contempt is heaped on the poor through the various mechanisms of the 'welfare' state and perpetual high unemployment.

As for reciprocity today, for community and place, the evidence is less clear. The cry of 'power to the neighbourhoods' in the 1960s seems somewhat muted now; for example, residents' groups in Toronto are less sure of themselves than in 1972. Yet the development of neighbourhood services in health and law are indications of strength. Even more so, the appearance of many small-scale housing and food co-operatives bringing people closer to basic economic concerns is certainly the strongest sign. The separation among people and of people from place and land brought on in early Pennsylvania by isolated farmsteads and land speculation is now being tackled by collective action at a local scale. Whether this action will succeed depends largely upon whether energy shortages and the failure of corporations to deliver force us to move together. Up to now North Americans have shown a propensity to believe that the frontier is still as open as it was in early Pennsylvania. The problem of uncontrolled growth is revealing that to us now.

36 James Henretta's 'Families and Farms: *Mentalité* in Pre-Industrial America,' *William and Mary Quarterly*, 3rd Series, 35 (1978), argues against my individualist view in favour of the lineal family. In a future response I will attempt to show that he reduces community to family and by and large ignores the problem of class.

37 Leiss, *Limits to Satisfaction*

The author wishes to thank Christopher Collier, Joe Ernst, William Gilmore, Ken Hewitt, Stan Johannesen, Roy Merrens, John Warkentin, and Michael Zuckerman for their critical reading of earlier versions of the present essay.

JOHN WARKENTIN

Epilogue

What do geographers attempt to accomplish? They hope to provide an understanding of the earth as the place where man lives, and some geographers go on themselves, in one way or another, actively and directly to use their understanding to make the world a better place in which to live. Geography, as F.R. Leavis argues for English literature, has an important dimension as a civilizing subject, and communicates with a very wide range of people.

Most persons who have read these essays form one kind of audience: scholars working in the field of geography. Through them knowledge grows and a discipline is built up through the research articles and monographs that they produce. Yet in the course of their work geographers make connections with disciplines other than their own and with the concerns of the everyday reader. The very nature of their study means that geographers sooner or later address themselves to every man. Recently there have been changes in the subject that also affect that general audience. What is the surface of the earth like? – that was the main question asked in the past. Now geographers increasingly ask: Why is it that way? How can it be altered? This came about because of the quickening pace at which the surface of the earth was altered through the actions of man and because of the new ways in which geographers approached their subject matter. In past ages land tended to change slowly; once major features were in place they remained for generations. Geographical features were described but their origins were often not properly investigated or explained, and little attempt was made to assess changes then in progress. Now geographers look at the forces underlying what they see on the ground: the design of cities, attitudes to landscape, arrangements of communication systems, the quality of housing, areas of poverty, the nature of communities and neighbourhoods, and so on – matters of concern to every person. People, geographers now clearly recognize, change the world.

Some geographers and kindred souls have attempted to work directly in helping shape the world in which man lives by being goads and leaders, administrators, and civil servants. The work of Patrick Geddes, Isaiah Bowman, and, more recently, that of geography graduates employed in governmental planning agencies exemplifies such activities. Yet all humans are involved in creating the environment, and they can be reached and influenced in many ways. In these days of literacy it is possible to broaden and deepen the public's understanding of the earth through articles and books. By reading and thinking about accurate, well-written accounts of the land and how it came to be, citizens' values may change, a sense of stewardship for the environment may be fostered, and new goals and priorities envisaged and their implementation supported through the proper planning of rural areas and cities. In this way geography is a subject of intrinsic importance in civilizing places and making them better habitations for man.

Andrew Clark was concerned about places. It was, of course, important to his career, as Meinig and others have pointed out in these essays, that he lived during a formative era in geography, the era when among other things the subdiscipline of historical geography took new shape. Meinig notes the vital role that Clark played in this development. Through his books and teaching Clark put immense effort into giving historical geography scholarly rigour and interpretive depth. Shining through all of this labour is his intent: to get to know and understand particular areas so that eventually through his writing and teaching others could understand them too. He worked, as we well know, in the scholarly tradition of addressing fellow scholars on the historical geography of particular areas, using methods such as investigating the transfer of cultures to newly settled lands and analysing what ensued. But something always happened to Clark as he worked on these lands. In analysing and presenting his material he did not tend to define a precise problem, study it, and build an argument to solve the problem. Rather, his approach was broader; it was regional. Deliberately, particularly when he took pen in hand, Clark would provide a full account of what the land was like, how man made it habitable, and how he fared in it.

Specialists on regions described and analysed by Clark will turn to his publications for years to come. So will the people who live in them; the thorough exposition of local geographical relationships means that Clark's work holds great value for local people. Only last week in London, England, where I am writing, a sociologist from New Zealand told me how much he had learned from Clark's book on South Island. Clark was very much aware of this wider audience. He was deeply concerned and complained vehemently that his book on Prince Edward Island was not properly distributed on the island itself. The book, he quite rightly assumed, although he did not use these very words, would be life-enhancing for the folk who lived in the land described.

Clark had a great and abiding affection for both his Islanders and his students. Working with graduate students was a joy to him, and he took a deep pride in their accomplishments. He was pleased to see them spread outwards, both in where they taught and in their interests. From the essays in this volume it is apparent how the students represented here have done research on many topics that go well beyond what Clark was doing. That is natural. Yet if one thought that these topics were outside his areas of informed concern one would be denying – at one's immediate peril were he still here to speak – Clark's omnivorous interest in all fields of geography. In fact, of course, most of the essays here contribute to our understanding of the geography of North America, a fact that would have delighted Clark because his research centred on that continent.

The essays fall into straightforward themes. Harris and Gibson examine broadly the experiences of the French and Russians in the settlement and exploitation of North America, Mitchell studies cultural regions, and Hilliard and Ray analyse some problems in economic geography. Themes in cultural and social geography, involving acculturation, urban images, and community are examined by McQuillan, Ward, and Lemon. Clark would have loved to get his teeth into each of these pieces. I do not mean to offend the essayists when I say that each essay would be different and improved had it been exposed to his copious and incisive criticism. I say this from my own experience. Well do I recall a letter that I received from Clark after I had not written to him for some time in which he hoped that my silence was not due to any offence that he might have caused in tearing something of mine apart. It was not; I always appreciated and benefited from his suggestions for improvement. Clark as an editor, in fact, participated in a project along with one, occasionally getting so carried away in his alternatives and speculations that one felt one had to pull *him* back into the theme of the manuscript.

My purpose here is not to summarize or review what has gone before in this volume. Taking the essays as points of departure I mean to remark on the state of historical geographical scholarship in North America, viewing it in the context of how it relates to work in other fields and considering what might be done to continue to advance our understanding of North America.

The essays are very much in the Clark tradition of examining change through time. It is wise, I know, to recognize that historical geographers use vertical or horizontal approaches in analysing their material and topics and to distinguish them carefully. Clark performed a necessary function for debate and growth in the discipline by stressing the value of vertical analysis, but I think too much can be made of the limitations of horizontal analysis in historical geography and not enough of its assets. Clark, of course, made effective use of the cross-section in his own work, particularly in *Three Centuries and the Island.* The cross-section, in my view, has been too harshly treated. It is often forgotten that it, too, is dynamic, dynamic in showing spatial relations that can be lost in the vertical approach if a geographer is not careful. In getting the most out of a horizontal or a vertical approach a great deal depends upon the geographer's mode of analysis and style of presentation. For instance, in H.C. Darby's *A New Historical Geography of England* Peter Hall's cross-section of *circa* 1900 has just as much dynamism, analysis, and explanation of relationships as J.T. Coppock's vertical treatment of the period 1850-*circa* 1900. There is a danger that geographers will ignore essential spatial relationships if they persist in looking at change through time alone. A constant placing of geographical phenomena into a dynamic spatial context is necessary because these interactions give a world-wide territorial perspective to geography.

There is little overarching theory in these essays (although Mitchell queries some conceptualizations and advances one), and I do not find this surprising. Theory in geography should not be dragged in, nor should it be eschewed; rather, it should be sought for and used where it can advance understanding. That takes discretion. Geographical reality is so complex that it resists easy theorizing; no theory will encompass very much of that reality. Although appropriate applications of theory are worthwhile, the fact is that the need for good, accurate, qualitative description and explication continues, drawing upon shaping processes and offering insights into forces that have created geographical patterns. And, of course, generalization is always vital. The important thing is that data and ideas must stand up to the test of scholarly scrutiny.

In recent years there has been a forced reassessment of what the social sciences can do to change and, one hopes, improve living conditions and society. The social sciences have had limited success in helping solve broad social problems, thanks to the inherent complexity of human affairs, and the fact that human values and aspirations change. As social scientists, with more and more chagrin, have finally become aware of this, they have also begun to realize that one of the most effective ways to help make a better society is to provide people with accurate information relevant to their concerns — containing as much understanding and interpretation as possible — then listen and respond to the reactions of those people and assist in bringing about desired changes. Because of the nature of our discipline, which is concerned with the total environment, geographers should be in the forefront of supplying basic information and interpretations to people, and responsive to the new processes of social change that are going on. In these essays there is much pertinent discussion leading to a deeper understanding of North American social development, and Lemon, of course, who ostensibly deals with colonial Pennsylvania, is writing as well about social reality today and tomorrow everywhere on the continent.

In a sense the historical geographers writing here are not enmeshed in theory nor cushioned by it, but pierce directly into process and the complexities of human society. This entails the direct confrontation and handling of immense amounts of diverse source materials.

Clark's teachings on the need for documentation and making certain that source material is adequate, appropriate, and accurate for studying a topic in historical geography can almost be viewed as a means of defining a place for historical geography within geography. Geographers from many fields delve into historical geography in doing their own researches, be they economic geographers, urban geographers, or any other kind of specialist in a systematic field. Usually this is just an occasional joyous foray to gain a deeper and more illuminating perspective on their particular main interests in current geography. Historical geographers cannot be so selective. It is essential that they be thoroughly imbued with the scholarly knowledge on the place and the era in which they specialize: its society, culture, industry, commerce, values, aspirations, prejudices, attitudes to landscape, architecture, literature, and art. This may sound pretentious and demanding but there is no short-cut to understanding, no room for false modesty, and no deviation from striving for the highest standards. By these means historical geographers will avoid imposing crude Whiggish interpretations of geography on a place and an era. But this still only achieves an appreciation of the geography of the place based upon what it was at a particular time. The restricted cross-section is not enough. It must be illuminated through knowing what went before and what came after, and that is why in historical geography as in history the perspective of time is required, and the thoughts of many scholars on what a place and an era actually were like must be sought.

Cumulative scholarship is a correcting mechanism in any scholarly field, bringing alternative hypotheses to bear on a topic and exposing different viewpoints. Historical geography in North America is still too young to possess a significant body of literature on any one topic. The problems examined are highly diverse. And the historical geographical regional works are so selective in what they cover out of the total source material available that they really are works of art — none the less true for that, it must be emphasized — but they do not lend themselves to scholarly comparisons. A few areas are only now beginning to get enough attention from historical geographers and others so that scholars benefit from exposure to many approaches and to informed criticism. A body of literature on the interpretation of the Great Plains environment is developing, material is accumulating on the settlement of Newfoundland, and there is much research on New France, as Harris's essay shows. The example of New France is particularly revealing. The need for historiography, the need to keep on testing and endeavouring to prove one's own work and that of others right or wrong, increases as scholars probe deeper for explanation. As new data are found in archives and analysed, and as new explanatory hypotheses are formulated, new interpretations and reinterpretations of New France unfold, the result of work done by scholars from a number of disciplines, including historical geography.

Research in historical geography will prosper in association with other disciplines. Certain fundamental problems badly need the basic research and imaginative insight of many scholars from a variety of fields. The significance of class and community in the historical geography of North America, alluded to by both Ward and Lemon, is an example. I hope that many first-rate scholars from diverse disciplines will converge on this topic and open up a productive dialogue, although heaven forbid that one massively financed research group should be loosened on this comprehensive sort of problem; I have much more confidence in the results of the cut and thrust of many scholars from diverse disciplines. It just takes time.

One of the most famous chapters in the scholarly study of Canada, certainly the most seminal, is the conclusion of Harold Innis's *The Fur Trade in Canada*, first published in 1930. Innis starts that chapter: 'Fundamentally the civilization of North America is the civilization of Europe and the interest of this volume is primarily in the effects of a vast new land area on European civilization.'[1] Meinig has told us how Innis was Clark's mentor at the University of Toronto (or 'Varsity,' as Clark fondly liked to call it) and Clark's empirical approach is reminiscent of Innis. Clark, however, investigated 'What happens in the New World to an Old World people' very much with a geographer's cast of mind, and he was deeply concerned with the full geographical experience that people have in a new environment. As people migrate from place to place within the North American continent and settle and develop new areas, similar broad questions arise. Harris, Mitchell, and Gibson examine such fundamental themes with the same breadth of approach as Clark.

---

1 Innis, *The Fur Trade in Canada: An Introduction to Canadian Economic History* (New Haven 1939), 386

Harris investigates the experience of a European people in the New World who had both settlement and mercantile objectives. In New France the settlement process was not the acculturation of a small group into an existing larger society but the creation of a new society. The French settlers were affected by the native Indians, but much more, as Harris demonstrates, by the transformation of their culture by extremely potent new environmental circumstances and the strengthening of the role of the nuclear family unit on the land for at least the first century of settlement. We see here a concern for social aspects that have not normally entered into broad geographical syntheses, common as they are in sociological studies. It is a good example of a new but vital factor being made a central part of a geographical study, and it makes other geographers take notice.

Mitchell examines what happens to cultural groups, such as Harris described, when they move into new areas in the continent, although he puts the question in such a form that he actually examines the ways in which cultural regions are created. His essay on cultural regions is a study of cultural processes deliberately viewed and analysed at a continental scale. Here we see the full complexity in historical and cultural geography that confronts anyone who tries to sort out how cultural regions are produced in large, previously unsettled areas. This is a revisionist study, demonstrating that the processes producing geographical change are much more complex than is sometimes thought and that great care must be taken in generalizing about cultural regions. It is very evident that a scholar cannot permit any break in either space or time in tracing what happens as new cultural regions emerge, lest essential local or national forces and transitional stages are overlooked. Mitchell provides a useful and cautionary perspective for scholars working out explanations of cultural origins in particular regions within North America.

Gibson in his study of Russian America is not concerned with cultural change within rural societies but with the New World experiences of a European commercial enterprise working through outposts and native peoples and taking away selected valuable local resources. The total Russian experience takes precedence in this study of physical and human encounters in the New World. In its very comprehensiveness of approach this is similar to Clark's work. But it differs in that Clark invariably attempted a geographical synthesis of a region in his book-length studies, and Gibson presents us with a geographical synthesis within the broad conceptual theme of resource exploitation. In analysing this theme overseas connections and local geographical conditions are very carefully interwoven.

Any reader of Clark is made to realize that the importance of local geographical conditions must never be forgotten, and that the physical environment must enter strongly into any appraisal of the settlement of North America. Clark's students are making numerous and considerable contributions to our knowledge of the geography of the colonial period of eastern North America from New France to New Spain. Much European exploitation consisted of people moving into middle-latitude North American lands. These lands, once they were cleared, were similar in many respects to those of Europe. Settlement was a matter of chopping trees and then establishing farms, using a known and appropriate agricultural technology. The study of this process is a classic theme in geography. In some areas, however, as in the region studied by Hilliard, man had to be innovative in appraising and utilizing a particular site and make heavy investments in improving land and managing water before agricultural production became possible. It is the intimate associations with the land, the field patterns, annual round of farm operations, and labour problems to which Hilliard gives particular attention.

Associations between man and the physical environment tended to be overlooked in geographical studies for many years. It is a complex and frustrating field to research at a sophisticated level because of the difficulty in determining how people in the past actually did regard and evaluate the physical environment. This problem is receiving more and more attention from historical geographers, but often the research is done, or at least presented, at a broad regional perspective rather than at the scale of detailed local impressions and appraisals of farmers who actually worked the land. Sources will be difficult to find, and will have to be very carefully interpreted, but it is at the local level that scholars should place more effort.

Mitchell does discuss and illustrate how landscape artifacts can be used in analysing cultural regions, but I want to draw attention to one aspect of the transformation of the land not covered in detail in these essays: the rural and urban landscape and the values and attitudes which underlie their creation. Much historical geographical research is needed on the patterns and origins of fields, woods, farmsteads, roads, fences, and styles of buildings in the countryside; on the streets, open spaces, trees, residential buildings, and service and industrial areas in towns and cities; and on recreational areas and wilderness. Links must be made with scholars in the humanities, with literary historians interested in attitudes to nature and wilderness, with art and architectural historians, and also with town and regional planners, and scholars concerned with recreation. The total landscape – wilderness, rural, and urban – and the quality of the environment, and man's reaction to it, need intensive research and imaginative thinking from the perspective of historical geography. Many people, regrettably, do not even realize that there is a landscape and land with people to be studied and understood and changed. More attention must be given to poverty and prosperity, the closing of resources, and the physical, economic, and social conditions in which man lives. Patrick Geddes and Benton Mackaye have shown geographers ways to relate man and environment.

Perhaps in no area in geography are changes taking place more quickly than in social and cultural geography. In Clark's *South Island* the links with anthropology were present but those with sociology were less well developed. An advance of great importance is the increasing awareness of the significance of the ideas of social sciences such as sociology in studying the kinds of problems historical geographers are investigating. The theme of man and the land must stay with us as a subject for study, but it is important as well that we begin to look in more sophisticated ways at man in society. Ray, McQuillan, Ward, and Lemon do this.

Although Ray focuses his essay on a problem in economic geography, it is readily apparent that by studying closely the trading transactions of Indian and fur trader he is able to illuminate much of what went on in the acculturation process between Indians and Europeans. Now, finally, through this sort of painstaking research we are beginning to see some of the economic and cultural processes of the vital contact period at work and thus gaining a fuller understanding of what happened. Ray amply demonstrates how Clark's emphasis on archival research pays rich dividends. His investigation is based upon a close analysis of documents in a magnificent archive on the early exploitation of North America by Europeans, the documents of the Hudson's Bay Company, now housed in Winnipeg. This archive holds material on the economic geography and social geography of northern North America that will keep researchers busy for years to come, and we can expect to see great progress in these areas of research in historical geography. Ray's essay, too, is a good example of the revisionist work that Clark always encouraged. In this instance the interpretations of two economic historians are being challenged, demonstrating the cross-disciplinary dialogue that I was discussing earlier.

McQuillan specifically is concerned with a problem in acculturation, focusing on the process itself and exploring it in analytical and classificatory fashion. He adopts the abstractions of the social sciences to throw light on a process that is of geographical interest, recognizing at the end of his essay the need for a fuller approach at a further stage of research to take account of the value systems involved in acculturation. As he points out, the functioning of communities and the expressed aspiration of people will have to be studied. These are neglected but vital areas of investigation in historical geography that will be of increasing importance as the phenomenon of culture undisguised enters ever more strongly into our historical geographical consciousness and research endeavours. We shall have to turn to the ideas of scholars in the humanities as well as in the social sciences to properly appreciate the kinds of life created by different groups in North America.

In parts of their studies Hilliard and Ray are concerned with blacks and Indians, respectively, peoples who for many years have been largely ignored by geographers. This is another area where research is needed, and historical geographers can contribute usefully, but it will be essential to take full account of the work done by scholars in other disciplines. Studies of the historical geography of blacks and Indians are worth doing in themselves, not as segments of other studies, and salutary beginnings have been made.

On the whole, Clark and his students have preferred to deal with the land itself rather than with how the land was perceived. There are exceptions, such as work done some years ago by Roy Merrens. Ward's essay in this volume is a perception study — not of the image of a distinctive environment but of the Victorian American city. A heartening aspect of the last generation of scholarly work in the social sciences has been the beginning of the thorough study of the city. Historical geographers are entering this field strongly. Scholars from many different disciplines are contributing, and Ward in this essay is himself working across the bounds of geography, sociology, history, and social and political thought, providing, furthermore, in his references examples of the close interaction across disciplines characteristic of the field of Victorian studies. Ward reveals some of the new concerns scholars have. Quality of housing, class differences, planning, and the ideological bases that motivate reforms are matters which underlie this study.

North American land promoters produced distorted idyllic images of the places to which they hoped to attract settlers; reformers in pursuing their social goals also failed to take account of local geographical realities and projected inappropriate images of what cities were like, tending to equate conditions in British cities with those in American cities. Possibly the reformers were taken in themselves. A failure to consider sufficiently local physical and human geographical conditions is endemic in much architectural practice and social and landscape planning. Self-defined stereotypes, not what exists, have been fought by ardent reformers; and too often people have not been given what they needed or desired but what was thought to be good for them. Frequently we are still tied up in stereotypes today as we try to cope with modern social problems. Ward's essay is not only an examination of the image of Victorian cities but a morality tale for today: we should turn sceptical and critical eyes on ourselves to see how dispassionately we view our own social geography.

A few geographers are now reversing things. First they try to understand society; then and only then do they relate problems of the land to that society. In studying social and cultural geography there has been a move in scale from large groups to community and neighbourhood groups. Harris, we saw, even looked at the family unit. Lemon's concern is with the relations of individuals within communities rather than with the relation of individuals to the land, while recognizing that community and place are associated. Conscious organization in communities to attain community goals within overriding wider societies and various social systems lies behind Lemon's thinking. He ranges freely in time, applying insights derived from the past to the present, and those from the present to the past. In doing so he is more geographical than historical, using those two terms in a strictly disciplinary sense. The work of historical geographers can give insight into contemporary problems, and Lemon does not hesitate to comment on present circumstances. Certainly he is academically interested in community but he also wants to reform society to permit community to survive. Here we enter the realm of the socially concerned academic. In many ways Lemon is the Patrick Geddes of the students taught by Clark. Geddes in his book on Dunfermline beautifully demonstrated his aim of producing a different world, stating that 'Social science is thus no mere abstract study, apart from practical problems such as those which have been before us; it arises from active life, and it returns thither with fresh suggestiveness, new invention.'[2] The important thing is that the geographer who does get involved in active reform must be aware of his own intentions and biases and so must his reader. Then let him have his say, and argue his case as well as he may. There is no doubt, for instance, where Lemon stands. Such explicitness is more useful than any hedging or surreptitious slipping in of a point of view.

In these essays one readily sees that Clark's students absorbed his basic teachings on methodology and on reaching out to other disciplines. Now they are going their own ways, well beyond their teacher, as capable students should. Yet there is a potent centripetal force which was at the centre of Clark's work and which also is a cohesive element in the research activities of the students represented here. That unifying element is the endeavour to understand how places on the earth's surface change and yet not lose sight of the individuality of a place.

Where does all this research activity lead? In the physical sciences it is often stressed that scholars must pursue their researches freely. Although T.S. Kuhn has shaken our faith in this ideal of objectivity, it still seems that the search for knowledge is justification in itself, that no one knows what practical technological applications may be made at some future time, be they beneficial or detrimental. Yet one trusts that physical scientists have a responsible approach to the world, and appreciate it as a complex interrelated system as geographers do. In the humanities the hope is that scholarly research and critical thinking will deepen our understanding of the thought, aspirations, and values of man, and of his greatest achievements in the arts.

2 Geddes, *City Development: A Study of Parks, Gardens, and Culture-Institutes, A Report to the Carnegie Dunfermline Trust* (Edinburgh 1904), 221

In historical geography we try to do something of both. We produce many sharply delimited pieces of research, which in most instances are of interest to only a few other scholars – knowledge seemingly for its own sake. Yet the topics studied are not as accidental as they sometimes appear. Prescribing guidance in geography is as constrictive and pernicious as in the physical sciences, but one can at least suggest that research should be related to significant processes that shape the earth's surface. In that way research is not narrowly antiquarian or precious. If the researcher has a grasp of the discipline of geography as a whole, as well as of his specific field, then the topics studied normally will relate constructively to the work of others, be cumulative, and contribute to the formulation of generalizations or to the verification of existing generalizations, and to theorizing. This leads to synthesis and a wider understanding and explanation of the character of the surface of the earth.

Historical geographers can also strive much more directly for another kind of synthesis and understanding by drawing on the substance, methods, and approaches of the humanities and the arts. To pursue this we must look at the relationship of historical geography to regional geographical writing. Meinig has already discussed Clark's interest in regional geography. Although there are exceptions, for years regional writing on North America by geographers has tended to be niggardly, and largely relegated to textbooks. Some texts do come alive because they are more than inventory and classification. There is more insight and stimulation in J. Russell Smith's and Griffith Taylor's old texts than in many later books because of the insatiable curiosity, insight, ability to see relationships, impishness, and sheer generalizing nerve of these men. With their perspective on space and time and emphasis on the forces that create an area, historical geographers have a great deal of leaven and insight to contribute to regional writing. The finer regional monographs have always revealed good understanding of the past and an artistic ability to incorporate this effectively into analysis and synthesis.

Meinig has indicated how Clark increasingly regarded his major historical geographical studies as regional interpretations, and he has illuminated Clark's approach in drawing a distinction between 'geographical change' and 'changing geographies.' I agree that Clark's last two books were essentially regional interpretations on historical geographical lines, and I would dearly have liked to have seen more. I have long felt that Carl Sauer could have given us a fine regional monograph on the American Middle West and Clark on Atlantic Canada as both regions developed in the nineteenth and twentieth centuries, and I very much regret that neither lived to do so. We can be grateful that the practice of historical geographers writing regional monographs on parts of North America has been well and worthily exemplified by Clark and by Meinig. Significantly, Clark himself continued to point the way – and to consolidate it – in the series of historical geographical monographs on North America that he was editing for Oxford University Press (now called the Andrew H. Clark Series in the Historical Geography of North America).

A good historical geographer has to be at scholarly peace with the region and era he studies, with his sources, and with his methodology. If the resulting ideas are presented with clarity and style, readers will find his work interesting, convincing, and worthwhile. This brings me back to what I started with — the fact that a geographer has a wide audience if he only knows it. The underlying motif of Clark's work, I have always felt, is to provide an interpretation in the round of a selected part of the earth on which man lives, and he accomplished this in his books and his regional essays. Not only scholars but general readers learn from Clark, and I want to end with the latter because they can be vital in democracies in bringing about geographical change. An effective way to assist people to live in closer harmony with their region and with their neighbours in the world is to assist them by means of good regional books to know their own regions better and through this, to a degree, even themselves. Then they can participate more wisely as citizens in attempting to change their region in ways that they think are right. Geography is indeed a civilizing subject.

Andrew Hill Clark and his work

Andrew Clark was born in 1911 in Manitoba, the son of a Baptist medical missionary. Following his graduation from McMaster University in 1930, he worked as an actuary in Toronto during the Depression before undertaking graduate work at the University of Toronto. Here he came under the lasting influence of Griffith Taylor and Harold Innis. In 1938 Clark went to the University of California at Berkeley to take a degree under Carl Sauer; his dissertation on New Zealand later became his first book. During the Second World War he served as a geographer with the United States Department of State; it was then that he acquired American citizenship. After five years at Rutgers University, where he attained the rank of professor, Clark moved in 1951 to the University of Wisconsin at Madison. Here he did the bulk of his teaching and research, supervising nineteen dissertations (eleven of which have been published) and writing two books and numerous articles, addresses, forewords, and reviews. Largely through his efforts, historical geography in North America came not only to thrive but also to win the respect of geographers and historians alike. He died of cancer in 1975 at the age of sixty-four, leaving his wife, Louise, three sons, and a daughter.

AWARDS AND HONOURS

1930   BA, McMaster University

1938   MA, University of Toronto

1944   PhD, University of California at Berkeley

1945   United States citizenship

1953-4 University of London Lectureship in Geography

1957-61 Editorship of American Association of Geographers Monograph Series

1961   Brittingham Research Professorship, University of Wisconsin

1961-2 Honorary president of the American Association of Geographers
Fulbright Research Scholarship

1962   John Simon Guggenheim Memorial Fellowship
Social Science Research Council Fellowship

1964   Chairman of Section VI of 20th International Geographical Congress

1966   George MacDonald Lectureship, McGill University

1966-75 Vernor Clifford Finch Research Professorship in Geography, University
of Wisconsin

1967   Erskine Fellowship, Canterbury University

1969   American Historical Association Beveridge Citation for *Acadia*

1971-2 British Petroleum Fellowship in American Studies, University of
Dundee, Scotland

1971-5 General editorship of Oxford University Press' Historical Geography of
North America Series (now the Andrew H. Clark Series in the Historical
Geography of North America)

1974   Canadian Association of Geographers Award for Scholarly Distinction
in Geography
Visiting professorship at Hebrew University of Jerusalem

1975   Co-editorship of the *Journal of Historical Geography*
Honorary fellowship in American Geographical Society
Honorary degree from Brandon University (posthumous)

1975-6 Claude Bissell Professorship in Canadian and American Studies,
University of Toronto (unfulfilled)

PUBLICATIONS

1942   'Prince Edward Island.' *International Journal* 6: 33-5
1944   'The South Island of New Zealand: A Geographic Study of the Intro-
       duction and Modification of British Rural Patterns and Practices
       Associated with the Exotic Plants and Animals of the Island.'
       PhD dissertation, University of California at Berkeley
1945   'The Historical Explanation of Land Use in New Zealand.' *Journal of
       Economic History* 5: 215-30
1946   'Field Research in Historical Geography.' *Professional Geographer*
       (Old Series) 4: 13-22
1947   'Physical and Cultural Geography.' In *New Zealand*, edited by
       H. Belshaw, pp. 20-47. Berkeley: University of California Press
       'Climatic and Edaphic Anomalies in the Pre-European Grassland of
       South Island, New Zealand.' *Annals of the Association of American
       Geographers* 37: 52-3 (abstract of a paper given at the forty-third
       annual meeting, Columbus, December 1946)
       'South Island, New Zealand and Prince Edward Island, Canada: A
       Study of Insularity.' *New Zealand Geographer* 3: 137-50
1948   'Legend and Fact in Historical Geography: An Illustration from Nova
       Scotia.' *Annals of the Association of American Geographers* 38: 85-6
       (abstract of a paper given at the forty-fourth annual meeting, Charlottes-
       ville, December 1947)
1949   Review of H.F. von Haast, *The Life and Times of Sir Julius von Haast.
       Geographical Review* 39: 510
       *The Invasion of New Zealand by People, Plants and Animals: The South
       Island.* New Brunswick, NJ: Rutgers University Press
1950   'Contributions to the Geographical Knowledge of Canada since 1945.'
       Geographical Review 40: 285-308
1953   'Ralph Brown's Beitrag zur Amerikanischen Historischen Geographie.'
       Die Erde 5: 148-52
       'Geographers Are Where You Find Them: Titus Smith of Nova Scotia,
       1768-1850.' *Annals of the Association of American Geographers* 43:
       161 (abstract of a paper given at the forty-ninth annual meeting,
       Cleveland, April 1953)
       Obituary of Harold A. Innis. *Geographical Review* 43: 282-3
       Review of H.A. Innis, *The Bias of Communications* and *Empire of
       Communications. Geographical Review* 43: 140-2
1954   'Careers for Geographers in Higher Education.' *Professional Geographer*
       (New Series) 6: 19-28

'Titus Smith Junior and the Geography of Nova Scotia in 1801 and 1802.' *Annals of the Association of American Geographers* 44: 291-314

'Historical Geography.' In *American Geography: Inventory & Prospect,* edited by P.E. James and C.F. Jones, pp. 70-105. Syracuse: Syracuse University Press

1955 'The Social Sciences in Historical Study.' *Professional Geographer* (New Series) 7: 34-5

1956 'The Impact of Exotic Invasion on the Remaining New World Mid-latitude Grasslands.' In *Man's Role in Changing the Face of the Earth,* edited by W.L. Thomas, Jr., pp. 737-62. Chicago: University of Chicago Press

'Use of a "Control Area" to Test Hypotheses in Broader Regional Studies.' *Annals of the Association of American Geographers* 46: 241 (abstract of a paper given at the fifty-second annual meeting, Montreal, April 1956)

'Canada and Australia: A Comparison.' *Geographical Review* 46: 421-3

Review of K.B. Cumberland, *South-West Pacific. Geographical Review* 46: 294

1958 'Changing Geographies of Cultural Origins and Religious Preferences in Nova Scotia.' *Annals of the Association of American Geographers* 48: 256 (abstract of a paper given at the fifty-fourth annual meeting, Los Angeles, August 1958)

1959 Editor of R. Hartshorne, *Perspective on the Nature of Geography.* Association of American Geographers Monograph Series, Number 1. Chicago: Rand McNally

Review of G. Taylor, *Journeyman Taylor. Geographical Review* 49: 599 *Three Centuries and the Island: A Historical Geography of Settlement and Agriculture in Prince Edward Island, Canada.* Toronto: University of Toronto Press

1960 'Old World Origins and Religious Adherence in Nova Scotia.' *Geographical Review* 50: 317-44

'Geographical Change – A Theme for Economic History.' *Journal of Economic History* 20: 607-16

Review of K.B. Cumberland and J.W. Fox, *New Zealand. Geographical Review* 50: 292

1962 'Geographical Diversity and the Personality of Canada.' In *Land and Livelihood: Geographical Essays in Honour of George Jobberns,* edited by M. McCaskill, pp. 23-47. Christchurch: New Zealand Geographical Society

Editor of D.W. Meinig, *On the Margins of the Good Earth.* Association

of American Geographers Monograph Series, Number 2. Chicago:
Rand McNally

'Land Use Pattern.' In *Great Lakes Basin*, edited by H.J. Pincus,
pp. 141-55 (with E.R. Officer)

'*Praemia Geographiae:* The Incidental Rewards of a Professional Career.'
Annals of the Association of American Geographers 52: 229-41

'The Sheep/Swine Ratio as a Guide to a Century of Change in the
Livestock Geography of Nova Scotia.' *Economic Geography* 38: 38-55

1963   Editor of L.M. Alexander, *Offshore Geography of Northwest Europe.*
Association of American Geographers Monograph Series, Number 3.
Chicago: Rand McNally

'Honing the Edge of Curiosity: The Challenge of Historical Geography
in Canada.' In *Occasional Papers in Geography*, no 4, edited by Walter
G. Hardwick and John D. Chapman, pp. 1-10. Vancouver: British
Columbia Division of the Canadian Association of Geographers

1964   'The Scanty Legacy of the French Occupation of Cape Breton Island.'
In 20th International Geographical Congress, *Abstracts of Papers*,
edited by F.E. Hamilton, pp. 262-3. London: Thomas Nelson & Sons

'Coordinates of Historical Geography.' *Annals of the Association of
American Geographers* 54: 417 (title of a paper given at the plenary
session of the sixtieth annual meeting, Syracuse, April 1964)

Review of A. Grenfell Price, *Western Invasion of the Pacific and Its
Continents. Geographical Review* 54: 291

1965   Review of Tryggvi J. Oleson, *Early Voyages and Northern Approaches.
Geographical Review* 55: 618-20

'New England's Role in the Underdevelopment of Cape Breton Island
during the French Regime, 1713-1785.' *Canadian Geographer* 9: 1-12

Review of N.C. Pollock and Swanzie Agnew, *An Historical Geography
of South Africa. Geographical Review* 55: 133

1966   Editor of (with Foreword and Notes) Isabella Lucy Bird, *The Englishwoman in America.* Madison: University of Wisconsin Press (first
published by John Murray: London 1854)

'Acadia and the Acadians: The Creation of a Geographical Entity.' In
Frontiers and Men, edited by J. Andrews, pp. 90-119. Melbourne:
F.W. Cheshire

1967   'The Three Worlds of the Canadian.' *Annals of the Association of
American Geographers* 57: 168 (title of a paper given at the plenary
session of the sixty-second annual meeting, Toronto,
August 1966)

1968   'The Roots of Canada's Geography.' In *Canada: A Geographical*

Interpretation, edited by J. Warkentin, pp. 13-53. Toronto: Methuen (with D.Q. Innis)

Acadia: The Geography of Early Nova Scotia to 1760. Madison: University of Wisconsin Press

'What Geographers Did.' Review of T.W. Freeman, *The Geographer's Craft. Economic Geography* 44: 83-6

1969 'The Strategy and Ecology of Man's Occupation of the Intermontane Northwest.' Review of D.W. Meinig, *The Great Columbia Plain. Pacific Northwest Quarterly* 60: 98-102

'Historical and Geographical Perspectives.' In *One Prairie Province? A Question for Canada*, edited by David K. Elton, pp. 325-36. Lethbridge: University of Lethbridge and *Lethbridge Herald*

1971 Editor of (with Foreword) D.W. Meinig, *Southwest: Three Peoples in Geographical Change*. New York: Oxford University Press

'The Canadian Habitat.' In *Man and His Habitat*, edited by R.H. Buchanan, Emrys Jones, and Desmond McCourt, pp. 218-46. London: Routledge and Kegan Paul

Editor of (with Foreword) D. Ward, *Cities and Immigrants: A Geography of Change in Nineteenth Century America*. New York: Oxford University Press

1972 'Some Suggestions for the Geographical Study of Agricultural Change in the United States, 1790-1840.' *Agricultural History* 46: 155-72

'Contributions of Its Southern Neighbours to the Underdevelopment of the Maritime Provinces Area of Present Canada, 1710-1867.' In *The Influence of the United States on Canadian Development*, edited by R.A. Preston, pp. 164-84. Durham: Duke University Press

'Historical Geography in North America.' In *Progress in Historical Geography*, edited by A.R.H. Baker, pp. 129-43. Newton Abbot: David and Charles

'Acadian Heritage in Maritime "New France." ' *Geographical Magazine* 45: 219-27

1974 Editor of (with Foreword) R. Cole Harris and J. Warkentin, *Canada before Confederation: A Study in Historical Geography*. Toronto, London, and New York: Oxford University Press

1975 'First Things First.' In *Pattern and Process: Research in Historical Geography*, edited by R.E. Ehrenberg, pp. 9-21. Washington, DC: Howard University Press

Editor of (with Foreword) D.R. McManis, *Colonial New England: A Historical Geography*. New York: Oxford University Press

'The Great Plains: Perception by Any Name.' Foreword to *Images of the Plains*, edited by Brian W. Blouet and Merlin P. Lawson, pp. ix-xiv. Lincoln: University of Nebraska Press

'The Conceptions of "Empires" of the St. Lawrence and the Mississippi.' *American Review of Canadian Studies* 5: 4-27

1976   'The Look of Canada.' *Historical Geography Newsletter* 6: 59-68

DOCTORAL DISSERTATIONS SUPERVISED AT THE UNIVERSITY OF WISCONSIN-MADISON

1959   A. Philip Muntz, 'The Changing Geography of the New Jersey Woodlands, 1600-1900'

1960   Stephen L. Stover, 'The Changing Regionalization of Sheep Husbandry in Ohio'

1962   H. Roy Merrens, 'The Changing Geography of the Colony of North Carolina during the Eighteenth Century.' Published as *Colonial North Carolina in the Eighteenth Century* (Chapel Hill: University of North Carolina Press, 1964)

1963   David Ward, 'Nineteenth Century Boston: A Study in the Role of Antecedent and Adjacent Conditions in the Spatial Aspects of Urban Growth'

1964   Leonard W. Brinkman, 'The Historical Geography of Improved Cattle in the United States to 1870'

R. Cole Harris, 'A Geography of the Seigneurial System in Canada during the French Regime.' Published as *The Seigneurial System in Early Canada: A Geographical Study* (Madison: University of Wisconsin Press, and Quebec: Laval University Press, 1966)

James T. Lemon, 'A Rural Geography of Southeastern Pennsylvania in the Eighteenth Century: The Contributions of Cultural Inheritance, Social Structure, Economic Conditions and Physical Resources.' Published as *The Best Poor Man's Country: A Geographical Study of Early Southeastern Pennsylvania* (Baltimore: Johns Hopkins University Press, 1972)

1965   Paul W. English, 'Settlement and Economy in the Kirman Basin, Iran.' Published as *City and Village in Iran: Settlement and Economy in the Kirman Basin* (Madison: University of Wisconsin Press, 1966)

Terry G. Jordan, 'A Geographical Appraisal of the Significance of German Settlement in Nineteenth-Century Texas Agriculture.' Published as *German Seed in Texas Soil: Immigrant Farmers in Nineteenth-Century Texas* (Austin: University of Texas Press, 1966)

1966   Sam B. Hilliard, 'Hog Meat and Hoecake: A Geographical View of Food Supply in the Heart of the Old South, 1840-1860.' Published as *Hog Meat and Hoecake: A Geographical View of Food Supply in the Heart of the Old South* (Carbondale: Southern Illinois University Press, 1972)

1967   James R. Gibson, 'The Geography of Provisionment of the Okhotsk Seaboard and Kamchatka, 1639-1856: Overland Supply and Local Agriculture.' Published as *Feeding the Russian Fur Trade: Provision-*

230 Andrew Hill Clark

ment of the Okhotsk Seaboard and the Kamchatka Peninsula, 1639-1856 (Madison: University of Wisconsin Press, 1969)

1968　Ralph D. Vicero, 'Immigration of French Canadians to New England, 1840-1910: A Geographical Analysis'

1969　Clarissa T. Kimber, 'Recent Historical Plant Geography of Martinique'
Robert D. Mitchell, 'The Upper Shenandoah Valley of Virginia during the Eighteenth Century: A Study in Historical Geography.' Published as *Commercialism and Frontier: Perspectives on the Early Shenandoah Valley* (Charlottesville: University Press of Virginia, 1977)

1971　C. Grant Head, 'The Changing Geography of Newfoundland in the Eighteenth Century.' Published as *Eighteenth Century Newfoundland: A Geographer's Perspective* (Toronto: McClelland and Stewart, 1976)
Arthur J. Ray, 'Indian Exploitation of the Forest-Grassland Transition Zone in Western Canada, 1650-1860: A Geographical View of Two Centuries of Change.' Published as *Indians in the Fur Trade: Their Role as Trappers, Hunters, and Middlemen in the Lands Southwest of Hudson Bay, 1660-1870* (Toronto: University of Toronto Press, 1974)

1973　Thomas F. McIlwraith, 'The Logistical Geography of the Great Lakes Grain Trade, 1820-1850'

1974　Robert Hoffpauir, 'India's Other Bovine: A Cultural Geography of the Water Buffalo'

1975　D. Aidan McQuillan, 'Adaptation of Three Immigrant Groups to Farming in Central Kansas 1875-1925'

Contributors

James R. Gibson is Professor of Geography, York University, Toronto

R. Cole Harris is Professor of Geography, University of British Columbia, Vancouver

Sam B. Hilliard is Professor of Geography, Louisiana State University, Baton Rouge

James T. Lemon is Professor of Geography, University of Toronto, Toronto

D. Aidan McQuillan is Assistant Professor of Geography, University of Toronto, Toronto

Donald W. Meinig (PhD, University of Washington, 1953) is Maxwell Professor of Geography, Syracuse University, Syracuse

Robert D. Mitchell is Associate Professor of Geography, University of Maryland, College Park

Arthur J. Ray is Associate Professor of Geography, York University, Toronto

David Ward is Professor of Geography, University of Wisconsin-Madison

John Warkentin (PhD, University of Toronto, 1960) is Professor of Geography, York University, Toronto

Subscribers

A.F. Burghardt
M.P. Conzen
J.H. Galloway
J.R. Gibson
Graduating class of 1930, Brandon University
R.C. Harris
C.G. Head
S.B. Hilliard
J.T. Lemon
T.F. McIlwraith
D.A. McQuillan
D.W. Meinig
R.D. Mitchell
D. Ward
J.H. Warkentin